The Quest for Grace

Manning Clark was born in Sydney in 1915. He was educated at Victorian State schools, Melbourne Grammar School, and then at the Universities of Melbourne and Oxford. He taught history at schools in England and Australia, at the University of Melbourne, and at the Australian National University in Canberra. Much of his life was spent in writing the six volumes of *A History of Australia*. He is married, with six children and seven grandchildren, and lives in Canberra.

Penguin Books

Other books by Manning Clark:

A History of Australia (6 vols, 1962–87)
Meeting Soviet Man (1960)
A Short History of Australia (1963) (revised illustrated edition 1986)
In Search of Henry Lawson (1978)
Occasional Writings and Speeches (1980)
Collected Short Stories (1986)
The Puzzles of Childhood (1989)

Manning Clark

The Quest for Grace

PENGUIN BOOKS

Penguin Books Australia Ltd
487 Maroondah Highway, P.O. Box 257
Ringwood, Victoria 3134, Australia
Penguin Books Ltd
Harmondsworth, Middlesex, England
Viking Penguin, A Division of Penguin Books USA Inc.
375 Hudson Street, New York, New York 10014, USA
Penguin Books Canada Limited
2801 John Street, Markham, Ontario, Canada L3R 1B4
Penguin Books (N.Z.) Ltd
182-190 Wairau Road, Auckland 10, New Zealand

First published in Viking by Penguin Books Australia, 1990
Published in Penguin 1991
10 9 8 7 6 5 4 3 2 1
Copyright © Manning Clark, 1990

Typeset in 11/13 Berkeley Old Style by Midland Typesetters, Maryborough, Vic.
Made and printed in Australia by Australian Print Group, Maryborough, Vic.

National Library of Australia
Cataloguing-in-Publication data:

Clark, Manning, 1915–
The quest for grace.
ISBN 0 14 014355 1.
1. Clark, Manning, 1915–   . 2. Historians – Australia –
Biography. I. Title
994.007202

For Sebastian, Katerina, Axel, Andrew, Rowland and Benedict

Contents

Contents

Preface

This book continues *The Puzzles of Childhood*. Like *The Puzzles* it is based mainly on memory, supplemented by the notes taken for a volume of *A History of Australia* which, alas, was never even begun. I have also made use of diaries begun in April 1941.

Once again I must thank Roslyn Russell for her help. I am grateful to Heide Smith for permission to publish the photograph of myself on the front cover, and the photograph of my wife and myself; to John Fairfax & Co. for permission to publish the photograph of my family and myself; to the *Canberra Times* for permission to publish the photograph of David Campbell with members of his family and myself; and to Collins/Angus & Robertson for permission to reproduce the extract from 'Night Sowing' from David Campbell's *Collected Poems* (1989). I must also thank Pat Dobrez, Don Baker, Ken Inglis, Bill Gammage, Don Watson, Peter Craven, Nicholas Brown, Kathleen Fitzpatrick, Suzanne Welborn, Helen Crisp, and Joan and Bruce Grant, for their help and encouragement. It remains to thank the unthankable one, my wife Dymphna. I say this because I can only hope that anyone who reads the work will see it in part as a hymn of praise to her and to my mother and father. I hope the students at Blundell's School, at Geelong Grammar School, the University of Melbourne, and the Australian National University, will notice how moved the old man always is when he writes about them. I never forget.

Manning Clark
Canberra
3 March 1990

But the little sticky leaves, and the precious tombs, and the blue sky, and the woman you love! How will you live, how will you love them? . . . With such a hell in your heart and your head, how can you?

I want to be there when everyone suddenly understands what it has all been for.

—F. M. Dostoevsky, *The Brothers Karamazov*

The Quest Begins

Anyone who has read *The Puzzles of Childhood* will not be surprised to be told that at the age of eighteen my favourite reading was the Book of Ecclesiastes. The preacher put into memorable words my response to life: 'Vanity of vanities, saith the Preacher, all is vanity ... that which befalleth the sons of men befalleth beasts ... as the one dieth, so doth the other ... so that a man hath no pre-eminence over a beast: for all is vanity.' All return to the dust from whence they came. There is one alone, and there is not a second. Childhood and boyhood left me in a dense fog. Many people offered to guide me out of that fog; many beckoned to me, saying they knew the path to the light. While in the fog I said many foolish things, hurt many people, and hurt myself. This book is the story of how I found my way out of the fog. It is a story of my search for wisdom and understanding.

I began this search early in 1934 at the age of eighteen. In March of that year I signed the matriculation roll at the University of Melbourne, and enrolled for the degree of Bachelor of Arts with honours in the School of History and Political Science. I also became a student of Trinity College. I was still a scholarship boy.

History, I was told, was a bible of wisdom. The beginning of wisdom, I was told, was to learn the benefits humanity had gained from the spread of British institutions over large parts of the world. So the first step was to study British history both at 'home' and 'abroad'. In the first year there was British history from the Norman conquest to 1660. This was intended to teach us about the origins of British political institutions, the rule of law, the birth of British liberty, the British genius for compromise, and the virtue of British pragmatism.

There was also ancient history. The Greeks, we were told, would teach us the wisdom of moderation in all things, of harmony between passion and reason, between the Dionysian frenzy and Apollonian restraint. The Romans would teach us by their example the wisdom of law, order and decorum. We first-year students were novices who were being initiated into membership of the club of the highly civilised.

I do not know now how soon I realised there was something lacking. I remember thinking at times there must be some other subject in which the lecturer discussed things that mattered. Just as people hope things will be different on the other side of the street, so I hoped there would be a lecture theatre where it was all happening. My lecturers were all people of distinction and achievement. But alas, I could not respond: it was though they were training me for a race in which I did not wish to run.

The Professor of History, Ernest Scott, was on leave during 1934. The acting head of the department was Jessie Webb, the senior lecturer in ancient history who also lectured to us in Professor Scott's subject, British history from 1066–1660, with special reference to the period 1642–60. The honours course was British colonial history from 1607–60 – the planting of the British colonies in North America. In addition, Miss Webb had to correct two three-thousand word essays from each honours student in first year, set and mark the exams in both first-year subjects, mark some of the papers, chair the examiners' meeting for those doing final honours, represent the history department on the faculty, the professorial board and other university committees, answer all correspondence (without the help of a secretary), and discuss problems with students. Now I marvel she was able to help us so much.

I was disappointed. I was searching for wisdom and understanding. I wanted her to help me to 'understand what it has all been for'. Miss Webb told me about recent research on Athenian tribute lists, and the latest reports from the diggers in Crete. I was interested in Miss Webb's face. There seemed to be another person inside her, whose grip on life was as fragile as the wisp of unruly hair swaying in front of her troubled brow. I never dared to speak to her: she was on the dais. I was down below. I looked up: she looked down.

Professor Scott lectured to us in Australian history in 1935. 'Scotty', as we called him, belonged to the Alfred Deakin–Herbert Brookes world of the Protestant ascendancy in Melbourne. He was an English migrant who, while working as a Hansard reporter for the Commonwealth parliament, had made his mark as a historian with the publication of *Terre Napoléon* (1910) and *La Pérouse* (1910). He was appointed to the chair of history in 1913. In 1914 he published a life of Matthew Flinders, and in 1916 *A Short History of Australia*. In his early years as a professor his attacks on the Catholics had led to protests from Catholic students. We were told that they, and not Scotty, had to apologise. Melbourne was a Protestant city: Melbourne had all the rectitude, all the confidence of knowing there were 'certain certainties'. So nuns went on sitting with heads lowered and pens down while Scotty lingered over strange goings-on in monasteries and nunneries on the eve of the Reformation. Looking back, I doubt whether Scotty had any real interest in the Galilean fisherman. Perhaps that was why I always felt like a stranger in his classes.

He was an entertaining lecturer. Every lecture was a creation. There was a challenging introduction, the announcement of the subject for the day, the development of that subject, and a peroration foreshadowing the subject for the next lecture. Scotty had many mannerisms which members of the class enjoyed imitating. He swiftly jerked his right arm from elbow to hand, like a railway signal which could not decide whether to stay up or stay down. In moments of excitement, and there were many of them, the right arm went on jerking long after he had stopped talking. At ridicule he was superb, especially of the follies, absurdities and extravagances of Catholic historians, and all 'foreigners' who made absurd claims, he told us, for Portuguese or Spanish discoveries of Australia.

Others enjoyed him. They waited each year for his description of one of Cromwell's parliaments as 'picked, packed and pocketed', or for his character sketch of Catherine the Great in European History B as having 'the mowwals of a suburban tomcat' (right forearm *molto agitato*). I wanted something more than these witty exercises in alliteration, something more than a recitation of the follies of the whole world outside the history classroom of the University of Melbourne. It was a British exile's version of the Gibbon view that history was a record of the crimes and follies of humanity without Mr Gibbon's pity, without Mr Gibbon's yearning for another creation, without Mr Gibbon's dignity and tenderness.

Perhaps I was expecting too much. In time I came to believe that the story of the Europeans, or the white man, or the British, or the Anglo-Celts in Australia – call them what you will – was one of tragic grandeur, that there were moments like what the Germans call

3

'*Sternstunden der Menschheit*' (the starry moments of humanity) in the story. I heard nothing of these moments from Scotty. Instead I heard much about dinners he had attended in Rome with the librarian of the Vatican Library at which he had wagered a bottle of wine that he was right about the Dieppe map. Scotty had won the wager, and what a good bottle of wine the two of them had enjoyed, ha, ha, ha! Academic history was a game played by gamesmen skilled in discovering errors in the books and articles of rivals. How stupid everyone else was – ha, ha, ha! (with many swishes of the forearm).

My fellow-students taught me much about life. Eddie Foxcroft, second son of the deputy librarian in the Public Library of Victoria, had all the gifts to rise to a place of prominence in the world. He wanted to write books: he wanted to leave his mark in public life. Eddie wrote his book; Eddie, in collaboration with 'Nugget' Coombs, Fin Crisp, Trevor Swann and others, created the welfare state in Australia. By then Eddie had three phones in his carpeted office. But just as he was about to reap the rewards he coveted, Eddie died. His life taught me much.

So did Margaret Kiddle. She was the daughter of J. Beecham Kiddle, and was big of body (she stood 6'3") and large of heart. I remember dancing with her at parties given by Yarraside for Yarraside, plus the scholarship-boy contingent, those who were expected to repay their scholarship debt to Yarraside by serving Yarraside all the days of their lives. I remember that dancing with her it was 'eyes up' if you decided to speak: with all others it was 'eyes sideways down'. I remember seeing her again sliding into her seat in the old history classroom wearing an English-style tweed suit, a buttoned-up blouse, with a camellia in the buttonhole on the coat, and her hair rising majestically from her noble brow. She had all the externals of a daughter of the Western District or of Yarraside. Her accent was more English than Australian, her stance was imperious, the stance of all those Melburnians who believed they drafted and enforced the rules for all of us. Yet her religion was not Christian, she believing, as she told me, neither in God nor in Christ. She was a Stoic, who believed in the will to endure and to bear with courage and dignity whatever cross chance or circumstance condemned her to carry. Hers was a very heavy cross. From the onset of adolescence she had been told she would die young. She had lost one kidney, and the other kidney was not functioning properly. So once a month she spent two days in bed.

At the time (1934) I, and, I guess, most of my male contemporaries in the Arts Faculty at the University of Melbourne knew very little about the menstrual cycle and its effect on the emotional life of women. There was, if I remember correctly, not much sympathy, very little of the eye of pity, and much irritation about otherwise inexplicable changes of mood. I remember noticing that for two or three days in each month the face of a woman in our class would look as if it were drained of blood, a face of laughter and gaiety would become haggard and remote. The lively would become listless; some, normally friendly and even flattering, would suddenly lash out, and before you could disengage you might find yourself the subject of an unkind character sketch. I found all this quite bewildering, and, in self-protection, decided it was wise not to come too near.

Margaret Kiddle taught me what went on in the heart of a woman. By her example she showed me that it was precisely on those days when a woman was suffering pain, and putting on remote looks, that she most needed sympathy and understanding. She taught me that a woman could have a full and satisfying life without marrying and bearing children. Over cups of tea in the caf (downstairs in the old Union building), during walks from the history classroom to the library, or further to the public library, she told me, in that circum-locutory language which the customs of the time dictated, that she would never marry because her doctor had told her she could never bear a child. She also told me she would die young. She told me then and later of how she hoped to conceive other children: for her there would be a child of the heart; she would write books, children's books, and a history of her father's tribe, the men and women who founded squatterdom's domination in the Western District of Victoria – the creators of the Melbourne Club, Melbourne Grammar School, Geelong Grammar School, Trinity College, Janet Clarke Hall, Yarraside with all its hangers-on, its servants, and its dependent territories in other Melbourne suburbs.

Margaret Kiddle had her flowering time. She began her life's work with the publication in 1950 of her book on the life of Caroline Chisholm. In *Men of Yesterday* (1961) she soared: she became more than a chronicler of her class, she became a historian. She gave birth to a child which would live longer than any child of the body.

When the time came for her to die she behaved with the same dignity and courage with which she had conducted the whole of her life. She was admitted to Bethesda Hospital, where blood transfusions were given to prolong her life. She decided she had had enough: she told the doctor there would be no more transfusions. She told me not to visit her again as she wanted me to remember her as she had been when we first pivoted on the polished floors of Toorak women rich enough to have a house with a ballroom, or on those walks to the library when she persuaded me that it was possible for a man to know what was going on in the heart of a woman; that between men and women there could be tenderness, pity, and platonic love. The bond men had with each other could also be forged with a woman. When she died in 1960, for me it was as though a mighty presence had disappeared from the face of the earth.

Not long before she died she visited me in Canberra. She had heard my wife was in hospital, and offered to help me. Weakened though she was by her own complaint she insisted on doing the washing. While we were pegging out the clothes together on the clothes hoist she, taking advantage of her great height, peered over the white sheet she was neatly pegging on the line and put a question to me, face to face. With her I never ducked, or looked at the ground. 'You knew Pat Colebrook well, didn't you, Manning?'

She was right. I had known Pat Colebrook well. She was another one of the students in the honours school in history and political science. Her real subject was women's life and love. But no one gave lectures on that subject at the university. When we started to speak over tea and biscuits in the caf she told me she was interested in minds. She flattered me. She told me three or four of our fellow students – she cited Eddie Foxcroft as an example – had brains, but I was the only one amongst the honours students who had a good mind, a mind which would one day be quite productive. She was like my mother: she believed, or rather she claimed she knew ('Women have those special insights, you know, Manning') that I was a person who must be protected against corruption by the world, taught and persuaded not to 'seek salvation in the muck'. She wanted a communion of minds. So far I had only heard of the communion of saints, and all I knew about saints did not make membership of that communion very appealing.

It was not minds which drew us close together one night on a dancing floor in a mansion on the hill in Domain Road, South Yarra. Or if it was the mind then the mind must have taken up temporary residence in that part of the body identified by my mother as 'down below, Mann dear'. She drew very near. I did not know what was overwhelming both her and me. I realise now I made a most inadequate response to her great need. I laughed in embarrassment, perhaps in fear of finding myself the object of a passion I did not understand. I knew nothing of love, or rather every time I had timidly dropped the mask and allowed someone, either man or woman, to see, as it were, the man within, there had been a recoil, a curl of the lip, a look of disdain, or wounding words. I remember thinking of this intense moment in a South Yarra ballroom when years later I read the words in a poem by Thomas Hardy: 'God kept our fleeting bodies apart.' Well, I have never been vain enough to believe that God, if He is there at all, would take interest in a young man and a young woman (the young man all togged up in Yarraside's idea of what a man should wear to a dance, and the woman outwardly just as conformist in choice of dress, hairdo, and make-up) visited suddenly by a wild sensual passion. It seemed to me much later it was not God but the lore of Yarraside which kept our bodies apart. By then I was punishing myself for not noticing how much the moment meant to her.

Perhaps I was frightened. Shakespeare had alerted me to what often happened in the relations between men and women – 'Phyllis was loved. She liked Corydon.' Here I was liking someone who loved me, and I did not know what to do. In love, simulation is more obvious than a counterfeit coin to one of Her Majesty's inspectors in the Mint. Literature, music and philosophy could not help. She continued to believe in me: I continued talking to her, even though I knew it was agony for her, but I needed her faith, needed her vision of what might be if I were to resist all the tempters met along the road during my search for the medium in which to say those things she believed I would one day say. I had sinned: I was prepared to use another human being and not even notice the price she paid for her sacrifice.

Ten years later she died suddenly of pneumonia. But it was many years before I became aware of my guilt. By then it was too late. It was like my behaviour to my mother and my father. By the time I realised what they had lived through, it was too late to speak to them: they were dead. It was the same with Pat Colebrook. By the time I realised my obtuseness, my insensitivity, and my lack of imagination, it was too late. I could only torment myself in the watches of the night, or send up the appeal to intercessors who were probably not there: 'Have pity on all of us for our great folly . . .'

Rohan Rivett was an enthusiast. He was the grandson of Alfred Deakin, and son of Sir David Rivett, executive head of the Council for Scientific and Industrial Research. He was never able to identify for us the reasons for his enthusiasm. He held no firm political opinions: he told us he held no religious beliefs. Perhaps that was why he chose Camille Desmoulins as the subject for his long essay (20 000 words) in his final year in 1937. Camille was *the* enthusiast among the revolutionaries of 1789, and it was never quite clear what he stood for. Thomas Carlyle in *The French Revolution* summed him up: 'one did not almost love thee, thou headlong lightly-sparkling man!'

By contrast Hyrrell Ross, the daughter of a Gippsland farmer, always stood on entrenched ground. Later, she fell in love with Judah Waten, born in Odessa, son of a Russian Jewish labourer and a mother who believed in culture. Judah converted Hyrrell to Marxism. Within a year the virtues of a girl from the bush were blended with the virtues of political belief. At that time the Communist Party was for many the conscience of Australia. While we liberals who could not make up our minds stood in the sand, believing we were the representatives of higher civilisation, Hyrrell was to stand on firm ground. I envied her, but could not share her faith, because no matter how strong the desire for a new creation I could never believe such things as they believed in could ever be.

I was still wearing the heavy blinkers of all members of the Protestant ascendancy – I still believed British institutions and the Protestant religion were the essential conditions for a high standard of material well-being, liberty, the rule of law, tolerance, fair play and decency. They brought you such a prize – riches in this world, and a place of honour on the resurrection morning at the beginning of the life of the world to come. Hyrrell believed such hopes were based on a lie. She and Judah never gave up hope for me until they died. They were models of political virtue, guardians of the Russian revolution. I always wanted to ask them: how do you know it is true? I had the thirst to believe: I was looking for a light to guide me out of the fog. Judah and Hyrrell never tired of offering to show me the way. But I must find my own way out.

There were many other lantern-bearers in the fog. There were the members of the Evangelical Union, the women who always wore stockings, and fastened the top button of their blouses, the women who wore smiles on their faces even on a hot north wind day in Melbourne, because smilers bore witness to their joy in being part of God's creation. They used to tell me they were praying for me, and I wanted to say they would need to pray a very long time, as their smugness grated on the mind of a young man who believed life was much more of a mystery than anything acknowledged in their philosophy. There were the followers of the Student Christian Movement, who ran weekends at Chum Creek where they dispensed Christian cheerfulness, Christian mateyness, and anything which papered over all the evil in the world. They were the dispensers and distributors of the physic of Christian goodwill as a cure-all for the ills of the world. There were the members of the Newman Society, claiming the Catholic Church had the keys to the kingdom of heaven, and that outside that Church there was no salvation. Their confidence both attracted and repelled me. I was not ready to perceive that their members had a compassion for all, often lacking among the smilers.

There were the men who heeded the divine command to fear God and eschew evil. I remember two of them very clearly. One was Dick Hamer and the other was John Leach. Both had been to Geelong Grammar School. Both were reluctant to reveal the man within. John Leach was killed during the war when flying over enemy territory and I believe he would have been as calm in that plane as he was when confronting an opponent on the football field. Dick Hamer went on to become a Liberal Party premier of Victoria. They were both models of Melbourne bourgeois rectitude, both kind, both sympathetic with those who could not manage the world. I remember thinking at the time that their example and their behaviour would be most commendable if the rest of humanity either could or wanted to follow their example. But what if others could not?

I also asked myself why such upright men should put their talents at the service of a corrupt, unjust and evil society. I was to discover later that the advocates of the universal embrace were capable of the most abominable cruelty. I was to discover also that upright men and women, free though they were of self-laceration and doubt, and attractive as they were because of their capacity always to do the right thing, their capacity never to give offence, were exotics in Australia. Their model was 'Englishmanism'. They were seeking perfection in what was rapidly ceasing to be relevant in Australia.

College life taught me many things. The warden of Trinity College, Dr J. C. V. Behan, invited to musical evenings in the Lodge those likely to respond. The women from Janet Clarke Hall wore evening dresses; Dr Behan wore the gown of a Doctor of Laws. Those were the days of the gramophone needle. Coarse souls used steel needles: the sensitive, such as Dr Behan, used a rose thorn, sharpened to a point with a special cutter. Dr Behan was a majestic figure. He stood behind the gramophone, clasping the collar of his gown with both hands, and told us, after a medicinal glass of sherry and a dry biscuit, that he proposed to play the Adagio from Beethoven's *Quartet in A Minor*, performed by the Budapest String Quartet. He told us with a twinkle in the eye that although he knew he should probably not say this in a Church of England College he always found Beethoven more inspiring than any religious service. No one said a word, though the Janet Clarke Hall contingent looked as though they understood. At the end of the first side (in the days of the 78s a twelve-inch record lasted three minutes) and while Dr Behan was silently winding the gramophone, Kathleen Brumley sighed deeply, and said, 'That was heavenly, Dr Behan.' Dr Behan looked over the tops of his spectacles, and replied, 'Better to come, Miss Brumley, better to come.'

On another night Dr Behan played excerpts from *Swan Lake* by Tchaikovsky. I was strangely moved, and began to weep. I had no idea at the time that the ballet was a story about treachery, about the betrayal of an innocent woman, and about the forces of darkness and their malevolence towards the innocent. I wanted to ask why a note of melancholy pervaded the whole work. That struck a deeper chord inside me than all the optimistic, shallow talk of the time about material progress, and the role of the British. But for a Prufrock in the drawing-rooms of our teachers at the University of Melbourne to rise and say, 'I am Lazarus come back from the dead, come back to tell you all', would be seized on by the upright and the straiteners as evidence that you were peculiar, certainly never likely to get things straight. So I held my tongue.

By then Ross Wilson, a resident in the 'Vatican' at Trinity College, had introduced me to the poetry of T. S. Eliot. 'The Love Song of J. Alfred Prufrock' made an immediate appeal. I remember another Trinity student, Michael Thwaites, a classical scholar and a poet, wrote a witty poem in the form of a letter to T. S. Eliot, ending, if I remember correctly, 'Dear Thomas, please write me something I can understand.' I laughed. Ross Wilson was incensed. As it turned out, Michael Thwaites did understand certain elemental things. He joined Moral Rearmament, and later worked for the Australian Security Service. I never understood then, and I do not understand now, why such a lovable, gifted, high-minded man should work for Security.

Ross Wilson was a theological student, then in his final year in the history school. He was an Anglo-Catholic who made scathing comments about all low-church Anglicans. One of them in Trinity, Ken Prentice, was so low, he said, he had never been able to get up from the carpet. I was puzzled by the vehemence of his remarks. Ross was a brilliant student of history. I still remember him telling me after he finished his final exams at the end of 1934 that in the paper on the history of the thirteen British colonies in America he wrote like an American, he *was* an American.

I remember also being puzzled for a while by his talk when he was slightly drunk. His eyes were on fire with life. James I, he said, had his Steenie (the Duke of Buckingham), Christ had his beloved disciple John, and he, Ross Wilson, had his ——. He also told me with wild enthusiasm that all the men of genius belonged to his fraternity – Socrates, Christ, Shakespeare, Leonardo da Vinci, Michaelangelo, Byron, and many others. The trouble was, Ross always fell passionately in love with the most normal men, and convinced himself that his passion was reciprocated. He elevated smiles into shy confessions of love, and saw gifts of books as symbols of a desire to make the gift of the body. He drank to excess to give him the confidence to declare his passion, only to hear the wounding words from the love object that the latter did not know what he, Ross, expected from him, or that he, the loved one, was engaged to be married, or even something more bizarre.

This would trigger off a wild frenzy in Ross. I remember once calling on him in the 'Vatican' after one of these many rejections. He had smashed every piece of china in the room, trampled to pieces the gramophone records which had fuelled his fantasy, torn to shreds the paper on which he had written poems about his love. Again, as with Pat Colebrook, I felt inadequate. Here was another human being reaching out for help, and I was quite powerless. That will happen to me many times in my life. The misfits, the ones who cannot stop, women possessed by a wild passion for scoundrels, and men with some private hell in their hearts, will tell me of their pain, believing I could help them, believing I knew the answer. But no one knows the answer. They need the divine, but maybe that is the greatest delusion of all – that there is someone, somewhere, who can help. All I can ever do is to offer them protection against their persecutors and tormentors, and to advise them to beware of those who believe they know the answers.

I was already fumbling towards the idea that no one could help them, that there is even a refined cruelty in suggesting that things could ever be any different for them. Those who profess themselves followers of the universal embrace or medicine men for social evils, I was to find, were often most lacking in charity, pity and understanding for all the ones whom God seemed to have forgotten. No one could stop Ross Wilson rushing on to his destruction, or the huge waste of his vast talents as a writer.

Not long after the scene in Trinity College I asked him how he, a candidate for holy orders, reconciled his sexual behaviour with the teaching of the church. He became very excited. He told me God made special dispensations to those who were not of the marrying kind, that because of the cross they carried during their lives God compensated them with special favours, granting them dispensation from the teaching of the church on chastity. But when I asked him what authority he had for this opinion he told me it was a question between him and God: Christ understood. He had had his beloved John, and Christ was the son of God. And didn't I know that in the Book of Samuel the love of a man for a man was deemed higher than the love of a man for a woman – 'the soul of Jonathan was knit to that of David'. No – Ross insisted in that shrill voice of his – the members of his fraternity were God's elect.

That astonished me. It seemed to me then, and it seems to me now, that people like Ross never knew the peace of God which passes all understanding, that they were never quiet, that there was uproar in their souls, terror of the police, terror of being found out by the 'hearties'. I remember at the Trinity dance that year at the Palais de Danse in St Kilda, Ross, with a wild look in his eye, the look of a man whose soul was never quiet, grabbing me by the arm and shouting at me in a voice of wild despair, 'He's dancing with a woman: he should be dancing with me!' What could I say? What could anyone say? Who could ever rescue Ross from the delusion in his heart?

Ross left Melbourne to study in Cambridge, England. He was received into the Catholic Church, but to his dismay they wisely (as I believe) decided not to accept him as a candidate for the priesthood. This rebuff stung him into quite reckless behaviour. He became a park prowler in London. The inevitable happened. He was trapped by a police decoy, and charged before a police magistrate with unnatural sexual behaviour. He commissioned a Q.C. to defend him. On the latter's advice he grew a beard, and the magistrate upheld his counsel's plea of mistaken identity.

The ordeal broke Ross. Soon after the acquittal he threw himself under a truck in a London street. He was not killed. He became a cripple for life. I called on him in London in the summer of 1956 and we went for a walk in a public garden. Ross threatened women who came near with his walking stick, and shouted obscenities at them, accusing them of being responsible for all the pain and suffering and terror he had lived through. Back in his room he told me he no longer believed in God. He now knew what Christ meant when he cried out on the Cross: 'My God, my God, why hast thou forsaken me?' God had let him down. I asked him whether he could endure life without God's world – the world of caring, of forgiveness, of love. He replied that he would spend his days writing advertisements for the whisky firm for which he worked. He felt murderous towards humanity, he would use his gifts to lure men and women on to their destruction, and laugh as they drank themselves to death. This revenge on humanity would be some compensation for what they had done to him. Again I was deeply aware of my own inadequacy to help. I wondered then, on my way back to Oxford, as I wonder now years later, whether anyone can ever grasp the hand held out for help, held out for relief. Perhaps that was one of the reasons why I was always such a doubting Thomas with those who claimed to have the answers, who talked as though they, usurping God's role, knew how to wipe away all tears from human eyes, as though a time would come when pity and compassion would wither in the human heart because they had removed the need for pity.

Oddly enough, while Ross Wilson was giving me a lesson in the follies and passions of human beings, others tried to persuade me they knew the answers to human suffering. That happened in a rather bizarre way. In November 1934 Victorians celebrated the centenary of the arrival of white people in their State. Among the special guests invited to mark the centenary, and to dedicate the Shrine of Remembrance in the Domain, was Henry, Duke of Gloucester, third son of the King of England. Prince Charming was coming to preside over the celebrations organised to commemorate the founding of a British settlement in Melbourne in 1834. Victorians would learn that, without the monarchy, there could be no British Empire, and that, without the Empire, Australia as they knew it would cease to be.

I cannot claim to have been disgusted by the grovelling and the sycophancy lavished on the Duke by the politicians of Spring Street and the hostesses of Yarraside and the Western District of Victoria.

The monarchy and the Empire, the British connection, and the local cult of Englishmanism, were for me at that time rather like the mountains, the sea and the sky: they were from eternity and would not change. Yet the occasion opened up a new world for me. John Masefield, the English poet laureate, was one of the guests of the Victorian Centenary committee. I knew him as the author of a book on Gallipoli in which he had praised the Australian soldiers as worthy descendants of the heroes of the Greek army at the siege of Troy, and of poems I had been told I should like when doing English literature for matriculation. He came to Trinity College as the guest of the warden, Dr Behan, to talk to the students.

I do not remember much of what he said. Fifty-five years have passed since he spoke to us. But I do remember the face of the man, the florid complexion and the white hair – the face of a man who was magnificently alive. I remember also he had a message for those who wanted to hear. Art, he told us, was one of the three great comforters of humanity, the other two being alcohol and religion. To illustrate his point he took the example of a cat sitting on a mat watching a rat enter a room. He distinguished between the way the empirical observer, the prose writer and the poet would create the scene. The artist saw things others did not notice. Perhaps that was what my mother always insisted lived in me, namely this special vision, this awareness of something extra in the scene of a cat sitting on a mat waiting to pounce on a rat. I can still remember the exaltation on hearing John Masefield speak, the revelation of a kingdom quite different from the kingdoms of this world. He spoke of the eternal city, and of the dogs prowling outside the walls of that city. I wondered then whether I had the gift to be a citizen of that eternal city, or whether my divided self would mean that one half of me would always live in that city while the other half joined the dogs threatening to convert it into a kingdom of nothingness. Perhaps art was a lamp, a light to guide me out of the fog by which I was surrounded.

At the time another lamp lit up the fog. It was the light in which 'Bluey' Carter had tried in vain to interest me during the Belgrave years. A pamphlet written by Joyce Manton, 'The Centenary Prepares for War', was a revelation to me. The writer urged Australians to be sceptical of all this mystical talk about Australia and the Empire. The centenary celebrations, the dedication of the Shrine, the royal visit, and all the display by the matrons of Toorak, were a smoke-screen to conceal the true purpose of the coming together of all these imperial celebrities in Melbourne. The real purpose was to prepare for war. The survival of capitalist society depended upon war: capitalist society needed both war and fascism: Australians must destroy capitalist society, and create a society in which the freedom of each was the condition of the freedom of all. In June 1934 the Nazis butchered radicals and homosexuals in their Party on the 'night of the long knives'. In the same year Sergei Kirov was assassinated in Leningrad. The world was once again turning nasty. I wanted to know whether those professing to know salvation for society knew anything about my hunger for individual salvation.

I had given up all hope that God would work a great marvel in this world. Here was a group of people in Melbourne telling me they could do what God had failed to do. They could build a heaven on earth. Straiteners, conformers and heart-dimmers would be replaced by life-enlargers. We would all have life and have it more abundantly.

I began to haunt the International Book Shop in Exhibition Street and the Communist Party Book Shop opposite in the same street, and to spend a portion of my pocket money buying the *Guardian*, the *Tribune* and the pamphlets on culture in a communist society. It seemed as though here was the light to guide me out of my fog. I remember feeling exalted when reading the words: 'I gave my life to the noblest cause of all, the liberation of mankind.'

When I risked revealing my great expectations, my thirst and hunger for the day when men neither hurt nor destroyed, the communists put on black looks like those put on by the self-appointed standards men in the bourgeois world. I noticed, to my discomfort, that there was no room for any difference of opinion within the ranks of the builders of this new world. You were either 'correct' or you were 'not correct'. Those who erred and strayed from what was 'correct' were hounded with the same ferocity, the same character sketches, as the nonconformers in the bourgeois world. This was not a movement for the liberation of mankind from spiritual bullies: this was a movement to give another gang of spiritual bullies a chance to draw up the rules of how we were all to behave.

I had always been uncomfortable with those who claimed they knew all the answers. Accepting another man's view of the world meant the loss of the right to decide for oneself. That I could not abide. I already believed passionately I must make my own decision even if I were wrong. The spiritual bullies wanted to take that right from me. I believed there was a mystery at the heart of things. Wordsworth had

15

put it into words for me: there was 'the burden of the mystery'. The self-appointed engineers of the human soul acknowledged no such mystery, or dismissed it as reactionary mysticism and nonsense. They talked and wrote as though it were possible to measure the passions of the human heart by the methods of the bookkeeper.

I was also ill at ease with their rejection of Christ. At that time I had not read Nietzsche, and had not heard of the argument that pity was a sign not of strength but of weakness. I knew Karl Marx had borrowed a phrase from Charles Kingsley and dismissed religion as 'the opium of the people'. I knew too, at second hand, that Lenin, the architect of the Russian revolution of November 1917, had criticised Christ for preaching forgiveness, turning the other cheek, and for talking of a kingdom which was not of this world. I knew too that the followers of Marx and Lenin had accepted the teaching of the Enlightenment that the doctrine of original sin and the doctrine of innate human depravity were infamous, and both infamies must be erased from the human mind. What bothered me was that in their moral indignation at such an insult to humanity – an indignation which did great credit to their hearts – they slid into ignoring humanity's oldest problem, namely the origin of human evil.

They did not want to acknowledge the dark side of the human heart, or, if they did, they said in reply that it was evil conditions which had been the breeding ground for human evil. I was never able to accept that proposition. It was not just the influence of my child-hood, of hearing the words in church that the heart was deceitful above all things, and no one could know it. It was a knowledge from personal observation and personal experience of what could come up from inside a man, a knowledge of all the madness and folly in the human heart and a conviction that, like the mountains, the plains and the sky, evil would never go away.

So I was just as divided about the future-of-humanity men as I was about the believers in the kingdom of God. I wanted to believe, indeed needed to believe, because life as I knew it till then was little more than a continuing drama of pain. Any doctrine, any remedy, which promised relief for all the sufferings, the humiliations, the absurdities, the contradictions, the agonies of human beings, attracted me. It was like being in love: it was food for a great hunger. Just as love transcends all offences, can overlook all flaws, taints and blemishes so there was always the desire to believe any doctrine, any teaching claiming to liberate human beings from these chains.

16

One encounter with a future-of-humanity man towards the end of 1934 taught me they were not for me. I walked with him from the University of Melbourne to the Flinders Street railway station. He was a Marxist, a dialectical materialist, and an uncritical supporter of the Soviet Union. He flattered me, telling me his Party needed young men with brains and drive to develop a revolutionary consciousness in the Australian working class. He and his Party would be the vanguard: they needed intellectuals and artists to spread the word. But there was something in the way he talked, or the way he looked, which held me back. He knew all the answers. That was something I could never accept. I went silent. As his tone became more and more hectoring, I asked him how he knew that he was right. He looked at me as though I were a hopeless case of bourgeois prejudices – an obscurantist wearing the mask of a child of the Enlightenment. We parted at Flinders Street, he to catch one train and I another. It was like a parting of the ways, one of those moments in life when a man discovers where he stands.

There were distractions to divert my mind from the question I will never answer: What then can we believe? It was the era of dances in the home. The wealthy held their dances in their own ballrooms, and paid for their own bands. The Varsity Melodists were the much-sought-after band. We, the young men and women, slid gracefully over the polished floors as Dick Bentley (later famous in many B.B.C. comedy shows) crooned to us, or sang, 'When we dance together cheek to cheek', as bold young men pressed their left cheek to their partner's left cheek, and encouraged the women to draw closer.

I remained the observer. I could never draw near. I had been told that no gentleman ever displayed such passions in public to a member of his own class. The women of the Toorak and South Yarra ballrooms were painted and powdered Madonnas. If you must indulge in that sort of thing you ought to look elsewhere. The Palais de Danse, and not the dancing boards of Lady So-and-so's, was your hunting ground. I noticed also that others chatted in a lively manner with their partners. I remained silent. There was always the fear that if I revealed what was going on in my mind my partner would say: 'How very peculiar' or 'I don't know whether I quite like that. It sounds rather unhealthy' or 'That's rather unsavoury'. So I held my tongue, and did all the fancy steps of the time, pivoted with the discretion demanded, and dreamed of all those things that could never be.

Cricket was another distraction. I had seen Jack Gregory's leap just before delivering the ball, walked out on to the Melbourne Cricket Ground at the end of a day's play and gazed at his footprints in the turf as though they were some religious relics. I had seen Percy Chapman moving with the grace and beauty of a ballet dancer. He was as beautiful as one of the horsemen in the friezes on the Parthenon, of which at that time I had seen only reproductions. (Five years later I saw him at Oxford when his once-beautiful face had degenerated into a collection of stalactites dropping down from his swollen cheeks, in which gullies had taken over the places which were once smooth. I wondered then what had been the moth fretting away the rich garment he once wore to my delight.) I had seen Harold Larwood run up to the wicket at the Melbourne Cricket Ground with a lightness of tread and a daintiness I would never forget. I had heard A. N. Barlow, the test umpire, tell us in the Melbourne University cricket team that Larwood was the only bowler for whom he had to look round to see whether he was moving towards the bowling crease. I had seen Stan McCabe hook Larwood off his cheek for four. I had seen Walter Hammond take catches in the slips with an air of indifference.

At the university things were going well for me. I was picked out as a promising cricketer. Selectors, and men claiming to be close to the selectors promised great things for me if I worked hard at my batting. But I knew that such could never be. It would be pleasing to believe that my nervous disorder was the only hurdle between me and success. That hurdle could never be jumped. But I also knew that I was not as good as they believed. Cricket taught me what I could and could not do. Cricket played a part in teaching me to face the truth about myself, to resist the temptation to nourish a delusion, and not feed a life-lie.

By an odd irony my nervous disorder became quite unruly just at the time when I was embracing life. Acting on medical advice I withdrew from the university. At the time it all seemed quite unfair, something which mocked my idea of the fitness of things. Again there was the temptation to brood over the unanswerable questions: Why did this happen to me? What had I done to deserve all this, to be called on to walk through life with this fatal flaw in my clay? I listened to the fifth symphony of Tchaikovsky and, for a time, took many a bath in the soupy waters of self-pity.

I turned to alcohol as a crutch. Alcohol had a very strong attraction for me. One glass of beer and I was free of an attack by the savage monster. But nature had played a rather cruel trick on me. I was not a weeping drunk, or a fighting drunk, or a lecherous drunk. I was a disintegrating drunk. One glass and I began to get my own back, to settle scores for the agonies suffered from concealing such a weakness as minor epilepsy, that agony of resenting that everyone else could walk without the fear of falling down. That disorder had presented me with an insoluble problem. I found it difficult not to be envious of the happiness of others: I found it difficult to forgive others their happiness. So for years I derived a perverse satisfaction from needling the virtuous, the happy and the good. I played for the applause of those who had quite different reasons from mine for their hatred and their mockery.

I fell for the temptation to believe that those who carried a cross were entitled to take liberties. I was tempted for years to believe that those with strong spiritual aspirations could wallow in the gutter without doing themselves or others any harm. I did not foresee that what stood between me and what I wanted to be was a stroke of great fortune. It never occurred to me that a flaw could be a means of grace. There would be much thrashing around in the fog, before I learned that Australia did not have to belong to the tough: that Australia could and should belong to the lovers and believers.

During the spell from the university I read many books. Once again I read Ecclesiastes, and had a good wallow in the preacher's cry of despair. Happily I remembered 'Lofty' Franklin's remark to me at Melbourne Grammar that one day I would be interested in the works of Dostoevsky. So I bought the Modern Library edition of *The Brothers Karamazov*. Perhaps it was a measure of my obsession with God's world that at the first reading I scarcely noticed Dostoevsky the great wit, or Dostoevsky the man who knew so much about love.

Young Russians, he told the reader, when they met in the tavern, talked about those things I had wanted to talk about in the bars of Carlton, but had never taken the risk. They talked about the eternal questions of the existence of God and immortality. Those who did not believe in God talked of socialism, and of the future transformation of human society and life. They wanted to know why evil was part of God's creation. Dostoevsky knew my longing. He put that into words for me. I read the words of Ivan Karamazov: 'I want to be there when everyone suddenly understands what it has all been for.'

I wanted that, and will go on wanting just that all through the wild years and the calm-down years. I too will always both thirst to believe, and be tempted to reject God's world. That contradiction will never be resolved.

It never occurred to me then that any words by an Australian writer would answer my desire to be there when everyone understood what it had all been for. From what I had heard from Scotty in the first half of 1935 I gathered that Australian historians wrote of the number of stadia, and how many parasangs explorers travelled in a day. Australian historians did not address the great issues of their time. It never occurred to me then that a man or a woman could advance in wisdom or understanding while writing a history of Australia.

I was a child of my time. I accepted the silly inference of those days that we Australians were paupers in things of the spirit, that we could invent a stump-jump plough, or a wheat harvester, but we would never write a *Brothers Karamazov* or a *Mayor of Casterbridge*. We lived in Australia, but our minds were elsewhere. We were exiles, isolated by thousands of miles from those centres where men and women explored the passions of the human heart. Our feet stood on foreign soil, not the soil out of which the sources of our wisdom had ever sprung – the 'ghastly' country of Palestine, the mountains, plains and seas of Greece, the eternal city of Rome, England's green and pleasant land, the glens of Scotland, the emerald isle of Ireland, America (where a human being had written the words about the rights of all human beings to life, liberty and the pursuit of happiness), France (the birthplace of that revolution of 1789 which had begun a new era for humanity), and Russia (where, bearing the Cross in Slavic dress, Christ had once wandered). But there were no legends that the sacred feet of Christ had ever trodden Australian soil, or that any of his disciples had planted the faith so far away. We were borrowers, parasites feeding on food produced abroad. I was young and foolish at the time. A time would come when I would discover the error of my ways.

But not then – not in 1935. Then I was reading L. H. Myers, *The Root and the Flower*, a debate at the court of one of the Mogul emperors of India, between the apologists for the Christians, the Muslims, the Hindus and the Buddhists. I was not even ready for the idea that there was wisdom in the East. Europe was my source of wisdom: Europe, not Australia, was my place of 'holy wonders'. Forty and fifty years later the bookshops in Australia will display many books on eastern wisdom, Australians will travel in the Zen country, in the lands of the Buddha. The young and those of riper years will read the *Kama*

Sutra, the news will spread amongst the sensitive souls searching for something more than a house, a car, a refrigerator, a word processor, a holiday on the Reef, or ten days in Bali, that the *I Ching* or the words of an Indian guru can give what no material possession, no sensual pleasure can give – namely, a quiet heart and a peaceful mind. But not then.

My eyes were always turned towards England, Ireland, Scotland and Europe. I did not realise then that what I was looking for could be found in Australia. My generation for a while believed the age of discovery belonged to the past, to the mighty men of renown in previous centuries, to Columbus, da Gama, Magellan, Tasman, Cook, and others. We regretted that there were no north-east or north-west passages to discover. We did not know our past: I did not know then that a knowledge of our own past would help to liberate us Australians from being spiritual exiles, and second-rate Europeans in a strange land.

Like most of my contemporaries I was then an Austral-Briton. For me then there was nothing odd in Arthur Streeton borrowing a line from Wordsworth's poem, 'The River Duddon', as the title for his painting of a stretch of the Nepean River – 'Still Glides the Stream'. There was nothing odd, nothing to be explained in the frequent use on Australian war memorials of the words 'Lest we forget' from Rudyard Kipling's poem 'The Recessional'. I assumed no words by an Australian could do justice to the high solemnity required.

In 1936 I was allowed to return to the university – not cured, because minor epilepsy does not go away. It has to be lived with. It was to be a lucky year for me. I attended lectures by Professor Kenneth Bailey on British constitutional and legal history. Kenneth Bailey was a fine flower of the Austral–British world. He was a liberal, a man who was reluctant to be decisive on any questions except those concerning solecisms in the use of the English language. They at least provoked him to mirth, if not to some wilder passion. He wore a gown and a mortarboard, taking the latter off his head just before the lecture, and placing it on the rostrum. I remember in one of the early lectures to us he threw back his head, laughed, and said, 'Oh, happy solecism, oh, dislogistic syllogism'. I remember also once asking Keith Aitken, a gentle spirit from Melbourne Grammar who made his name later as a judge of the High Court, whether he was going to a lunch-time lecture Bailey was to give in the Public Lecture Theatre on the League of Nations. Keith replied, 'Manning, I don't think it would be very profitable to spend an hour listening to Bailey saying, "Yes ... and No".'

There was more to Bailey than the liberal who scrupulously presented both sides of a question. I remember watching him dance with his wife at one of the university 'hops', as they were called, and being astonished by the ease and grace with which he moved over the floor, and the glow of life in his eye. Kenneth Bailey was a man of passion, a man concerned for his eternal salvation, a man who confounded bourgeois society with the good life. I remember once he told me there were dogs outside the eternal city. At the time I thought he meant Australian larrikins were the dogs – but, after the cold war and the Petrov Commission of 1954 I wonder whether for him the dogs outside the eternal city were the communists, the atheistic materialists, the self-professed enemies of God's world and the British Empire.

He always looked so worried, as though he were always sober and vigilant because his adversary, the devil of communism, was prowling around seeking to devour capitalist society. I suspect Kenneth Bailey also feared that if human beings did not believe in Christ's kingdom, then they would accept the proposition that everything was allowable and indulge in the favourite sport of goats and monkeys. He knew that in Australia civilisation did not rest on solid foundations. So he was never at ease: he was on guard all the time. When talking to you his eyes darted round the room searching for the enemies of civilisation. He was probably always anxious and worried because he knew he had dedicated his vast talents and his vast knowledge to the defence of a doomed society. He was yet another gifted scholarship boy who became an apologist for bourgeois society in Australia. Kenneth Bailey was a moral man defending an immoral society.

Kenneth Bailey belonged to the generation who had fought in the First World War. Perhaps that explained the expression in his eyes, of a sensitive, gentle spirit who had seen feral cats on the battlefields of Flanders and France licking blood out of human skulls. He always looked as though he wanted to cry out to us, 'The horror of it, the horror of it'. He was already being superseded by another generation of lecturers and professors at the University of Melbourne, who were too young to volunteer for the Australian Imperial Force, but old enough to know about the horrors and the abominations.

In 1936 I attended the lectures of a man who had something to say. He was W. MacMahon Ball, and the lectures were on modern political institutions, a course which covered Great Britain, Australia, France, Germany, Italy and the Soviet Union. Mac was not a 'dry as dust', 'yes and no', 'it's all as difficult as Hell' type of university lecturer. He was an actor in academic dress, decorating the confessions of a passionate heart with the apparatus of academic scholarship. He wanted to know the answers. He wore the expression of a puzzled man on his face. I could imagine him, when lecturing, pausing in full flight and asking us all: Will someone please tell me who I am? Scotty did not seem interested in whether we liked him or not. Ken Bailey wanted to turn our minds to higher things. But Mac Ball played for our approval, played for our applause. He was like a conjurer with a pocketful of coloured handkerchiefs which he displayed to the audience, one by one, to see which one they liked.

He had a commanding presence. His hair – silvery grey, with attractive waves – was backdrop to a noble brow. His eyes at times teemed with life, yet at other times they had a glazed look, as though they were shields against intruders. He had all the gifts and tricks of the showman. He paced up and down on the rostrum as though he were winding up some machine inside himself. Taking a stand, like a Napoleon of the antipodes, well to the left of the desk, he summarised for us in lively language the left-wing view of his topic for the hour. Then pacing up and down the rostrum again he came to rest at the right of the desk, from which he presented the conservative or right-wing view of the same topic. After some solemn pacings up and down, and side glances at all of us who were hungry for the denouement, and maybe with a hint that he despised himself for being such a spell-binder and despised us for succumbing to the spell he cast, he stopped in the dead centre of the rostrum, grasped the reading desk firmly with both hands and presented the W. MacMahon Ball view. This was always presented with the confidence of a man who knew all the answers. Yet, looking back now at this superb performance in the Mac Ball show I suspect that what attracted me to him was that deep down he was consumed by doubt about everything.

When Mac Ball stood in front of the blackboard with a piece of white chalk in his hand I believed that everything was about to be made plain. I remember to this day the lecture on the British Liberal Party's Yellow Book of 1928 in which the party presented the case for a mixed economy – a mixture of private and public ownership.

I remember also brilliant lectures on Marxism, on Leninism, and on the issues between Stalin and Trotsky.

I noticed that Mac Ball was never able to resist the temptation to score, to dominate and to shine, without working hard. Had he worked hard, had he marked out a field or a subject for himself and perfected himself in it, he would have shone in the honours classes, and in publication. He found the satisfactions he was looking for in giving public lectures. At that time he was a spell-binder. He found his satisfactions giving talks to weekend conferences organised by the University Extension Board, where again, with little or no preparation, a spell-binder could have the members of the audience looking at him with adoration and expectancy, as though he were about to reveal some great truth about the human situation, or teach them how to live. But he knew that he did not know the answers. So I suspect now that he was tempted to despise his listeners for their gullibility, and to despise himself for giving them expectations he could not fulfil.

I do not know when he feared it was all slipping away. I remember the faraway look in his eyes as he gazed out of the window during classes, as though there must be another life than the one in which he found himself engaged. Perhaps in time he was the victim of enjoying easy successes. Who knows? He was a very great teacher. But by 1944 his great days as a teacher were over. He started a new career in public life. Melbourne University lost one of its great teachers, just as in the 1950s and 1960s other universities lost teachers who were seduced, not by the bitch goddess of success or fame, but by the idea that it was more important to write a book than to teach a class. Mac Ball was one of the last of the great teachers in the humanities in the Australian universities. He belonged to the era of John Anderson in Sydney and Max Crawford in Melbourne. We were all lucky to hear him during the flowering time of his life. He was lovable, so warm in his reaching out to all of us that we forgave him his foibles. After all, love, we have been told on high authority, transcends all offences. In 1936, the year of his high tide as a teacher, I did not see him as a 'haughty man', or as a Humpty Dumpty who was sitting on a wall and would one day have a great fall.

I did wonder a little what would happen to a man who had charisma but not the patience to persevere. At that time I had not read La Fontaine's fable, 'La Cigale', about what happens to animals who do not work hard enough to build up a store to keep them through the winter. If I had it would probably have struck me as an irrelevant piece of puritan piety, a tract to provide spiritual refreshment to the life-deniers. Time will teach me the error of my ways in the days of my youth. Time will teach me what happens to a man with the gifts and the flaws of a MacMahon Ball. In 1936 I gazed at him with the admiration and the laughter of approval and delight. By 1956 when I began to write the first volume of *A History of Australia* I was looking back at him with the eye of pity – not knowing then that perhaps he could not tell anyone what had happened to him, or ask himself: why did this happen to me?

In the following year, 1937, I studied economic history under Herbert Burton, who was then a lecturer in the Faculty of Commerce. The subject was not my cup of tea, but lovable 'Joe' Burton was certainly my cup of tea. He was not judgemental: he was a man who seemed to be nursing some private sorrow about which he either could not or dared not speak to anyone. The pain was too deep to be healed by the standard bar-room confessionals for the secular humanists of Melbourne, or late at night at a would-be Bohemian extravaganza when the nonconformists could let off steam against the straiteners of the Melbourne suburbs. No, 'Joe', as he was known to his friends, had an inner dignity which did not allow him to seek any easy cure for that wound of his, of which none knew, when the doctor told him he and his wife Barbara would never be able to have children.

The dullness of content in his lectures was redeemed by his sincerity of manner. Besides, I had my fantasies to keep me going while Joe Burton wrestled with the question posed by F. W. Maitland in his lectures on English constitutional history: what is baronial tenure? Answer: the tenure enjoyed by him who is entitled to a seat in the House of Lords. Who is entitled to a seat in the House of Lords? Answer: he who holds his land by baronial tenure. Years later I read the remark by Henry James: 'There's always so much to say.' It seemed there was not much to say about baronial tenure – as indeed there never is about any subject in history from which human beings are missing. That was why economic history made no appeal to one side of me – the side searching for grace.

I could always enjoy my own fantasies. We were introduced by Joe Burton to the proposition: the rise of the middle classes began in the fourteenth century. I had my little daydream, my private question and joke. If the middle classes started to rise in the fourteenth century, how high are they now? Perhaps they are out of sight! Did that mean those life-deniers of Yarraside were on the rise?

There were always two sides of me. There was the observer, the one who stood always a pace or two apart watching the human scene, puzzled by what he saw, striving to impose an order on the chaos. That young man was still in a deep fog, still excited by every shaft of light which pierced the fog from time to time, only to be shattered again when the fog quenched the light, and the darkness returned. There was the other side of me, the young scholarship boy who had to get on, had to do well in exams because a poor performance would mean the loss of the scholarships which paid fees and board both at Trinity College and the University of Melbourne. That side of me had to survive in the jungle of life.

There also had to be a mask to hide the man within, to protect the seeker from the world. It was sometimes the mask of a buffoon, a young man who behaved like a clown, or, in the eyes of the harsher judges (especially women) like a show-off, a young man of many hungers with an insatiable desire to draw attention to himself. It was sometimes the mask of a young man who derived satisfaction from being witty at the expense of other people, a young man with an almost feminine eye for the weak spot in another person, especially a rival or a competitor, and a flair for composing the wounding words – and sometimes, be it confessed, a perverse pleasure in watching the squirms of the victims.

Now, I remember that person with shame and horror – because a time does come when, even if the mask must stay on, the methods used to defend the man within from a public scan, from scrutiny, do change. A time comes when it is no longer necessary to fight like a savage. That side of me, in search of the means of grace, in search of loving and being loved, was my eternal city. I live now with the guilt of past follies – of all the mad, wild deeds when I foolishly believed I would find 'precious metal in the dirt'.

That man within had to be shielded: no one must know about the man within; we were all solitaries living within our own skins: there could not be excursions in search of other people. No one must know of that other 'wound'. Who would ever suspect it of a clown and a coiner of witty, if cruel, phrases about other people, especially the pretentious, the pompous, the know-alls, the ones who claimed to know the answers? All ideologues were on my hit list, especially the wearers of the lawn sleeves. So were those who were concealing some truth about themselves from the world, those who were terrified they might be uncovered, the secrets of their hearts revealed.

Homosexuals, driven by the lore and the law in bourgeois Melbourne to practise a gigantic cover-up, sometimes dressed up in white tie and tails, a flower in the buttonhole, and escorted 'horsey' women to dances. They joked with each other about their designs on 'the whore of Melbourne town', and asked men of their persuasion, 'If I did, old boy, do you think I would be torn limb from limb?' They could be terrified by a hint that you knew, that you might drop a hint in the right places.

In that jungle we were all tempted to be betrayers and betrayed. We all entertained the mad hope of winning the approval of the men and women who awarded the prizes and the blanks in the great lottery of life, and earning membership of their tribe by acting as informers on those who had 'erred and strayed' from the ways of Melbourne. I despised myself for even entertaining such an idea, and then tormented myself for being tempted. I did say to myself that such a deed of darkness could be a justifiable revenge for what I had to endure because of my 'shadow': those with a 'primal fault' were entitled to get their own back. That side of me caused me later an infinity of anguish in the years when I had to face what I had done in the past. I could never forgive myself, never be forgiven by those I had mocked and wounded. But, thank God, I was not a betrayer.

I had to get on. Economic necessity alone was enough to make me a hard worker. The bitch goddess of success lured me on, as it has lured so many of the sons of the clergy. Fame was always a spur, at least for that side of me which believed the university, as a microcosm of society at large, was a jungle in which only the tough, the ruthless and those with luck came to the top. That side of me drove me to work hard in economic history. Besides there was always the chance that Marx was right, that he who understood the laws of history might also understand the laws of life. The means of production and distribution, I had learned from Marx, were the sub-structures of a society. They explained the structure, politics and government, and super-structure, ideas, ideologies and art. A knowledge of the sub-structure of society might illuminate the political and intellectual history of any period, might deepen my understanding.

So in the weekly honours class in economic history in the first half of 1937 I studied a section of P. Vinogradov, *The Growth of the Manor*, hoping to find a light at the end of the dark tunnel. Later in the year I studied each week a few chapters (I forget now how many) of J. H. Clapham's *The Economic History of Modern Britain*. It was not great fun: it was a hard slog each week. The class discussions were not very lively. Who could be excited by the early railway age in Britain; who could be excited by the history of canal transport? Clapham in economic history was like H. A. L. Fisher in European history or F. W. Maitland in constitutional history, without the grandeur of Maitland. Clapham was above the search for a pattern, or a meaning: he was content to tell his readers what happened. He was not interested in pattern-seekers, or warm-hearted young men and women combing over the past to find ammunition for their own political campaigns. I found it all very puzzling, but the deeper the puzzle, the more my examiners applauded.

At the end of the year, despite all the warnings that only those who had studied economics could expect to receive a first-class honour, to my surprise and to my satisfaction, that year the examiners placed me first in the final honours examination in economic history. I was pleased, but also felt a bit of a fraud. I remember being told later of a boy at Melbourne Grammar School who was so embarrassed at winning a divinity prize, he being an unbeliever, that he deliberately failed the divinity examination in the following year. That option was not open to me. I had to win scholarships to stay afloat in that stormiest of seas, the rivalry between the gifted and the triers. It was always possible to try so hard in the honours school of history and political science that you could be mistaken for a gifted person. You might even deceive yourself. Who knows?

Becoming a Melbourne Boy

One day in March 1937 in the old history classroom I knew a moment of exaltation. On that day I heard a man lecture in the Old Arts building who knew all about the tragic grandeur of human history, knew about the *Sternstunden der Menschheit* (starry moments in human history), knew of all the follies, all the passions, all the abominations of human beings, but still entertained a shy hope, Rabelais's *'grand peut-être'* (the great maybe). He was Max Crawford, the new Professor of History at the University of Melbourne.

Max Crawford told us on that memorable day that historians had mistakenly labelled the movement of people in Asia and Europe from the fourth to the tenth centuries as 'the barbarian invasions'. The better word would be *'Völkerwanderung'* (what a magic moment when he wrote that word on the blackboard!) or 'migration of the peoples'. He urged us to read the relevant pages in A. Toynbee, *A Study of History*, saying as an aside he found Toynbee most illuminating on such set subjects, even though he had reservations about the latter's theory of challenge and response as the key to human history. What a contrast to Scotty! Scotty had rubbished Toynbee as an historian who wrote a second book in his voluminous footnotes. Scotty had put the question to us: when the Romans delivered the Christians to the lions, where was the economic motive? *Exeunt* Arnold Toynbee and Karl Marx. Survivors: British institutions, the Melbourne Club and Yarra-side. By contrast, here was a teacher with a reverence for life.

After their lectures Scotty and Jessie Webb wound their gowns around themselves, collected their notes and swept out of the room, with the air of saying to us sinners the words the post-resurrection Christ had used to Mary Magdalene: 'Touch me not'. Maybe that was not their intention. But for me they were always the great 'Touch me nots', to whom I never dared to speak. But this new Professor of History, Max Crawford, stepped down from the rostrum, and asked me did I have a match, because he was dying for a smoke. I was so delighted that my fingers trembled and some matches spilled on the floor. He had a light in the eye: he wore on his face the expression of a man who knew much about melancholy. He said that if ever I wanted to sort out any puzzles I should just knock on his door, and, if he was free, he would be delighted to talk things over. Being friendly and democratic at Melbourne University in those days was as rare as a display of generosity and understanding by either side in the sectarian dog-fight.

A smaller number of students turned up for the honours lecture later in the week. That year the honours syllabus was the history of Spanish, Portuguese and French colonisation during the sixteenth and seventeenth centuries. Again there was the exhilaration of setting out on a voyage of discovery. We were urged to read W. H. Prescott's *The Conquest of Mexico and Peru*. Either then, or quite early in the course, Max Crawford recited from memory the words Charles V had spoken to Martin Luther at the conclusion of the Diet of Worms:

My predecessors the illustrious kings and emperors of the House of Habsburg have up to now been proud defenders of the Catholic Faith, defending and extending the same to the best of their ability. It is absurd that a single monk led astray by private judgement should set himself up against a body of doctrine which has been held as absolute truth for a thousand years and more and I will use all my vast dominions, and the wealth of the New World, to drive this damnable heresy off the face of the earth.

History was a drama. History was what Thomas Hardy said it was – a rattling good yarn in which the mighty men of renown were brought to ruin by some mole in their being, some fatal flaw wherein they were not guilty.

Max Crawford advised us all to look at how the artists of the Catholic Reformation had portrayed the scene. I did that immediately, and allowed my own imagination to expand on the magisterial words of Charles V. In the paintings I found the artists gave Charles the face of an apologist for an old order which was doomed to die. They gave him both the air of refinement, of being *comme il faut* (proper), and, at the same time, the air of a fop, a hint of decadence, that charm of the over-ripe. Charles addressed Luther in Latin, the language of the upper classes in both secular and ecclesiastical society. Luther replied in German, the German of the people. The painters gave Luther a coarse face and dressed him in an ill-fitting cassock. Luther emitted the air of a man of the people.

History was full of such confrontations, moments of illumination. Years later I saw in a book a photograph of the German general, von Paulus, confronting a Russian soldier on 31 January 1943, the day of the German surrender of Stalingrad. Once again an old order was confronting a new. The Russians labelled the photograph 'Konyets' (The End). Here was an officer of the German army, immaculately dressed, his face a history book of the German patrician class and the officer caste, the eyes wearing the puzzled look, and all the pain of belonging to an order which has had its day, an order which has just suffered a humiliating defeat. Here was a Russian soldier, his face a map of the great hope of November 1917 – that the Bolshevik revolution had begun a new era in the history of humanity.

Max Crawford strengthened my hunch that there was another kind of history than the one I had heard but not responded to in the classrooms of the University of Melbourne. Hungers are sometimes satisfied. Someone – I forget who – asked me whether I had read John Henry Newman's, *A History of My Religious Opinions*, sometimes entitled *Apologia Pro Vita Sua*. What insights some people have into what is going on behind the most carefully adjusted mask! Much of what Newman had to say made no appeal, like some of the malice directed against the Church of England. In another essay by Newman I read the sentence: 'The thought of a Church of England service makes me shiver.' Well, I was a shiverer at Church of England services, but not for the reason Newman probably had in mind. For him the Church of England was a travesty of Catholic truth: for me it was then a confidence trick to persuade the simple-minded that their God would let them suck their favourite lollypop through all eternity.

I knew there was the law: that repelled me. I knew there were the prophets. Newman was a prophet. He prophesied the future of Western society in the *Apologia*:

Liberalism [i.e. in religion] is too cold a principle to prevail with the multitude. Evangelical Religion or Puritanism ... had no intellectual basis; no internal idea, no principle of unity, no theology. Its adherents ... will melt away like the snow-drift. It has no straightforward view on any point, on which it professes to teach, and to hide its poverty, it has dressed itself out in a maze of words . . . It does not stand on entrenched ground, or make any pretence to a position; it does but occupy the space between contending powers, Catholic Truth and Rationalism. Then indeed will be the stern encounter, when two real and living principles, simple, entire and consistent, one in the Church, the other out of it, at length rush upon each other, contending not for names and words, or half-views, but for elementary notions and distinctive moral characters.

I cannot claim that on reading those words, I knew that this would be the subject for a history. Nor can I claim that on reading it an idea sprang up in my mind: that is a theme for a history of Australia. At that time it never occurred to me that Australia had a soul. I was one of many spiritual exiles who looked to London, Paris, Berlin, Rome, or Moscow as birthplaces of the things of the mind. The discovery of Australia came later.

Newman had reminded me of the questions I will never answer. Rome had kept alive the image of Christ. The Protestant churches, into one of which I was born and educated, have corrected Christ's work. The Protestant churches have been captured by the Pharisees. Church of England worshippers appear so confident of their virtues, so smug, have such a cocksure air that I wonder whether they believe the Resurrection morning will occur on the Melbourne Cricket Ground, where they will have reserved seats in the members' stand, sheltered from the heat of the sun if it happens in the summer and the icy winds from the Antarctic if it happens in the winter – yes, and the members' bar will be open in case there is any delay. But what if Rome is based on a lie: What if Christ did not rise from the dead? What if God did desert Christ on the Cross? What if even He, that most perfect being, could not overcome the sharpness of death and open the Kingdom of Heaven to all believers?

That left Man as god, Man becoming god-like, both as a creator, as a lover, as a dispenser of mercy, as a forgiver, and as a carer. For years I have wanted that to be true. As with belief in God, the desire to believe in Man is strong, but so are my doubts – doubts which persuaded me in dark moments that I understood why St John wrote of Christ: 'For he knew what was in man.' I heard the overture to *The Magic Flute* by Mozart; I heard the lovers in that opera sing of their hopes for human beings after their minds have been liberated from ignorance and superstition. I began then to yearn for that to be true – that men and women could, without help from a God, achieve for themselves what Christ once offered them, namely, have life and have it more abundantly. Years later I learnt that Mozart wrote his *Requiem Mass* in the same year as he wrote *The Magic Flute*, that the idea of the Madonna, the 'Agnus Dei', and the passionate need for someone to take pity on all of us for our great folly, lived in him side by side with the longing for the day when the great dream of the Enlightenment was fulfilled.

I read a work which was not one of the prescribed books in history subjects, nor on any of the reading lists our teachers handed out to us. That was *The French Revolution: A History* by Thomas Carlyle. I bought the Chapman and Hall three-volume edition of the work at a second-hand bookshop in Melbourne for three shillings and sixpence. I do not remember now why I bought the book, Carlyle being then one of the authors of the nineteenth century held in scorn and contempt by the self-appointed standards men of the Melbourne literary community. They dismissed Carlyle as a forerunner of the Fascists, a man who was all 'piss and wind', but no substance. Carlyle, the bar-room lefties were quick to tell me, was sexually impotent, ha, ha, ha! At an afternoon tea party at his house in Cheyne Walk, London, ha, ha, ha, the great man was denouncing the absurd suggestion that women should have the vote. There was no need to give them the vote: they already had it in the bedroom. His long-suffering wife Jane dropped the acidulous remark, 'He hasn't given me a ballot paper for twenty years' – ha, ha, ha! That floored him. Exit Carlyle.

Like marriage, Carlyle must not be taken lightly, but reverently. Yet, happily he does not ask the reader to forsake all other historians and cleave to him. He paints the picture of a society about to be shaken to its foundations: he portrays the character of the principal protagonists doomed to destruction, and how ill-equipped they all were to survive the tempest that engulfed them. He counsels the reader to view all the actors on the great stage of history with the eye of pity and a little love. He knows all the abominations committed by the old regime, and by the new: he has heard the 'shrieks of despair'. He has resisted the temptation to take sides, to interrupt from time to time with a 'Woe is me' or a 'Cursed be ye'. He has heeded what is for a historian Christ's most difficult command: 'Judge not'. He has heard the wild cries and the ragings of humanity, and watched them sail away into 'the Deep of Time'. The knowledge has given him great wisdom. He has risen above the struggle. He has eyed the human scene as Heraclitus had eyed it two thousand years earlier: 'To God all things are fair and good and right, but men hold some things wrong and some right.'

He has done the god-like deed with human history: Carlyle has imposed an order on the chaos of human history. Like the fox in the Greek fable he knew many things: and like the hedgehog in the same fable he knew 'one big thing'. 'One thing, therefore,' he wrote, 'history will do: pity them all; for it went hard with them all. Not even the seagreen incorruptible [Robespierre] but shall have some pity, some human love, though it takes an effort.'

I remember much from that first reading: his eye of pity for poor Marie Antoinette, dancing on in the Palace of Versailles, not knowing that within a few years her head would be in the basket. I remember the portraits of the proud, vain men such as Necker and Loménie de Brienne, vain enough to believe they had the answer to the problem no one could answer – the problem of the government's finances. But there was more to it than a bankrupt treasury. France was rushing towards a great explosion, during which 'poor mortals' would be 'swept and shovelled to and fro'. Necker suffers from a dullness so deep no one can fathom it. Voltaire comes to Paris to die. His presence rouses hope:

Is not this . . . our Patriarch Voltaire, after long years of absence, visiting Paris? With face shrivelled to nothing; with huge peruke à la Louis Quatorze, which leaves only two eyes visible, glittering like carbuncles . . . sneering Paris has suddenly grown reverent; devotional with Hero-worship. Nobles have disguised themselves as tavern-waiters to obtain sight of him: the loveliest of France would lay their hair beneath his feet.

Voltaire was their 'Prophet and Speaker'. But, Carlyle hints, Voltaire has nothing to say: the prophet and speaker is one of the 'dry souls' of the Enlightenment.

It never occurred to me at the time that a historian could do a Carlyle with the history of Australia, or do a Thucydides with our mighty men of renown: our William Charles Wentworth, our Alfred Deakin, our John Curtin, our Jimmy Scullin, our Robert Gordon Menzies or our Gough Whitlam. I lived in Australia: my spiritual life was centred in Europe: my wisdom, such as it was, came from the Bible, from Shakespeare, Hardy, Dostoevsky, Tolstoy, Melville, Prescott, Carlyle, from Thucydides, from Plutarch, but not from any Australian writer. Carlyle had uncovered the field of the possible in history; Carlyle had lifted my eyes from the Melbourne obsession with the 'lowdown', from Melbourne mockery, and taught me a man should write about things that matter.

An experience during 1936 helped me to understand why Emily Brontë had written that for a lover the universe could never 'turn to a mighty stranger'. I was in love. That began in the winter of 1936, when I noticed that every time I saw Dymphna Lodewyckx on a seat beside the north wall of the Old Arts building, I gulped. I wondered: What if I dared to speak to her – would the gulping stop, would the beauty of her face and body be consumed away by the trivia of acquaintance? What would happen if the voice, the sentiments expressed by that voice, did not match my vision of a woman who could be all in all to me?

I did speak – but it took me a long time to make the move. Like me, she often worked at night in the university library (which now houses the law school library). I knew she was the daughter of Associate Professor Augustin Lodewyckx, the head of the Department of German. I knew, too, she always came top of every examination for which she sat in Germanic and French languages. Life so far had taught me the truth of that remark in the Book of Ecclesiastes that there is one alone, there cannot be another. But I never wanted to believe that was true: there must be someone to whom it was possible to speak.

One night in June 1936, shaking from I knew not what, I did take the risk: I spoke to her by one of the book-stacks in the library. That, I believed, should stop the gulping. Vain hope, the gulping became more frequent. The talking began. By that book-stack at the University of Melbourne we began together the journey over the stormiest seas of all – the journey to discover the heart of another person. At the start she was not sure she wanted to go on board that boat, only to find she was out on the high seas before she had time to decide whether she wanted to launch out into the deep.

We talked about everything. It all tumbled out over a table in Tate's tea and coffee shop in a Collins Street basement. It all gushed out of me. Before I knew what I was doing I was telling her things the poet Robert Burns advised me not to 'tell to any'. I was telling her about my father and my mother, about my minor form of epilepsy, about my wanting to be a writer. I was telling her how excited I had been by reading Carlyle's *French Revolution* because he had shown history was humanity's greatest story, which could be told by creating scenes and portraying people, making them come alive. I told her that so far I had not found a subject; yes, and how Scotty had quite failed to know what interested me by forcing me to write my long final-year essay on that dreary subject, 'The Victorian Electoral System 1842–72'. What could a man do here in this desert of the human mind? She understood everything. She was like my mother: she knew, she said, that one day I would do it.

She introduced me to a new world. Her father, Associate Professor of Germanic Languages at Melbourne University, was the gifted son of a Flemish peasant; he was selected for the priesthood, lost his faith, and joined the Dutch Reformed Church. Being a Fleming and being the son of a peasant were the two barriers to getting on; he had added a third by renouncing the Catholic Church. He went to Ghent University, joined the Flemish nationalist movement, and was awarded a university medal for his studies in Germanic languages. His quarrel with the Church forced him to look outside Belgium for a teaching position. He became an exile, a worker in the colonial areas of Dutch language and culture. He taught at the University of Stellenbosch in South Africa, where again he was the victim of the puritans, this time the puritans of the Dutch Reformed Church. He married Anna Hansen at Cape Town on 24 January 1910.

With a characteristic display of his dedication to scholarship and learning he sent his bride to Flanders to learn Dutch and French, and gave her a copy of *Webster's Dictionary* as a birthday present. After Stellenbosch he worked in the Congo. In July 1914, while on leave in Belgium, he decided to travel by boat to America via the Cape of Good Hope, Australia and New Zealand, probably in search of a position teaching Germanic languages in an American university. By then he spoke eleven languages. His boat steamed into Port Phillip Bay on 4 August 1914, the day Germany invaded Belgium. He decided to stay. He took a position as language master at Melbourne Grammar School, and sent for his wife, who was busy brushing up her Norwegian with her father's relatives. She sailed from Bergen in 1915 with their son Axel on a voyage in which the first stop was Melbourne. She and her husband bought a house in Millswyn Street, South Yarra. There, on 18 December 1916, a daughter was born. Her parents christened her Hilma after her Swedish grandmother, and Dymphna after her other grandmother and the Flemish and Irish patron saint of lunatics. Once again there was a bond, I being named after Dr Manning, a gaol chaplain and guardian of the lunatics of Sydney, and she after the woman who had ministered to the lunatics of the Low Countries.

There was also a bond of which neither of us knew at the time. Our two fathers were victims of the walnut-hearted men preposterously claiming to represent Christ on Earth – my father of the life-deniers in the Church of England, and her father of the harsh elders of the Dutch Reformed Church in South Africa. All we knew at the time was that there were puzzles in the lives of both our fathers. We had been told, 'In my beginning is my end.' We both grew to feel in our bowels the meaning of the words by T. S. Eliot. We both lived in the shadow of the avengers and the punishers: there were ghosts in the past of both of us.

We both had something to teach each other. In Beatty Street, Mont Albert, where her family took up residence in 1921 her father and her mother built a 'little Europe'. A high cypress hedge became the frontier between their family and Australia. Her father planted European shrubs and trees: an oak, not a gum tree, was the focal point in the garden. They spoke to each other in Dutch. They celebrated Christmas on Christmas Eve: they did not feature a roast, or a fowl, or a turkey, or a goose. They started with Norwegian fish pudding (*fiske* pudding), and *sild salat*, and moved on to meats cooked in the Flemish or Scandinavian way, to sweets of *blaue Beeren* (blueberries) and creamy rice – very different from the milky rice our maid Marge used to cook with such love and care. The Christmas tree in the sitting-room was decorated with a crib carved in Stockholm, and Swedish and Belgian flags. Before the distribution of the presents Hilde Streich, an immigrant from Stuttgart, played 'Stille Nacht, Heilige Nacht' (Silent Night, Holy Night) on the piano. I enjoyed the food and the drink, especially the drink, but remained an outsider.

Something held me back. I did not want to be an honorary citizen of Europe in Australia. I could not be a European. I was an Australian. I could not be part of this *'Eten klaar!'*, *'Wel te rusten!'* (Dinner's ready! Sleep well!) world. That was alien to me. I was an Australian. I did not want to assume another identity, or pretend to be what I was not. I knew only one language: in Australia I did not want to use any other language than Australian English in which to say things to other people. For me to use any other language, any other words, would be false, a betrayal of what I was. So I stood apart, an uneasy observer, resisting, maybe quite irrationally, this offer, this temptation to become something different.

For me there was more to it than the phobias of old Australian families. It was one of those moments when a man discovers who he is, and where he belongs. Around the Lodewyckx dining-table, in the sitting-room, and under the shade of the European trees in the garden, there was much talk of the follies of the British. That did not upset me; that did not precipitate a rush of blood to the head, or provoke lip trembling when I was granted a limited right of reply – a right I never exercised. There were lengthy lectures on the follies and stupidities of Australians. I remember one example – or what Barry Humphries calls 'a case in point'. Professor Lodewyckx scorned the Australian obsession with sport. To illustrate this he told a story of how in 1930 he was having lunch with some colleagues in the staff dining-room in the University Union. It was the winter of the record scores by Don Bradman in the test matches in England.

I tried to interest them in the economic problems confronting Australia – the fall in prices for their primary products, the growth of unemployment, the number of beggars in the streets ... but no, these professors do not want to discuss such things: they only want to talk about Don Bradman. So, I say to them, 'Will someone tell me, please who is this Don Bradman?' They were silent. I know I should not make myself unpopular in this way but ...

And away he went on a mini-lecture on the indifference of Australians to things of the mind.

Sometimes he paused, and put this direct question to me: 'But you are an Australian. Tell us what you think. I would be interested to know.' I remained silent – not out of rudeness, or boorishness, but, I suspect now, for a deeper reason. At that time (1937–38) I lacked the intellectual culture with which to give substance to my sense of being an Australian. My brain was full of the literature and history of the ancient world, of Russia, France, Germany, England, Scotland and Ireland (but only smatterings from America at that time). My heart was full of *Hymns Ancient and Modern*, of the 'hits' from the musical comedies such as 'Can't Help Lovin' Dat Man o' Mine'. In moments of resignation, and acceptance (there were not very many of those at that time!) the words and music of 'Abide with me' or 'Sun of my soul, Thou saviour dear', or 'Jesu, lover of my soul' would well up inside me, just as certain to moisten the eye as many pots of beer in those days when Dymphna and I discovered each other. Dymphna set me an example I admired but could not follow. She forgave those who trespassed against her.

I had no alternative to her father's 'Europe in Australia'. At that time Europe in Australia was not a dead tree: it was a tree kept alive by feeding off the giants in the forests of European culture. I knew little of what Henry Lawson labelled 'the Young Tree Green' of Australian culture. At that time I had not read a line of poetry or prose by Henry Lawson. Culture was 'over there'. We were the wild cherry trees in the bush – parasites. But why accept a life sentence of mediocrity; why be a second-rate European in Australia? Why not be an Australian? Dymphna's father was a fine representative of the Old World. Yet I did not want to be merged in that world. I had to find out who we Australians were – I did not realise that at the time. My eyes were already cast 'over there' – though paradoxically, one side of me was jibbing at the idea, saying this is not it, this is not it at all. But at the time I knew of no other possibility. There was only the dimmest intimation that this Europe in Australia was not for me.

Yet Dymphna's world was a source of constant delight and wonder. I read poetry – English love poetry, it never occurring to me at that time that Australian writers might have written about love in Australia. Australians, I believed then, did not go in for that sort of thing. I read Sir John Suckling's 'The Constant Lover':

> *Time shall moult away his wings*
> *Ere he shall discover*
> *In the whole wide world again*
> *Such a constant lover.*

I pondered over the words of Edmund Waller:

> *Go, lovely Rose –*
> *Tell her that wastes her time and me,*
> *That now she knows,*
> *When I resemble her to thee,*
> *How sweet and fair she seems.*

That could not be true of my Dymphna. She would never know such a cruel fate:

> *How small a part of time they share*
> *That are so wondrous sweet and fair!*

That could never happen to my Dymphna. How could such a 'fancy' ever pass away? How could I ever be 'quite myself again'? She worked the great marvel: for the first time since childhood I often had very tender and gentle feelings towards everyone. As ever in life I found an experience to match my mood. The Australian Broadcasting Commission had begun a series of celebrity concerts. In 1936, the year in which I took the risk of speaking to Dymphna, Elisabeth Rethberg and Ezio Pinza were billed to sing in the Melbourne Town Hall. The self-appointed judges of distinction in the Melbourne musical world put Rethberg in the first class. They were in raptures of anticipation, but were not able to explain to an outsider like myself: 'Ah, Rethberg', the women sighed, closing their eyes as though they were experiencing some ecstasy known only to initiates, 'she's not of this world'. But this Pinza, they had never heard of him.

I bought a ticket, took' my seat not far from the stage in the Melbourne Town Hall and waited for Rethberg to walk on to the platform. There was an epiphany that night, but Rethberg was not its medium. When Pinza walked on to the stage, he looked more like a buffoon than a concert artist. He wore a huge black cravat, a butterfly collar so grotesquely large that the stud could not press on his voice box, a loose-fitting dress-suit, and shoes so highly polished they could be used as mirrors. He could not stand still: he took his handkerchief out of his pocket and polished the top of the grand piano. What's this, what's this, I thought, a clown pretending to be a singer?

Suddenly he bowed deeply to Raymond Lambert, an exaggerated bow, because everything about the man was an extravaganza, he seeming to be an overtreater of everything. Lambert played a chord on the piano (I learnt later he always played a chord because he never knew and Pinza never knew where he, Pinza, would start). Pinza was transformed, as the music changed the buffoon into the artist. He began to sing. I, who a moment earlier had had difficulty restraining my giggles, was lifted from mockery to worship. He sang of love. Like all great artists he made plain to me what was going on in my own heart. His voice, his gestures (he was by no means niggardly with those either), made clear what was happening to me, why the world of human beings, previously almost always a 'vaudeville of devils', a world of hostile faces uttering words I wished I had never heard, had become a place of many delights, of wonders which stretched for miles and miles.

There was another magical moment. After the interval Pinza and

Rethberg sang the duet from *The Magic Flute* about '*Mann und Weib*' (man and woman). Dymphna had drawn my attention to the last words in Goethe's *Faust*, spoken by the *chorus mystieus*:

> *Das Ewig Weibliche*
> *Zieht uns hinan.*
> (The eternally feminine
> Draws us upward)

Well, yes, that was one way of putting it. But here was Mozart's music suggesting something I had always looked for, but never previously known. A man was not doomed to wander alone over the face of the earth. By becoming one flesh a man and a woman become whole, the two of them know grace, they know a peace which passes understanding.

There were other concerts by other performers, all reminding me of the great miracle which had been worked inside me. I heard Lotte Lehmann sing 'An die Musik'. Now I knew why Schubert wanted to offer thanks, to cry out with joy, '*Ich danke Dir*' (I thank you), because I, too, wanted to thank someone, but lacked the words and the music. I had never written a line of poetry or a bar of music in my life. So what was welling up inside me would one day come out in prose, be splashed on the page in one long, never-ending confession about life.

I heard Hubermann play Beethoven's *Violin Concerto*, and felt the chill when those five taps of doom were struck on the drum, and the violin soared, as I was soaring then, but the drums of doom would not be silenced. Why should a man who has begun a walk in the paradise gardens heed the drums of doom? Love liberated me from dependence on the last quartets of Beethoven and the slow movement in his '*Archduke*' *Trio*. I turned to Mozart's *Magic Flute*, to Bach's *Brandenburg Concertos*, to the music for those who have known and given the glory, and a rejoicing in being free at last from the need of some crutch, some consolation prize for the defeated.

The whole world became one never-ending delight. There were visits by Ian Fitchett to the room in Trinity College I shared with Ian Mackinnon. Late at night, after he had drunk quite enough to see the world as the world is not, he often dropped in for a chat. It was not an exchange. He talked and we listened. He was a colonial version of Dr Johnson, who, alas, so far had never found a local Boswell. He

41

loved blasphemy – the blasphemy of a man who inwardly wanted his faith back. His father, the son of W. H. Fitchett of *Deeds that Won the Empire*, and first principal of the Methodist Ladies' College in Melbourne, was a Methodist; his mother was a Catholic. Fitchett had a thirst to believe – and hence our understanding. But in his years in the kingdom of nothingness he did not suffer gladly fools, or the pompous, fraudulent, and pretentious. He demolished quick-smart any pretenders to a social standing to which they were not entitled by birth. Melbourne horse-breeders were not the only ones to keep stud books.

I remember his greeting the night he entered our room and was introduced to an unlikely-to-marry Anglo-Catholic theological student. Fitchett loathed those who flirted with but did not have the guts to break with the Anglican respectability-mongers of Melbourne: 'Ah', he said, 'an Anglican Borgia.'

I remember also a scene in the Trinity junior common-room on the morning the women's page of the Melbourne *Argus* announced that a well-known daughter of a country gentleman had married the son of a farmer. In those years the self-appointed judges of 'good breeding' in Yarraside would never dream of allowing the name of a man or a woman from the trading or the working classes to be written in their stud book. Waiting till there was silence in the room – his timing always being superb – Fitchett lowered the *Argus* and thundered, '——'s married the greatest outsider since Murray King won the Sydney Cup at two hundred to one.'

There were at least three voices inside Fitchett. One was the Catholic who had lost his faith, and did not want anyone to know the pain he suffered from that loss; another was the Western District country gentleman, who had, by birth, an entrance ticket to the drawing-rooms of South Yarra and Toorak, the man also with the eye for those who were there under false pretences. He had an encyclopaedic knowledge of the 'best' families. Yet another was the shy, almost muted voice of a man who knew his mother's family, the Irish Catholics, the licensees of pubs, had kept alive something the members of the Protestant Ascendancy most obviously lacked – the image of Christ, and the purity of the worship of the holy mother of God.

There was also the conversation of Tampion Daglish, a law student, and a graduate in the honours school of history. He was widely read in those parts of history which did not endear him to his examiners in the History Department, but which were a constant delight to his listeners at a Trinity supper party, especially if tongues had been loosened by a few beers at Johnny Naughton's, and a gin and tonic just before six o'clock closing to keep the glow alive till bed-time. Tampion had the most entertaining explanations for some events in British history. Our teachers told us William of Normandy won the Battle of Hastings because he had the better archers, and because one of the arrows of those more skilful archers had pierced the eye of Harold Hardrada, and so put the leader of the Saxons out of action. Not so, said Tampion. Harold Hardrada dallied with Edgar the Aetheling in London, enjoying himself so hugely that he arrived too late at Hastings to expel the Normans. Tampion was also witty about the low-church theological students in Trinity:

I cannot understand why the parents of —— should have had children. Tell me, because you, beautiful boy, you understand so much about the human heart, why did his father not say to his wife, 'Let us forbear, my dear, and put a silk handkerchief over it'.

Much laughter in our room, while Tampion slowly lowered his tumbler of beer. But as the 'beautiful boy' did not reply, Tampion went on, as we all knew he would expect us to give him the floor, and said in his high-pitched, girlish voice, 'But perhaps his father and mother were carried away by the poetry of motion.' Much laughter, as my room-mate, Ian Mackinnon, complimented Tampion on being in such good form.

Tampion had his terrors, though he was much more discreet than Ross Wilson. He was lucky. The 'hearties' of Trinity found him lovable and amusing, a court jester who could liven up a supper party. Tampion was worried about trivial things. He feared he could never be a *comme il faut* Trinity man. His father had been in trade: he had been to Ivanhoe Grammar School and not to Melbourne or Geelong Grammar. He was short – standing not much higher than five feet. His voice was not manly: he played no sport. But these were the worries to which he owned up to cover up a much deeper fear. I remember years later he told me he had enjoyed his time in the army because his working-class camp-mates did not make him feel peculiar because he took no interest in women. They called him 'Butch', and joked with him: 'Eh, Butch, how about lending me that piece of equipment dangling between your legs for the night? You don't seem to have much use for it.'

Later he also told me he decided during the war to ask a priest to receive him into the Catholic Church:

I know the priests are not gentlemen: I know the priests will be after my money [Tampion was rich, even if he was not *comme il faut* in other ways], but, my dear Manning, they do understand what I am, and they do not condemn me.

Tampion was never reckless, never seduced by alcohol into dropping his defences. He survived unscathed. He was the brilliant jester to the men and women of Melbourne whose spiritual ancestors had drafted the laws which taught him early in his adult life to place a very special meaning on the words: 'the price of liberty is eternal vigilance'. Tampion always remembered the words of the Prayer Book: 'Brethren, be sober, be vigilant'. His adversary was not the Devil, but that numerous tribe of the 'normal' in Melbourne.

I had already received many lessons in tribal loyalty. There had been the initiations at Melbourne Grammar. I had heard times without number that sentence of exclusion: 'He's not one of us.' Early in 1937 I had a refresher course in tribal loyalty. On 23 March I attended the debate on the Spanish Civil War in the public lecture theatre at the university. The subject of the debate was 'That the Spanish government is the ruin of Spain.' Speakers for the affirmative were S. J. Ingwersen, B. A. Santamaria and K. T. Kelly, and for the negative Nettie Palmer (as a measure of the mores of the times we referred to her as Mrs Vance Palmer), Dr G. P. O'Day and J. W. Legge. I entered the lecture theatre in a mood of elation. Max Crawford was still delighting me with his lectures; the wonders of Dymphna increased every day. There could not be much wrong with the world.

To my surprise I entered a room occupied by two howling mobs – one for and one against the Spanish government. It was like being in the outer at a game between Carlton and Collingwood. Well before the debate began the public lecture theatre was so tightly packed that the only way to get in was to be lifted over the heads of those standing near the two lower floor entrances. Before the chairman and the speakers entered the theatre the exchanges between the barrackers for Catholic Christendom and the barrackers for, yes, for what? socialism? communism? secular humanism? dialectical materialism? were lost in the uproar. Some students ran over the roof to add to the hubbub and noise in the theatre.

The entry of the chairman and the speakers incited the rowdies to wilder displays of approval or disapproval. The chairman, C. A. Scutt, the Professor of Classics, called for order. A liberal this Scutt, a man who had seen the horrors of the Balkan wars, and the even greater horrors of the Somme and Passchendaele, a cricketer, an Englishman who believed in decency and fair play. But his appeals fell on deaf ears. When he asked the opening speaker for the affirmative, Bobby Santamaria, to begin the debate, there were chants of approval from one side, boos and hisses from the other.

Bobby spoke in that voice which from that day to the present has always suggested to me the man within was about to reveal some higher truth. His information that night, as ever after, was voluminous, the argument as tidy as a theorem in geometry, but it was the quantity of felt life which attracted me. One passage in his speech lived on in my mind: 'When the bullets of the atheists struck the statue of Christ outside the cathedral in Madrid, for some that was just lead striking brass, but for me those bullets were piercing the heart of Christ my King.' Wild shouts of approval from his supporters, hurrahs, stamping of feet, much whistling. Angry cries from his opponents, some calling on him to keep it clean, or speak to the motion. Calling for order, Scutt asked both sides to give each other a fair go. Nettie Palmer, speaking for the negative, presented the case for cool reason, asking those present to face the facts: this is a class war, a war between the haves and the have-nots. Stan Ingwersen and Kevin Kelly will have none of that wishy-washy liberal soft-soap: General Franco is fighting for Christian civilisation against the barbarians of the east. Jack Legge and Dr O'Day spoke as sons of the Enlightenment.

I was bewildered – and staggered to find how fickle was my heart. One moment I was carried away by Bobby Santamaria's world: a moment later I was carried away by the Nettie Palmer world in which ignorance, superstition, poverty and domination were to be no more. From that night to the present day I will never be able to decide which side I am on – the side of Catholic Truth, or the side of the Enlightenment. I will go on wanting the Marxists to discover the image of Christ, and the Catholics to see the need to destroy our corrupt society, that being the essential condition for us all if we are to have life and have it more abundantly.

A family crisis taught me another lesson. In the second half of 1937 an infantile paralysis epidemic broke out in Melbourne. Of the many children stricken by the infection most survived. The adults were not so fortunate. Late in October my mother told me my sister Hope, then a nurse at the Children's Hospital in Carlton, had caught infantile paralysis. Within a few days complications set in, and my sister's face swelled to the size of a soccer ball. The doctors were at a loss, having neither a medical nor a surgical answer to the problem. The doctors talked of death, and confessed they were powerless to stop the swelling. My sister would die. My father and my brother Russell were convulsed with grief. They were like most human beings when confronted with such a situation: they did not believe it should happen to them, death at twenty-one mocking their idea of the fitness of things. What had they done that they should suffer in this way? They wanted to be rescued: someone should help them; otherwise it was all unfair. I said not a word, believing that we were all in the presence of something which we did not understand.

My mother did not give way to despair or to any railing against the mysterious powers in charge of the universe. She had her faith. In all the crises of her life she always asked the Father, believing that if she was worthy He would answer her prayer. This time she did not say aloud, 'I wonder what I have done in my life for God to punish me in this way.' In the room in which my sister lay, her face so swollen that she was no longer recognisable even by those who had known her for all her twenty-one years, with my father and my brother crying, overwhelmed by their sense of the disaster and the loss to come, my mother did not give way to such despair. My mother said, 'I am going to pray. I am going to ask the Father.' She knelt down by the bed- side. She did not pray aloud. When she rose again her face was transfigured: God, she told us, would answer her prayer.

My sister survived. My brother said to her, 'Good on you, Hopie, I always knew you would be all right.' My father was soon quite himself again, laughing and joking with everyone. He will go on laughing and joking, and telling people 'at least we can all have a good laugh'. My brother will inherit my father's gift for telling jokes. He will inherit too the strong pastoral tradition in my mother's family. He will become a jovial, almost Friar Tuck vicar in the Melbourne diocese. He will become a 'carer'. My sister will have another strength – the strength to survive. Nature has been kind to her by planting in her a loving heart. Her terrible suffering strengthened her compassion. She will be much loved.

My mother never recovered from the ordeal which she had endured with such dignity, courage and faith. It was as though she had poured out her spirit to God as a sacrifice for my sister's recovery. I was puzzled why this should happen to her. One side of me looked on putting faith in prayer as being as bizarre as Bobby Santamaria's talk about 'Christ my King'. The man within who wanted to get on in the world thought of this terrible illness of my sister as a misfortune – not the sort of thing to prepare a man to face Laurie Nash at the South Melbourne Cricket Ground on the following Saturday, or, more seriously, to prepare for the final examination in history in November. All-night vigils in a sick room were not the ideal preparation for what I was after – a result in the final honours examination which would at least give me a chance of a travelling scholarship.

There was another man within who learned much from the experience. The believer had strength: the believer never gave way to despair: the believer never broke down. So I was encouraged by my mother's example, I was strengthened for the ordeals to come. I was helped to face Laurie Nash without flinching. I found the strength to sit for the final examinations in history. My world went well. The results in the examinations qualified me for a travelling scholarship. But I was never able to tell my mother what her example meant to me.

The year had taught me chiefly two things – one was about love, and the other about belief. Those lessons will live on. So, alas, will my regret that my mother and I never spoke to each other about what mattered most. I still do not know whether she ever realised the depth of my debt. She would be shocked to know that in time I would break forever with the Church of England, partly because they could not satisfy the 'femina' in me – the hunger for a mother as well as a father. She, who looked to the Father alone, taught me by her example that day that a man must also look to a woman. Why then, did we not speak?

An Australian
in the Land of Holy Wonders

The year 1938 was, in some ways, like Charles Dickens's description of 1789: it was the best of times, it was the worst of times. It was the best of times because the University of Melbourne awarded Dymphna and me free first-class return passages to Europe by the Orient Line shipping company. Our life together would start on a journey. There was the hope that the blinkers fastened over the eyes by the conformist world of Melbourne would fall off. The tyranny of opinion, the oppressiveness of living in a society in which life-deniers were in charge, all the dead weight of a colonial and provincial past and present would be lifted from the minds of both of us. We would escape from dullness into an exciting world. Culture, I believed at the time, was over *there*, not *here*. Over *there* they knew something we did not know here. I believed I was about to receive something I could never receive in Australia. As a clergyman's son I knew the words of grace before meat: 'For what we are about to receive may the Lord make us truly thankful.' I was about to take a seat at the banquet of life. I was ready to be thankful to someone, even to the English, for the great benefits I was about to receive at their hands.

It was also the worst of times. Europe was moving rapidly towards war. The Jeremiahs of the Left in Melbourne, the self-appointed prophets of doom, plastered their slogan of the year on the walls of Melbourne University: 'Fascism means War'. Short-wave Moscow radio began its news service to the south-west Pacific with the words: 'The crisis of capitalism deepens every day.' The *Guardian* in Melbourne lectured its readers on the plot of the capitalists to plunge Europe into another war, on how the gnomes of the financial world were scheming for a war of annihilation against the Soviet Union. Why travel to a future battlefield? In March 1938 Hitler achieved one

it, or rather gave me the confidence in my own powers to open that door and then walk with another sort of confidence in that mansion of many rooms. Chis also had a heart. Chis spoke like an Australian. But the eyes of Chis were turned towards Europe. Chis recited a line by Mallarmé:

> La mer est triste, hélas,
> Et j'ai lu tous les livres.
> (The sea is sad, alas,
>   And I have read all the books.)

I understood the first line, thanks to those days at the Pyramid Rock, Phillip Island, when I looked for a sign in that ever-restless, ever-complaining sea, but found, alas, that for me there was to be no such sign. I was going to Europe: there I could read *tous les livres* – all the books. And thanks to Chis I would be able to read the French: maybe, with Dymphna's teaching, her love, her care, I would be able to read *Bücher in der deutschen Sprache*. I was going to Germany – the eternal Germany, the Germany of Bach, Mozart, Goethe, Heine and Schiller. Dymphna told me that lived on, despite the thugs and angry men who had seized power.

In March 1938 Max Crawford, the teacher to whom I already owed so much, invited me to attend his honours class on the French Revolution. Lively arguments broke out about the causes of the uprising. A minority, mainly gifted Catholic students, attributed the Revolution to the ideas of the *philosophes* – to Voltaire, Rousseau, Diderot, d'Alembert and others. They saw them as evil men. As they talked I recited to myself the words of Carlyle that these men were dry souls, men without any visions. But I did not dare to say that out aloud. An orthodoxy now reigned in the Melbourne history school: evil conditions made men and women evil; good conditions would make them good. Marx had written the liturgy for secular humanists. It begins, 'All history is a history of class struggles.'

Historians must study class struggles: historians must study the substructure of a society, because that was the key to the political and cultural life of every period in human history. The French Revolution was a class revolution, the revolution of the middle classes and the wealthy peasants against the feudal aristocracy, the monarchy and the hierarchy in the Church. Religion was a comforter for human beings living in misery, degradation and oppression. Enlightenment would end all superstition and ignorance. All men and women could perceive the truth: all men and women would follow that truth. Anyone who opposed these self-evident truths must be either mentally or morally defective. There was a virtue of the historian: there was political virtue: there was personal virtue. All men of good will had virtue. This was the new commandment of Melbourne: 'Get virtue'; find virtue in human history; find it in how men and women produced wealth; do not snoop around the human heart in search of virtue; find virtue, wisdom and understanding in discovering the laws of human society. All virtuous people saw the same truths in history. The second Melbourne commandment was 'Be correct', for being correct is a measure of a man's virtue.

The orthodoxy was only beginning in 1938. I had the impression that Max Crawford was already ill at ease with some of the behaviour of his disciples. He himself was a disciple of Arnold Wood, former Professor of History at the University of Sydney. Max Crawford, I suspect, believed a man's virtue did not depend on his material environment. A man was not born with virtue: he acquired virtue, by his intelligence and his soul. Max Crawford let slip remarks about another journey which the guardians of the new orthodoxy dismissed as chimerical. I remember once he told us in class a story of how Thomas Hardy had once seen a beautiful woman sitting disconsolate in the tray of a dray. Hardy asked himself: the American declaration of independence of 4 July 1776 offered to all men the right to pursue happiness, why then did this woman, living over one hundred years after that delaration, look so desperately unhappy? I suspected Max Crawford never accepted the simplistic view that evil conditions were the cause of unhappiness. He was like a man driving a team of horses who found to his dismay that one horse after another was breaking from a trot into a canter.

There was another man in the class of 1938 who was ill at ease with the new Melbourne orthodoxy, but fearful lest by opposing it he be pushed off the ladder on which he was fast climbing to the top. He was Zelman Cowen. To characterise him as a man for whom fame was the only spur would be a travesty. He had a Grecian nose, an olive skin, and the eyes of a man who was magnificently alive, and yet fearful lest words be said which reminded him he did not belong to the Yarraside version of the Protestant ascendancy. He was an outsider who by charm, sheer ability and hard work was destined to be a distinguished and loyal servant of Yarraside. He struck me then as a man who was as hungry for sympathy and understanding as he was for success.

I still think of him in that way. I remember the beautiful smile spreading over his face, and the eyes which usually darted all over the place like small fish startled in a rock pool, coming to rest for a moment when I told him his name was probably derived from a Hebrew word meaning a man of God. He told me he was an uncomfortable agnostic. He gripped me warmly by the elbow and told me it was most perceptive of me to detect that side of him. I did not need to tell him that when we talk about other people we often talk about ourselves. He knew that. That exchange forged a bond between us which not even later developments could shatter. Behind the robes of high office, behind all the pomp and ceremony, all the attraction of climbing to the top, there was the man with wondrous eyes pleading to all of us, 'Please tell me what it is all about'. There was the man who feared that unless he went on talking, someone might say wounding words.

Fear of hearing such words cannot be the only cause of a man or a woman becoming a non-stop talker, because, if it were, then in the Melbourne I knew in 1938 there would have been a plague of non-stop talkers. I remember it was fatal to drop a word such as 'immigration' into a conversation with Zelman if your last tram was to leave in ten minutes, because immigration or any such word usually triggered off a thirty- or forty-minute lecture – full of learning, full of wit, and full, shyly, of the wisdom of his people, but, alas, non-interruptible. Not to listen would have hurt him as much as the words of abuse. So I always hoped one of the many women who adored him would not flutter her eyelids and put a question: 'Zelman, what is democracy?' or 'Zelman, what is Fascism?' They were both at least one-hour jobs.

He was not always able to hold his tongue, or curb his exuberance. Once, at five minutes to one, after fifty minutes of a Crawford–Cowen duet (both of them were inclined to turn the class into a duet for unaccompanied teacher and student) – when our stomachs wanted food, but certainly not any more of this food-for-thought act with which we were being entertained – Zelman, after a characteristic nervous laugh, said, 'Well, with all due respect, don't you think that is rather a silly question for a professor to put to a class?' Max Crawford was not amused. He delivered a thirty-minute *apologia pro vita sua*, telling us his teachers were the humanists of the Renaissance, John

Bunyan, John Milton and John Stuart Mill, while our stomachs singularly failed to persuade him to stop, and our minds were visited by the dark thought, 'What if Zelman insists on a right of reply?' Happily that did not happen. Zelman knew who his future judges were. Pleasing them, winning their approval, was more important than winning an argument. But I doubt whether either of the two verbal gladiators was ever at ease with the other again.

Zelman was always magnificently alive. I remember a scene in a Toorak drawing-room on one of those occasions when young men wore dinner-suits, white shirts and butterfly collars, black ties, black silk socks held in place with suspenders, and dancing pumps. Zelman spilt cream all over the lapel of his dinner-jacket. Lesser men might have left the room in embarrassment or even shame. Not so Zelman. He converted a mistake into a triumph – at least into moments of high comedy, until one of the sharp-tongued matrons of Toorak asked in a stage whisper, 'Who is this clown in our midst?' A shadow fell across Zelman's face, though not for long, because within a few seconds he was telling us all that the cream and the dinner-jacket were a perfect study in contrasts, and on he went to lecture us all on the clash of opposites in human history, of the *yin* and the *yang*, citing himself as a living example of Toynbee's theory of challenge and response. His adorers (and they were always numerous) intoned a chorus of 'Brilliant, Zelman, brilliant', while others objected, 'Don't encourage him, or he'll go on all night.'

So I knew that behind the Zelman who came to the top there was a warm-hearted man, a man with a tempest in his blood, a man with the eye of pity, a man who, despite the public professions of certainties would go on seeking, as I would go on seeking to find out what it is all about.

During those first two terms of 1938 Max Crawford opened my eyes to the wonders of the French Revolution. In one class I remember he told us about E. Condorcet who, during all that uproar, sat down and wrote his *Esquisse sur l'histoire de l'esprit humain*. In the middle of a brilliant summary of that work Max Crawford paused, and said, 'That might be a good research topic for you when you go to Balliol College in October.' It was like 'Lofty' Franklin's advice to read Dostoevsky. Crawford was right about one side of me, the side which was attracted to the idea that one day all men would be brothers. But there was another side of me which was sceptical of all writers, preachers, teachers and publicists, who painted pictures of future harmony.

I had begun to read Alexis de Tocqueville's work, *L'Ancien Régime et la Révolution*, which persuaded me to dip into his other works. The asides of Tocqueville attracted me. I remember one: 'The field of the possible is much more vast than those who live in a particular era generally conceive.' But there was more to him than these asides. He was a historian in the grand tradition. He did not write of causes: he gave no explanations: he did not badger the reader, he never said the equivalent of 'Think of that!' He had no signposts, no scaffolding, no memos for his readers. Like Carlyle he told the story so that the reader had moments of illumination, moments when he said to himself: ah, so that's why there was a revolution in Paris in July 1789; that's why there was a Tennis Court Oath; why there was a civil constitution for the clergy; that's why there was a Terror.

In the hands of a great artist all the pieces in the jigsaw puzzle of history fall into place. The question was: Could a future-of-humanity man tell a story with an eye of pity for all human beings? Could a future-of-humanity man write a story in which the narrator knew that what human beings wanted they would never get? Future-of-humanity men believed good would win the victory against evil. Future-of-humanity historians wrote an epic. I was moving towards a tragic view of the human situation. I wanted to sing a hymn of praise in a minor key and was already ill at ease with those who wanted to write about the past like a theorem in geometry. Can a man with nothing to say write a story?

Perhaps exile from the narrow conformist world of Melbourne might give me something to say. Thucydides had taught me of that society in Athens on the eve of the Peloponnesian War where men did not put on black looks with their neighbours when they behaved in a manner which was displeasing to them. Dostoevsky had taught me that in Russia during that 'momentary halt in the tavern' the conversation was not about liquor and women and sport but of the 'eternal questions, of the existence of God and immortality', and those who did not believe in God talked 'of the transformation of humanity in a new pattern'.

Max Crawford has told us in class about *The Revolt of the Masses* by Ortega y Gasset. His face lights up when he tells us the question Ortega y Gasset put in his book: Can high culture survive in the age of the masses? Tocqueville wants to know whether there can be a historian in a democratic society. Max Crawford tells us historians do not give answers: they ask questions. Karl Marx tells us all previous philosophers have assumed that their task was to describe the world: he believed the duty of the philosopher was to change the world. That also excites me, but another voice inside me chants the melancholy words of Housman: 'It rains into the sea, but still the sea is salt.' Yes, I still hear still the voice of the preacher in Ecclesiastes: 'All the rivers run into the sea, but the sea is not full. From the place whence the rivers come thither they return again.'

I have been reading D. H. Lawrence – Sons and Lovers, The White Peacock, and The Rainbow. He has a message for me: he puts into words my feelings about life. At the marriage of Tom and Anna Brangwen, Will Brangwen speaks lyrically about a heaven different from those of the theologians and the self-appointed engineers of the soul. He speaks of the union between a man and a woman, how that they twain shall be one flesh. Lawrence puts it into words for me: 'For she was woman to him: all other woman were her shadows.' He speaks of life as a journey in which two human beings discover each other. I am about to start such a journey.

On the departure wharf at Port Melbourne on 16 August 1938 all was well. Dymphna and I had our free first-class passages on the Orama. I had little money – but that did not matter, because a clergyman's son, a scholarship boy, knew how to be poor in the society of the genteel and the rich. Had not one of the Renaissance Popes boasted he proposed to enjoy the Papacy? Well, I proposed to enjoy all that an Orient Line voyage in first class had to offer.

So did Dymphna. She loved the sorbets, all the exquisite, recherché offerings on the dinner menu. I was unmistakably from the Australian bush, a man with a taste for a roast of beef or mutton, some roast potatoes, some beans, or peas and carrots, some apple pie and cream, rounded off with a greedy man's slices of cheddar cheese. Dymphna chose the coq au vin, sweets I had never heard of, and a cheese platter of Camembert, Danish Blue and Brie – names, again, which were foreign to me. I was British: I had a British passport in my cabin: I was an Austral-Briton, a man born in Australia and educated as though he were British. I was shocked by what I saw in Colombo and Bombay. But I was a Melbourne man: I had simple solutions for every human problem: abolish exploitation; end 'imperial domination', and poverty, squalor, superstition, and degrading practices would disappear. The whole sea of humanity would become like the members of an Oxford common-room – polite, civilised, witty, charming, adequately fed and housed. Q.E.D. Next problem, please.

We were too poor to pay for a tour of the pyramids in Egypt; we stayed on the ship. I was not interested then in how close we were to Mecca. For me what had come out of Mecca was another one of those superstitions which would melt like the snow-drift at the first rays of the sun of Enlightenment and material progress. Nor did I see the sphinx, or inspect the tombs of a people who spent so wantonly on their dead to provide for their journey into another world. Well, Enlightenment would liberate them from all such vulgar superstitions. I was not ready then for ancient Egypt. I was British. I was a child of the Enlightenment. So I missed out on Herman Melville's remark that ghastly countries produce ghastly theologies. I did not ask myself then whether in Australia the inhabitants of another 'ghastly country' would one day spawn some 'ghastly theology'. That will come later. I was British: I was on my way to 'England's green and pleasant land'.

The day the *Orama* dropped anchor in the beautiful bay of Naples the government fell in Prague. The ship's news-sheet wrote of a crisis in Europe. Would Hitler order the German Army to invade the Sudetenland to liberate Germans from their oppressors? If so, would England and France then declare war on Germany? Panic. I bought all the Italian newspapers I could find, and with the help of Latin and French, and spurred on by the childhood fear of annihilation, I pieced together what was happening.

There was another shock. The poverty was appalling. But of course I have my cure for that. I am a Melbourne man: I have my faith. I have my litany: evil conditions have made people evil, and good conditions will make them good. I am Pangloss in shirt, shorts and sandals – a latter-day Pangloss silencing his conscience with the knowledge that after the great change everything will be for the best in the best of all possible worlds. Another voice inside me says: God will be very busy on the resurrection morning when this sea of humanity around me has to be changed 'in a moment, in the twinkling of an eye'.

I go into a church – I forget now which it was – and am bewildered. At the altar a priest dressed in rich vestments is saying mass in Latin. I remember the words of Macaulay about 'the series of pantomimic gestures and the unintelligible words which pass for religion in the Church of Rome'. I smile the smile of an arrogant member, long since retired, of the Melbourne Protestant ascendancy. Another thought darts into my mind: are all these ornamentations behind the altar, all the gorgeous vestments worn by the priest, designed to fool the ignorant and the superstitious, those who have not had a Melbourne course in the Enlightenment?

I hear for the first time in my life the tinkle of the sanctuary bell at the elevation, and a louder, deeper bell tolling in the tower of the church. A reverend hush pervades the whole church, as the priest raises the wafer high above his head and recites the words: 'Ecce corpus Christi . . .' And I wonder if this is the bell of salvation. But not for long.

In the bright light of the Naples sun, the intimation vanished. There were other things to think about. As the train carried us to Pompeii my eyes were glued to the pages of the Corriere della sera. Maybe the cities of Europe might soon look like the ruins of Pompeii. Maybe there would be another sack of Rome by the barbarians. Maybe Great Britain would not survive as a great power. Maybe salvation would come from Russia and a new society, like the Phoenix bird, would rise out of the ashes of the corrupt society of Europe, or maybe the British, the French, the Germans and the Italians would call for a crusade against Russia and destroy the world's first communist society?

So on to Toulon, where the barrows in the streets were filled with the fruits of a rich harvest, where the tiny segment of the sky visible above the narrow streets was a rich sensuous blue, as the hawkers, shop-keepers, stall-holders and shoppers, and the anthropologisers from our ship, contributed to an uproar about buying and selling. We joined the pagans in the market-place, the eaters and drinkers who seemed unaware of the drama being played out in Berlin, London, Paris, Moscow and Prague, of the never-ending grand opera in my mind on the fate of humanity. On to Gibraltar, which the English passengers on board, with a most infuriating arrogance, called 'Gib', as though they owned the 'bloody place'.

On towards the Bay of Biscay. Just north of Gibraltar we saw on the horizon a squadron of General Franco's destroyers lying in wait for a Spanish government destroyer to put out again on the high seas. I wondered for a moment why the powers of progress, the powers of Enlightenment seem to be losing this ghastly civil war in Spain, why had Moscow walked out on the Spanish government? Nothing I have read or heard in Melbourne has prepared me for this. It was all so bewildering. There were the words of the preacher in Ecclesiastes reminding us that the race was not to the swift nor the battle to the strong. There was the promise of England's green and pleasant land, if only we could get there before we two and all of us on the *Orama* were blown sky-high.

After Gibraltar there was another shock – the English passengers who had boarded the *Orama* in Toulon and Gibraltar. I had been taught that the English were models of behaviour: they were *comme il faut*, so copy them. But these men and women did not seem to possess the gift of tongues, or, if they did, seemed determined not to practise that gift with raw colonials. They made it plain by facial expressions of disdain and contempt that everything we Australians did – the way we spoke, the way we walked, the way we dressed – was all vulgar, crude, coarse, loud-mouthed, and lacking in both subtlety and refinement. England might be a finishing school in behaviour for the likes of us, but we were never likely to pass the examination set by Englishmen and marked by Englishmen at the end of the course. That was an examination no Australian could ever pass unless he ceased to be an Australian, or was prepared to curry favour by living up to the English idea of an Australian – a vulgar, loud-mouthed boaster, a man or woman who hadn't any opinions, hadn't any ideas, but had huge appetites and gross, animal ways of satisfying those appetites.

The white cliffs of Dover lacked the grandeur I had expected. They looked like smudged chalk rising out of the mist and gloom. I stood with Dymphna on the bow of the *Orama* waiting for what could never be. At Tilbury docks there was another shock. The clouds – so full of moisture that they kept unloading what they did not need on us as we moved towards the customs and immigration shed – hovered just above our heads. The air was dank, and miles around there was this well-ordered forest of chimney pots rising out of roofs on which the slates were glistening with moisture.

London was quite unmanageable. My mind lost its maps. My host was Horace Crotty, one-time bishop of Bathurst and now, thanks to his gifts as a preacher, vicar of St Pancras Church in Bloomsbury. His wife, Meta, was my mother's cousin. Cousin Horace, as I call him, was quite a performer. He told me over tea and a sandwich of bread and butter, both slices so thin that the two together were no denser than lavatory paper, not to worry about what was going on in Germany. The Jews, he said, would never be happy unless they stuck with music and God. Without those two they were enemies both to themselves and to humanity. I was puzzled because I remembered my grandfather telling me once, 'Your cousin Horace Crotty would have made a brilliant career in the church if he had believed in God.' I asked myself: could I, in this world of tea-cups of such fine porcelain that they seemed to be transparent, and all this spiritual talk, dare to ask, 'And about God, Cousin Horace, do you think He is there?'

I wanted to know whether there was going to be a war. Cousin Horace looked as though he ought to know, but I feared he did not. The English newspapers and weeklies were not helpful. The *Times* was unctuous and self-righteous; the *New Statesman* passed judgement on the political morals, or absence of, amongst English conservatives, while in its literary pages there was much of that chatter of over-civilised men and women who wrote of themselves as paragons of the civilisation a war would be fought to preserve. Yet often in the sentence following this appointment of himself as a knight of the Round Table, as a guardian of higher standards, the writer confessed that, unlike the vulgarians with their 'certain certainties', he was consumed by doubt about everything. The *Daily Worker*, the organ of the British Communist Party, called on the British and the French governments to negotiate a mutual defence agreement with the Soviet Union. Then Hitler would not dare to invade Czechoslovakia. They always wrote with the certainty of a theorem in geometry, or the confidence of men who knew history was on their side.

From the conservative press, and from conversations in the vicarage at St Pancras, I gained the impression that the conservatives were more interested in a crusade against Bolshevism; that, like the conservatives in Germany, they believed Hitler could be used for that purpose and then dropped. I wondered at times how the forces of evil in Germany could be defeated by 'darts of brown paper', or the debate for the human mind be won by the spiritual eunuchs of the *New Statesman*. Dymphna was going to Bonn University as a Von Humboldt Scholar. Should she set out? Could that be endured? So panic within, and panic without, and no one to whom to turn for succour. We parted, Dymphna to Bonn, and I to Oxford, just as Neville Chamberlain returned from Bad Godesberg and talked of 'peace in our time'. He and Herr Hitler, Signor Mussolini and Monsieur Daladier were to meet in Munich to work out the details of the agreement. The conservatives went down to their temples to pray: the radicals talked of treachery and betrayal, the mavericks called for someone to speak for England. I remembered the first chapters of Carlyle's *The French Revolution*. I was an observer of a society which was rushing towards an explosion, towards some great upheaval. No one could stop it. Change of government, negotiations, fiddling here and fiddling there might delay but could not avert the catastrophe. But I could not find anyone who shared my sense of doom.

Oxford was like an oasis in a desert. The dons of Balliol College were warm, eccentric and ultimately unknowable. A. B. Roger, the tutor for admissions at Balliol, told me I would be a welcome addition to Balliol's cricket team. Thinking I was planning to do research on a medieval topic he sent me off to talk to Richard Southern, later president of St John's College, Oxford. That was a pleasing error. With Dick Southern there was immediate recognition: we 'spoke the same language'. Within five minutes we had left history far behind and had started a conversation which would go on from then to the present day, he being a believer, who guessed belief was what mattered most to me. He asked me whether I was a 'sampler', and what I thought of the various samples – Rome, High Anglican, Low Anglican, Quaker, and so on. He asked me whether Australians were quite as coarse as they were portrayed in D. H. Lawrence's *Kangaroo*. I said I hoped not. He said perhaps I was full of doubt about that too, and we smiled, and decided we must talk some more. We would do that for over fifty years, to my great benefit and delight. Dick Southern was like my mother: he was a believer, and like all true believers he was not a bully in things spiritual: they were for God to decide, not man. We will meet again, and he will ask me, 'What is it this time?', knowing 'samplers' tend to move on. And I will tell him I am still travelling, still a pilgrim for the means of grace.

Dick Southern sent me on to talk to Humphrey Sumner, a senior fellow at Balliol in modern history. On my way up the staircase to Sumner's rooms I passed a man with a face which from that time occupied a prominent place in the picture gallery of my mind. It was Christopher Hill, a secular humanist with a pleasing blend of Marx the prophet, Marx the discoverer of the laws of history, and a pilgrim who hoped someone, someday, would tell him what it was all about. At that time he believed the old society must be smashed, bourgeois institutions replaced, exploitation cease, and all men and women be both free and equal. Christopher had both a face of hope and a face of sadness.

Humphrey Sumner had a sorrowful countenance, which, in very rare moments, gave way to controlled gaiety. He looked like a pre-

Raphaelite who had survived into the age of the masses. He wore his hair long. He had eccentric habits. He kept spills in a bowl on his mantelpiece, with which he lit his pipe. Yet he wore suits, shirts and ties which studiously conformed to the prevailing orthodoxies in men's clothing. I could not imagine then, nor can I imagine now, any man or woman confessing to Humphrey Sumner that they (the confessors) had a passionate heart. Sumner's passion was books. For him a book was not *in* the Bodleian Library, 'It *lives* in Bodley'. He was one of the few men I ever met who had an encyclopaedic knowledge of the past. I remember once quite early in our weekly talks telling him in an essay that the constitution of the second republic in France resembled the constitution of New South Wales as created by the Australian Colonies Government Act of 1850. 'Clark,' he said, 'the Australian Colonies Government Act always reminded me of the constitution of Siena in the fourteenth century.' His eye lit up, he lit a spill in the flame of his fire, puffed once or twice at his pipe, and talked with immense learning about constitutions and representative government.

He was not a show-off, or a man who paraded his learning as evidence of his own superiority, as evidence of his being one of the *gens supérieurs*. He could be withering with those who were not 'solid mandalas'. I remember once A. J. P. Taylor was talking to Sumner when I entered the room. Taylor was then in his first year as a don at Magdalen College and a university lecturer in history. I had heard him give the first three or four lectures on the history of the Habsburg Empire in the second half of the nineteenth century. Taylor was a brilliant showman. Well over three hundred students hung on every word he uttered in the Examination School's lecture room. He did not use a note. Facts, stories, anecdotes, jokes, asides about other historians, and bitter remarks about the whole human race, poured out of him in lively bursts of language. I was puzzled at the time by the bitterness. Taylor wanted the recognition his peers and colleagues would never give him. He would enjoy an international reputation for his gifts as a writer and a lecturer, but the judges for whose approval he craved never admitted him to their fold. The shape of things to come for Taylor was acted out in Sumner's room. Taylor, I could see, was not at ease in the presence of Humphrey Sumner, who was one of the judges whose approval Taylor coveted. So Taylor, anxious to impress, said to Sumner: 'Humphrey, we will have to write the history of Denmark for the Danes. They are making a terrible mess of it themselves.' Sumner: 'Alan, I didn't know you could read Danish.'

Taylor must try again. Taylor will spend a lifetime courting the good opinion of the ones who award the prizes and the blanks in the Oxford lottery. He will never get what he wants: he will become sadder and sadder, crankier, and more quirky in his judgements on history and life. He will gain the whole world, but that is not what he wants: he wants the nod from the Humphrey Sumners of Oxford, but that nod will never be given.

My talks with Sumner revealed quite quickly how well he understood me. I told him Max Crawford had suggested I might choose Condorcet as the subject for my thesis for the B.Litt. Sumner looked doubtful – but he left me guessing why. He suggested I write an essay for him on *Les Souvenirs* by Alexis de Tocqueville. I did that, and read it to him, but he made no comment on its quality, except, if I remember correctly, a mumbled aside that I understood the man. Tocqueville, he said, is your man: he is interested in what you are interested in – the effect of a mass age on a culture, the question whether equality and liberty are compatible with each other. And, he added, there was more to it than that: 'Tocqueville, like you, Clark, wanted to believe.' But before I could even say a yes, let alone ask him how he knew so much about me in such a little time, I was made aware that I was not to ask questions about what went on in his mind. From that day we understood each other, but I never dared to make a personal remark to him.

He urged me to start by reading French literature from about 1760 to 1860. So I began with Montesquieu, Voltaire, Rousseau, Diderot and St Pierre, and went on to Chateaubriand, Lammenais, Lamartine, Louis Blanc, Michelet, Stendhal, Balzac and Hugo. Hugo took me back to the time when I heard my father preach on *Les Misérables*, but in 1938 in Oxford my mind was still too stuffed up with the Melbourne obsession with the material setting to notice the message about forgiveness.

I also read Marx's *Class Struggles in France*, the *Eighteenth of Brumaire* and the *Civil War in France*. Marx was exciting: he made history like unto a theorem in geometry, decorated by his own taste for mockery and hatred. I was drawn to him at the time, but no sooner had I fallen under his spell than I read Balzac's *Une Ténébreuse Affaire*, *La Cousine Bette*, *Le Père Goriot*, *Eugénie Grandet* and *Illusions perdues*. I read Stendhal, who also persuaded me that history was much more complicated than the gospel according to Marx.

I was supposed to be a student of human society. I was really much more interested in the behaviour of the human heart. My attention wandered when I read Voltaire or any of the dry souls of the Enlightenment, but never when I read a work by Balzac or Hugo, or Pascal. *Les Paroles d'un croyant* meant more to me than all the arguments of the political philosophers and the political economists.

The lectures in that first term (Michaelmas term) were not the eye-openers I had been led to believe were performed each term at Oxford. A. J. P. Taylor provided good entertainment, but little more. R. G. Collingwood was a surprise. I decided to attend his lectures, because as a reader I knew him as joint author with J. N. L. Myres of the monumental *Roman Britain*, the first volume in the new *Oxford History of England*. He was advertised in the university lecture-lists to lecture on theories of history. Under his gown he wore a polo-necked sailing sweater, dark blue in colour, with some yachting title inscribed on the front in red letters. I did not know then that these lectures were a trial run for his book, *The Idea of History*. All I knew was that Collingwood, like Taylor, seemed to be bitter about the attitude of his colleagues. Nor did the theory excite me. A historian, I believed then and now, has something to say: a historian has a 'quantity of felt life': a historian tells a story.

Listening to R. G. Collingwood I thought of the story of Mary and Martha. Like Martha the man of theory was 'much cumbered': unlike Mary the man of theory seemed to lack the one thing that was 'needful' for a historian – the eye of pity and a little love for all the characters in his story.

England soon became one of my many lost illusions. Before contact my mind was stuffed with many contradictions about the English. The uproar stirred up in Australia in 1935 by Professor G. K. Cowling's article in the *Age* ridiculing the idea of an Australian literature, had not touched me at all at the time. Nor had P. R. Stephensen's brilliant if somewhat erratic reply, *The Foundations of Culture in Australia*, meant anything to me. (I do remember hearing about it at the time.) That would come later. I had not read the words of Henry Lawson asking Australians to choose between 'The Old Dead Tree' and the 'Young Tree Green'. I knew nothing of Australian literature. I only knew that literature, music, painting, religion, were all produced 'over *there*': Europe was the land of 'many wonders', Australia a cultural desert, and Australians were borrowers, and readers of books written in foreign lands.

Australia was the 'haggard continent': England was the 'green and pleasant land'. Australia was dead: England was the 'land of hope and glory', the 'mother of the free'. God had made England mighty. In His manifest bountiful goodness to all those who were British, God might make England 'mightier yet'. We all sang those words at the time, perhaps with a hint of sarcasm and cynicism and mockery, but there was also a shy, sentimental hope that England was worthy of the lofty role such admirers had cast her in. The world was facing a crisis – a crisis of belief and of society. The world was threatened with a double breakdown – a breakdown in its beliefs, and a breakdown of social order. The world was in a mess.

Maybe England had the answer. I had seen the film of Noel Coward's *Cavalcade* in Melbourne in May 1933. I had heard the song of a people who had lost their way – the 'Twentieth Century Blues': a song about a people who had nothing 'to strive for, love, or keep alive for' Yes, the world was in a mess, and maybe the English had the answer. The English stood for human dignity, the English way of life was the answer to the 'moral drift and decay' and all the 'decadence and unrest of the modern world'. So let us all, Australians as well as English, drink a toast to Old England, may she triumph over the Babel of the modern world, provide an alternative to all the strange gods, to that worship of idols by corrupt hearts. Or so I hoped.

My mind was also stuffed with the criticism of England in the books of the Left Book Club. I had read John Strachey on *The Nature of the Capitalist Crisis*, I had read in *The Cousinhood* a witty attack on the English land-owning and merchant classes. I had enjoyed the *double entendre* in the family motto of the Dukes of Devonshire: *feci quod potui* (I have *done* or I have *made* what I could) – they having certainly made a pile. But I had not read the literature of the victims of British imperialism. I had not read the Irish criticism of the English – I knew Adam Smith had dismissed the English as a 'nation of shop-keepers', and that Napoleon had popularised the epigram. I knew the Germans were bitter about 'perfidious Albion', the Swedes were repelled by English 'dirtiness', and the Russians in their novels portrayed the English as worshippers of the 'golden calf'. But at that time I had not read the words of the victims of British imperialism: the words of Gandhi or Nehru, or the words of the Irish who were shot after the Easter Rising in 1916. I thought we Australians were the beneficiaries of the British expansion overseas. I thought of the English as an alternative to Australian vulgarity, mediocrity and cosiness.

In all the early encounters I was made to feel I was outside a gate which would never be opened. At the time I had not asked myself: Do you really want the gate to open? At that time I had no alternative to 'Englishmanism'. Americans, we were told when we were young, were brash, raw, boastful, lawless. The British had that priceless blessing of the rule of law; the British settled their disputes in the law courts, the Americans with the gun; the English bobby was the people's friend, the Americans lived under constant threat of gangsterdom. The English accent – ah, that was the thing to cultivate; the American voice was 'nauseating, nasal and inane', or so we were told until we gradually learned better after the coming of the 'talkies' in 1929.

My education had steered me away from the great American intellectual tradition. My school and university courses on America stopped on 4 July 1776 just when America was starting. So I knew only smatterings after that date. My America was a compound of Tom Mix, Charlie Chaplin, Greta Garbo, Claudette Colbert, Adolphe Menjou, Joan Crawford, Shirley Temple, Buster Keaton, Laurel and Hardy, and many other magical performers like Duke Ellington and Louis Armstrong. My America at that time provided much of the froth and bubble of my life, sentimental songs for all those, like myself, who yearned for what could never be; I was pleased to find there were other 'yearners' in the world, others who knew all about the longing in the popular song, 'You were meant for me'. America provided the pap for all swooners, all dreamers, all those who wanted to put a comforting, soothing sentimental poultice on their wounds, all those who either could not or would not face the truth about themselves and the human situation. America provided pop culture for the beautiful dreamers in the age of the masses, the Hamlets in the age of high rise and the concrete jungle.

During my youth in Melbourne, moralisers warned me against dancing my way to damnation. They warned me to beware of the woman of snares and nets, to take care not to be seduced by those who preached sexual orgasm, or revolution, or both, as cure-alls for humanity's ills. Do not listen to those who offer a peace which bourgeois society and bourgeois love could not give. I took no notice. I loved American pop culture. I answered the frowners with the words of an American song: 'Jes keep on doin' what yer doin'.'

At that time I had no culture of my own. My teachers had not told me about the Australian as someone different from the Austral-Briton.

So there was a temptation to become an Englishman, a temptation to join the club of the supercilious and the arrogant and enjoy the great benefits. But two months in Oxford showed me the error of my ways. It was not the case of a man discovering the face of a whore underneath the painted pomp, the splendour, and the jewels of the loved one. It was the case of a man who did not belong – or the case of a man who was in the wrong room.

The superciliousness was offensive. But the real shock was to discover what some of them were like. I remember late in October 1938 being taken to London with other Dominion students to meet the Minister for the Co-ordination of Defence in the Chamberlain government, Sir Thomas Inskip. I expected to meet a man of stature, not this elegantly dressed, stripe-trousered, flower-in-the-buttonhole nonentity, who tried in vain to conceal the hollowness within under a smokescreen of courtly manners, and very knowing 'Oh, I see's', and sage nods in response to the comments of the students. I said not a word. Sir Thomas and his minions withdrew, and I walked out into the gathering storm of a late autumn London dusk.

Back in Oxford I heard again the culture chatterers ask in their high-pitched voices whether there was any chance of Winston (i.e. Churchill) getting back into the government. Again I said not a word, although, as I listened, the words of Carlyle came into my mind: 'Necker is brought back. But what can Necker do?' Well, I did not know then that England was doomed, that England was on the way down.

I was a *naïf*: I believed then that England was safe because the Left Book Club books told me so. In childhood I knew one simple truth: 'Jesus loves me, this I know / For the Bible tells me so.' I now had a new Bible – the Left Book Club Books. Could the Nazis win a war? Answer: No, a thousand times no. And why? Answer: Their tanks were mainly made of cardboard or some *ersatz* material: they would collapse like a house of cards. Besides they lacked the fuel with which to drive their tanks. Their motorised division would be a pushover. England might not deserve to be safe – but it was safe. The Bible of the sons of the Enlightenment proclaimed it. Enough said.

I could not live without Dymphna. I read in the Bodleian: I tried to concentrate, but my mind was elsewhere. Letters were some help, but I wanted the real presence – I was like doubting Thomas, one of those who had to see, one of those who had to touch. I listened to all the brilliant talk in Oxford. I smiled when a witty scholar at Balliol told me he had finally managed to translate the adjectives of Macaulay. I tried to be understanding and comforting when one of my Australian friends confessed to me that he could not stop going to bed with other men. I did not know what to say when Michael Thwaites, of whom I was very fond, told me what comfort he had known since he became a member of Moral Rearmament. I listened to a Benedictine priest who discussed with wit and learning the candidates for a forthcoming Papal election. I wrote letters to my mother in which I said much but did not refer to the private hell in my heart, the separation from Dymphna.

The problem was how to tell Humphrey Sumner I wanted to go to Germany, without telling him why I wanted to go to Germany. Humphrey Sumner did not look as though he had ever gulped in the presence of a woman. He was a loner. It could be cruel to tell him it was not possible for me to be alone, that without Dymphna in my life I was incomplete. So I rehearsed all the arguments in favour of going to Germany, without mentioning Dymphna. It was a flimsy case: not even years as a debater, or all the skills one acquired as a clergy-man's son in preserving outer calm while seething inwardly like a ravening wolf, could possibly conceal what my heart was telling me, that the things of the mind were not the great passion of my life.

There was no need for the casuist to exercise his skills. Before I could get beyond the stammering of a man determined not to let the mask slip, Sumner reached for a spill, lit his pipe, took one mammoth puff, and said to me, with the twinkle in the eye of a god-like creature who understood, even if he did not share my foolish ways:

Clark, you'd like to see your fiancée. Why don't you take the foreigners' course in German at Bonn University over Christmas and the New Year? If you want to understand de Tocqueville you'll need to read Heine thoroughly, especially the prose works.

So Sumner gave me an intellectual reason for satisfying immediately the passions of my heart. But I knew the real reason why I must go straight away. One Psalm I could sing with gusto: 'Lord, I am not high-minded . . .'

Dymphna was there on the platform at the Bonn railway station when I stepped off the train early in the morning of 8 November 1938. We walked in ecstasy up the stairs of the Bonn railway station, out of the darkness below into the light. We were in for a rude shock.

It was the morning after 'Kristallnacht' – the night when Hitler's storm-troopers took their revenge on the Jews in Germany for the assassination of a German diplomat in Paris by Grünspan. Glass was everywhere on the footpath. The windows of Jewish shops had been broken, and their goods scattered over the pavement and the road. There were trucks with men in uniform standing in the tray. The men had outsize bums: they had faces which reminded me of the faces of the bullies who had made my life a hell during the first two years at Melbourne Grammar School. But there was a difference: the members of the Long Dorm at Melbourne Grammar School flayed the uninitiated with a wet towel: these men carried revolvers on the bulging right cheeks of their bums. The Long Dorm bullies might maim a sensitive soul for life: these young men could kill. These men with guns, these men who looked as though they would never be complete unless they had a whip in their hands, were an epitome of evil. How had they risen to power in one of the most civilised countries in the world?

Dymphna took me to lunch that first day in the cafeteria of the University of Bonn. The big-bummed men sat at a special table in the corner of the Mensa, the swastika flag prominently on display. They were watching all of us; they nodded to each other when a German student chatted with a foreigner. We sat with Hans Ehrenzeller, a sensitive Swiss who was doing a Ph.D. on the proem to the novel from Grimmelshausen to Jean Paul. In the next six weeks Hans told me much about himself. He was the eternal outsider. German students dressed unostentatiously. Hans was different. His winter coat was grey in colour, unlike the ruling sombre black worn by all conformers. The coat of the conformers ended just below the knees: Hans's coat ended at his ankles. He laughed in a high-pitched hysterical voice when I quoted a German poem, but I liked him so much I was not hurt.

There were two Irishmen at our table – Ievers and McCutcheon, both choosing Bonn for their research degree rather than Oxford, Cambridge, or London, because of their hostility to the eternal enemy of the Irish people. I had never heard such sentiments before. The blinkers on the eyes of a Melbourne secular humanist, with a nostalgia for something else, were being rudely whisked off. There was also a blond German, Karl Heyers, who, I was told, was the best tango dancer in Bonn. He patted his hair, maybe out of vanity, maybe out of fear of being seen with foreigners. Who can ever tell?

After lunch Dymphna, Ievers, McCutcheon, Hans and I (but not Karl Heyers) went for a walk along the east bank of the Rhine. I talked with enthusiasm about the castles on the other side of the river. Ievers agreed they were beautiful, but added, 'You wait. They will soon be destroyed by the Anglo-Saxon barbarians.' I began to sing a Schumann song about the Rhine and Cologne cathedral – 'Im Rhein im schönen Strome' (In the Rhine, that lovely stream). The beauties of nature, the pleasing company, had wiped away the terrors of the morning. The river, the trees, the buildings washed me clean. Hans whispered to me he had never met a sensitive Australian before, and asked whether there were many like me in Australia. On the footpath along the Rhine we began an exchange of minds which was to continue until he died in 1974. We did not need words to speak to each other.

Dymphna's landlady was Frau Unger, the wife of Joseph Unger, a senior civil servant working in Cologne. That night she invited us both to drink a bottle or so of Rhenish wine with some German guests whom she thought Herr Clark might like to meet. The Ungers lived at Dietzstrasse Nummer Vier, opposite the Elisabethkirche. As I sat there wanting my glass to be refilled at Australian intervals and not this tantalising wait, while the Germans chattered about such irrelevancies as the vintage and the bouquet, I heard a bell toll in the church. I was drawn to what the bell was saying to me: something about the vanity, the emptiness, the superficiality, the shallowness of creeds like the one of which I was then a part-time believer – the belief in material progress, the conviction that good conditions would remove all the evil in the world. Here was a bell transmitting a message about resignation, acceptance, about what could strengthen a man to face his tormentors, about a love and a grace which drove away all fear.

The bell tolled this picture of another world just as Dr Busslei was lecturing me on the fate of the English and the French if they were so misguided as to resist the Führer's demands for *Lebensraum* (living space) in eastern Europe. Dr Busslei lectured on the history of art at the University of Bonn. Dr Busslei, Frau Unger told me a few days later, was one of what the Germans called the *psychologisch hoch-differenzierte Leute* (psychologically highly differentiated people). Dr Busslei, she told me, wept when he played the Adagio in Beethoven's *'Apassionata' Sonata*. Dr Busslei was a sensitive flower. I had heard about him in letters from Dymphna. There had been a wine-drinking evening in the Ungers' living room when Dr Busslei had lectured her about the future of the English and the French. He had shouted at her:

Merken Sie sich wohl was ich nun sage, mein englisches Fräulein. Im Jahre neunzehnhundertneununddreissig oder vierzig kommt der Weltkrieg gegen den Bolschewismus und im Laufe dieses Krieges werden England und Frankreich von der Weltkarte verschwinden.

(Mark well what I am saying, my young Englishwoman. In 1939 or 1940 there will be a global war against Bolshevism and in the course of this war England and France will disappear from the world map.')

Late that night Frau Unger had knocked on Dymphna's door, and told her she must not be too worried: *'Wissen Sie, der Herr Dr Busslei ist etwas extrem'* (You know, Herr Dr Busslei is a bit of an extremist).

Here he was again at Frau Unger's wine-drinking evening, warning me about Germany's intentions. He called me *'Der junge Engländer'* (the young Englishman), but my German was then too primitive to explain to him that Australians were not Englishmen. In Dr Busslei's mind we all belonged to what he called *'das ungeheuere britische Weltreich'* (the monstrous British Empire). He told me in a menacing voice that unless Herr Chamberlain accepted the Führer's demands for the Polish corridor, the return of the German colonies, and German living space in eastern Europe, then the German army would destroy that Empire; London and the English provincial cities would be reduced to rubble. And what, I asked timidly, about Australia? *'Ach, Australien'*, he replied contemptuously, *'das macht nichts aus'* (Australia doesn't matter). Australia, I gathered, did not count – but Europe did, and Dr Busslei recited with a fiendish gleam in the eye what was and what was not a *Kriegsfall* (occasion for war). After he left Frau Unger said reassuringly that not everyone in her street agreed with Dr Busslei.

Dr Busslei spoke much of *'die Macht'* (power): Dr Busslei spoke much of *'das Schanddiktat von Versailles'* (the shameful Versailles Treaty). Dr Busslei believed, with Goethe, that the world belonged to the brave and the strong – *'dem Mutigen gehört die Welt'* (the world belongs to the brave). Thanks to the Führer, Germany was now strong: the German army would atone for the disgraceful surrender on 11 November 1918. The German High Command would never again repeat the errors in the Schlieffen Plan, or the mistake of General von Kluck. Next time the German army would invade Holland, Denmark and Norway, as well as Belgium and France; next time the

Germans would capture the Channel ports before marching on Paris. England would be isolated, and the Luftwaffe would raze English cities. The German army would then turn east – '*der Drang nach Osten*' would begin; Germany would save Europe and the world from Bolshevism; Germany would save civilisation from the Asiatic hordes. '*Wissen Sie, Herr Clark*', Dr Busslei shouted at me, '*Asien beginnt an der Wintergasse in Wien*' (You know, Herr Clark, Asia begins at the Wintergasse in Vienna). The Jewish plot against Christendom would be crushed.

Up to that time I had been an uneasy, restless tent-dweller in the worldwide camp of British philistines. Now in Bonn the pegs tethering my tent to the ground were being uprooted one after another. The myths planted in my mind at Melbourne University and from reading Left Book Club books were exposed for what they were – hollow shams. Germany, under Hitler, would not be a military pushover. Secular humanists and Left Book Club writers and readers had taught me that Hitler, Goebbels, Goering, Ribbentrop, Schacht, and Baldur von Schirach, were wicked and stupid. My teachers had a simple equation: the wicked were incompetent. Fatal error. In Bonn I understood why the Psalmist asked his God: Why do you allow the wicked to flourish? Why did you allow the wicked to win?

I learned another lesson. German conservatives, like Dr Busslei, believed the Nazis would achieve what no Weimar government had achieved: they would restore order, street fighting would cease; there would be no more terrors either in the noonday or by night in bourgeois Germany. The Nazis would tear up the Treaty of Versailles; and the disgrace of November 1918 would be atoned. The German bourgeoisie would heed Christ's command: they would make 'friends of the Mammon of unrighteousness', and once Mammon had performed his allotted task they would get rid of him. Vain delusion. They were nourishing a delusion as pernicious as the delusion previously in my mind. I must learn that the wicked were often very gifted and very powerful.

I have been deceived. Hitler and his ministers were wicked men: the imagination of their hearts was evil. But it did not follow, as I and many of my contemporaries assumed, that they were stupid, or lacked talent, or would be a pushover in any war which might break out over, say, Danzig (now Gdansk) and the Polish corridor. Previously I had believed good would always defeat evil. I had learned that as a child from the teaching of the Christian church. When I had put away childish things and had become a man and was baptised in

Melbourne into the church of the Enlightenment, I changed my mind about the battle between good and evil. Evil was not endemic to the human situation: evil was made by man, and therefore curable by man. The Enlightenment contradicted Christian teaching. As a child I had recited the words: 'Thou alone canst remove all the evil in the world' – not knowing quite what those words implied about human impotence. Now, as a man, I believed man alone, man without divine aid, could and would remove all the evil in the world. But, here in Bonn am Rhein, these experiences, these encounters, these confrontations, have planted a doubt in my mind – just as experiences at school and in the world planted a doubt in my mind about God's world. I began to doubt the teaching of the Enlightenment on evil. I opened a dictionary and read that the origin of evil was the oldest problem known to humanity. I must give up childish things: I must start another journey of discovery. I must shed some of the baggage from the past.

Bonn was a good place in which to start. Bonn was a fine flower of old Germany, the Germany of Beethoven (Bonn being his birth-place), Brahms, Schumann (buried in the Bonn Friedhof – the beautiful cemetery on the hill overlooking the Rhine, and, yes Mr Ievers, you were nearly right, the Anglo-Saxons will almost destroy this place of beauty), of Ranke, Treitschke, Curtius, and many others. Herr Klett was rapidly teaching me to read German. Dymphna spoke German so beautifully, as she spoke Dutch, French, Swedish and Norwegian, that I called her in those golden days 'Linguistic Lizzie' and sometimes 'Continental Connie', who was having trouble teaching a boy from the bush. In between classes, which went on almost all day, I bought a copy of F. Eckermann's *Gespräche mit Goethe*, and a very small German–English dictionary, and, using the index, worked out slowly what Goethe had to say about Byron, Mozart and Raphael (amongst others). I bought a second-hand copy of Heinrich Heine's account of his journey to England and Ireland. I began to read the love poetry of Heine.

One day I read with difficulty Heine's poem about Cologne Cathedral. I was already familiar with the Schumann version, but not with the precise meaning of the words. I used to beef out:

Im Rhein im schönen Strome
Da spiegelt sich in den Welln
Mit seinem grossen Dome
Das grosse heilige Köln.

(In the Rhine, that lovely stream
The waters mirror
The great and holy city of Cologne
With its great cathedral.)

I had never understood why the singers I had heard on the gramophone or the wireless adopted a hushed and reverent tone for the next quatrain – as though they were in the presence of something greater than themselves, greater than all of us, or were being vouchsafed a glimpse into the heart of the greatest mystery of all:

Im Dom da steht ein Bildnis
Auf goldenem Leder gemalt.
In meines Lebens Wildnis,
Hat's freundlich hineingestrahlt.
(Painted on golden leather
There stands in the cathedral a picture
That beamed a kindly light
Into the wild chaos of my life.)

Well, I knew all about life's wildness, but had never discovered any god, any man, any woman, any work of art either in music, literature or painting to calm the storm within. I had read about Gothic cathedrals, about the spire reaching up from earth to heaven as a symbol of man's hunger to be reunited with the divine, but at that time, late November 1938, I was impatient with, scornful, even contemptuous, of all god-botherers, all 'that-sided' people. From Goethe I had learned the distinction between those who were *diesseitig* (this-sided) and those who were *jenseitig* (that – or other-sided) . I believed myself to be a sound *diesseitig* man. My concern was here and now, not in or with some future time and place. I scoffed at and mocked all knee-benders, and all petitioners, all grovellers at the throne of grace.

One cold afternoon late in November 1938 Dymphna and I travelled to Cologne on the Rheinuferbahn. If I remember rightly, McCutcheon, Protestant Irish, and Ievers, Catholic Irish (but, like me, both Christians who had lost their faith), travelled with us. One of the party – I forget who – suggested we go into Cologne Cathedral. Impatient as ever, thinking we may as well have a look at this museum of a dying and doomed faith, I skipped up the steps, savouring, sampling, a possible blasphemy with which to amuse my companions, and, perhaps, show them I too was one of the new men, one of the builders of a heaven on earth.

Inside the cathedral I was strangely moved. Dymphna, noticing what was going on inside me, left me alone to feast on it all in my heart. I walked behind the high altar, and saw by a stone wall the painting of the Madonna, the one referred to in Heine's poem, 'Painted on golden leather'. The sight of that face worked a great marvel within me. The tempests within subsided, the ghosts from the past stopped tormenting me. I will go back there every time I return to Germany. I will read of many men and women who have known a moment of grace while contemplating the Madonna in Cologne Cathedral. But I could not speak of the experience then to anyone. Was there anyone who would understand? Many years later when I risked talking about the experience my whole body shook, as I tried in vain to recite the words, 'Im Dom da steht ein Bildnis'.

I will never forget that moment. I had been vouchsafed a vision of what I had previously searched for in vain.

Out in the gloom and the damp of a late November day in Cologne the old vaudeville of devils overtook me again. I lapsed into buffoonery. We went to a café for food. To regain my sense of being an Austral-Briton, of being a simple boy from the Australian bush, I ordered 'poached eggs on toast, and a pot of tea'. I said it first in English with a very strong Australian accent. I was really trying to shelter in a safe harbour, or settling for what the hymn called 'the trivial round, the common task'. But from the day I saw evil in Bonn am Rhein there would be no putting back to harbour: I launched further into the deep when I stood in front of the painting of the Madonna and Child behind the high altar in Cologne Cathedral.

The Native
Decides to Return

Just before Christmas 1938 Dymphna and I took the train from Bonn to Munich. She was hoping to renew her friendship with the girls whom she had known during 1933 when she was a pupil at the Reformrealgymnasium in the Luisen-Strasse. All, save one, were reluctant to be hospitable to foreigners. The one exception was Erika Wiener, half-German, half-Jewish, whose father had been a colleague of Goering's in the German aircraft firm Albatros. Goering had ordered his release from Dachau after the 'Kristallnacht' (Night of broken glass) early in November of that year. Erika was now married to a German doctor, and anxious to start a new life in China, thousands of miles away from the race laws of Germany. I remember still her sad face, and wonder whether she escaped the gas ovens.

In Munich there were bizarre scenes, and bizarre conversations. We drank tea with a Gräfin (countess), a survivor from pre-1914 Germany, who waved a thin wafer biscuit hysterically in the air around her, and began every contribution to the conversation with a '*Aber wissen Sie, wir leben hier unter einem Terror*' (We are living here under a reign of terror, don't you know). We dined with a young officer in the Reichswehr who screamed at me, as Herr Dr Busslei had screamed in Bonn, about Germany's destiny to save Europe from decadence and Bolshevism.

We drank beer in the basement of the Hofbräuhaus where, having forgotten (the mind is sometimes kind to the heart) that a litre was not a Melbourne 'pot' but a pint and two-thirds, I was quickly away into that state of being where flesh-pressing becomes even more urgent than when sober. Soon I was telling myself that after a few more of these *Biersteine* maybe the Munich beer would quieten the voice within, tell the Melbourne Grammar code of what was and what was not done by a gentleman, to shut up. Like the boisterous young Germans, I too would pinch the bottoms of the barmaids as they placed the *Biersteine* on the table with their '*Bitt' schön*'. I would give a drunken '*Bitte sehr*' in reply. Yes, I would link arms with my table comrades and sing, '*Ich hatt' einen Kameraden, einen bessern findst du nit*' (I had a comrade, a better one you could not find).

But I could do neither. I did not belong. I went on drinking. That gave me another sort of courage. I asked one of the German students, '*Wie geht's in Rotspanien?*' He spat at me, and shouted, 'That's what I think of Red Spain', and asked me whether I wanted to come outside, and have it out. No, no, a thousand times no: let's have another drink, let's sing together '*Du, du liegst mir im Herzen*' (Thou liest in my heart), let's put our arms around each other and sing again, '*Ich hatt einen Kameraden / Einen bessern findst du nit*', and above all let's have a lot more to drink – *Jawohl, jawohl* – and tell conscience to keep quiet for a while. But I still could not pinch the bottoms of the waitresses.

In between the clowning in beer halls there was much in Munich to excite a young man's fancy. There was a performance of Wagner's *Tannhäuser* at the Nationaltheater, with a Norwegian Wagnerian tenor singing the title role. Once again there was the battle between conscience and desire. Should a young man who had taken on board the values and outlook of the Left Book Club, enjoy the work of an anti-Semite, and a man Hitler loved to honour?

Well, I did. I was exalted by a man who knew all about the ecstasy of sexual passion. Later I will discover the Wagner who believed art could rescue humanity from the world of the money-changers. I will discover the Wagner who knew some wounds could never be healed. I will discover the Wagner who knew from bitter experience that in the world treachery, betrayal and power struggles will always expel lovers from the Paradise Gardens, that an *Urvergessen* (primal oblivion) is the answer for lovers who want to become 'one flesh', who want to be *einig* (one person). But not for me. I know that for me that way madness lies.

A visit to the Alte Pinakothek taught me a lesson about Wagner and the *Übermensch* (superman). Dymphna and I wanted to see the art of Europe before the breakdown, the lapse into doubt and decadence, the lapse the Nazis had promised to rectify. A piece of Nazi-inspired sculpture, a representation in stone of the *Übermensch* or Wagnerian Siegfried, the mighty man of renown, caught my eye. What intrigued me was the lack of interest Germans displayed towards the work. The world of the supermen seemed to touch them not at all.

There was another advance in understanding in the Frauenkirche in Munich. A Catholic bishop preached a sermon warning worshippers to be on guard against the secular myths of the day, the myth of perfectibility, the myth that human beings could, without divine aid, create a heaven on Earth, and the myth of the *Übermensch*. Be on guard, he urged the congregation, against these idols of corrupt hearts, be on guard against the kingdoms of this world, trust in Christ's promises, ask Christ and the Holy Mother to give the peace which the world cannot give. I wondered then what endowed this priest with the strength to fear no foes. I was not ready then to tell myself that only believers, either religious or political, had such a strength, or to ask myself why this was so, why the rest were like those who had their reasons for not attending the wedding feast in Christ's parable – the 'any other time, but not now' men and women.

Before New Year 1939 we were back in Bonn, Dymphna to prepare for her seminars for her Ph.D. and I to attend my last classes at the foreigners' course in the German language. I was back in the world of Herr Direktor Koperanov from Bulgaria, who had been told by his business superiors to master the German language, as had others from India, England, France, the USA and Scandinavia. All of us were struggling to acquire *fliessend Deutsch* as the world rushed headlong to another disaster. The civil war in Spain was almost over: Franco was about to win. Nothing in my scheme of values, my faith in who would win the big prizes in the struggle between capitalism and socialism explained why this was so. Stalin, it was rumoured even in Germany, had lost interest in the Spanish Republic. My mental map of the future, yes, and my map of the present, would have to be redrafted. The world was not what I had been told it was. But what to do? Should Dymphna stay on in Germany? But that, I knew, was not the question. The question was: could I live without her? To that the answer was no. I could not, and would not.

The truth cannot be told to those who presume to be my judges – the dons of Oxford, her family, and my family. A high-minded reason must be found. No man in that decade of anxiety, that decade on which W. H. Auden pinned the label, the 'low, dishonest decade', could risk letting the judges know the secrets of his heart. How could I confess to any one of them that without Dymphna my serenity would disappear as the colours of a butterfly vanished if human fingers touched the wings.

I hatched a plan: if war looked imminent Dymphna would come to Oxford and we would be married. She agreed. It never occurred to me that I was asking her to sacrifice her career in Germanic languages for my sake. It never occurred to me I was assuming a man had priority over a woman. I was a child of my times. Women were the servants of men, nurses to men who fancied they had a creative imagination, sources of inspiration to men who believed one day their light would shine. Many years were to pass before I asked myself the question: was I justified? Who can tell? Dymphna, I was to find, had all the gifts of the server. But was any man entitled to exploit those gifts for his own glory?

Events moved swiftly. Dressed in a fur coat, fingers decorated with rings, and a suitcase full of leather-bound volumes of German classics, all entrusted to me by Otto Wiener in Munich to take to London to raise money to support him and his family in their impending exile, I left Bonn early in January 1939 for Calais and Dover. My bizarre appearance excited the interest of the British Customs officers at Dover. I looked to be the English version of the Australian abroad – showy, vulgar, in for all the lurks. When a Customs man asked me in the taunting voice of a British Customs officer who has sniffed out a cheat whether I had anything to declare, I was tempted to reply that if I answered his question in my way he would be listening for a very long time. He was disappointed. He could find nothing amiss in the luggage of this leery Australian. I bought a block of Cadbury's chocolate, and savoured it with much pleasure, the temptation to revert to the familiar British world being still very strong. But a break with the Melbourne past had begun. From that time there were to be no safe harbours. The journey over a very stormy sea had begun. There must be no looking back. Lot's wife had looked back, and had been turned into a pillar of salt. Those who looked back accumulated dust in their eyes.

But what to say to those I knew in Oxford? What to write to those I knew well in Melbourne? The English people I knew showed no signs of liberating their minds from their delusions. The right in politics, like the right in Germany, believed Hitler was on their side, that he could spearhead a crusade against Bolshevism in Russia. The left still clung to the dangerous delusion that evil men were incompetent – that Hitler, né Schicklgruber, was a failed soldier, a failed painter, a failed Putsch commander, a talentless mountebank, a psychopath who would lapse into a tantrum if only the French and the

British had the guts to stand up to him. Tyrants were despicable: the educated Englishman knew his history. The tyrant, as W. H. Auden reminded them in his poem, 'Epitaph on a Tyrant', written in that January of 1939, 'knew human folly like the back of his hand'. The *New Statesman* knew all about the 'crimes' of the British governing classes and the 'folly' of the common man. Raymond Mortimer was writing exquisite reviews of recent books, sorting out the wheat from the chaff. *The Times* was asking who would hear the first cuckoo in spring.

The English were holding up the pole for the tent which protected civilisation from the barbarians. Young priests of the Catholic Church, members of orders such as the Benedictines and the Jesuits, J. Alfred Prufrocks in clerical garb, chatted exquisitely about the forthcoming election of a new Pope. The academics, the writers and the publicists spoke with that hushed whisper, the muted tones we postulants from the colonies and Dominions were expected to master if we were to be admitted to the club. They were the wise ones: they knew. The rest of the world, especially Australians, were very foolish, and could not be told what the English knew. This assumption of effortless superiority had maddened me before the journey to Germany. Now, when I knew what the German government planned to do, and had the power to do, I condemned such behaviour as criminally reprehensible. As for the *New Statesman* writers and readers, I could imagine Raymond Mortimer polishing the sentences in which he told us of the delicate beauty, and the fine conscience in a paragraph by Marcel Proust, as the day of reckoning came nearer and nearer.

Years later I read the words by Alec Hope, ' the chatter of cultured apes / Which is called civilisation over there', and understood why he wrote in such a savage vein. I wonder why generations of Australians wasted their substance trying to imitate the English upper classes, why they were prepared to demean themselves into objects of ridicule by the very people whose approval they coveted so desperately. At that time I would not have cited this as evidence of human folly or of the madness in the hearts of all of us. I believed then we could all be changed. Now I am not so sure whether we can be changed. I still believe in a change in society, but not a change in the human heart, because that can never be. Why should a lover wish to change the beloved?

There was no time for meditation on human madness and folly in January 1939. Events in Europe were making preoccupation with personal happiness and ambition almost obscene. Hitler was making threatening speeches about Holland. The resistance of the English was stiffening: even the conservatives have had enough. The Munich agreement must not be torn up like that famous (or infamous) 'scrap of paper' in August 1914. Fate might decide there would be a war, if so, so be it. What to do? I tell Humphrey Sumner of my anxiety about Dymphna, but I do not and cannot tell him I cannot live without her. Perhaps he guesses that – he tells me what I want to hear: 'You think, Clark, she ought to leave Germany.' I say, 'Yes, I do', trying to mask my passion and stress my concern.

So the telegram is sent to Bonn: 'Come at once', or some such masterful words. Dymphna is prepared to sacrifice everything for me – a brilliant career as a linguist, a teacher and a translator. I am not saying with Ned Kelly, 'I am Ned Kelly and my will must be obeyed.' I am a child and a man of my age. I belong to old Australia, the country of male domination, male superiority. I just assume the man comes first. I do not perceive what I am asking of her – let alone feel any guilt. My one anxiety is that the 'others' (as my mother called them), the judges of this world, will weigh me in the balance and find me wanting – that they will see me as a man who is ruled by passion, that the tempests within must be quietened even if that meant the woman he loved never finished her doctorate at the University of Bonn. Would there be others who would be called on to make a similar sacrifice? I did not foresee then that a price must be paid by all those who assume that what they want they must have at once, even if that inflicts pain and loss on other people.

Dymphna arrived in Oxford from Bonn on 29 January. The chaplain of Balliol College, the Reverend T. M. Layng, agreed to marry us by special licence. His wife invited Dymphna to stay with them at 147 Banbury Road until the morning of the wedding. We were married on 31 January at 11.30 a.m. in the Church of St Michael at the North Gate, which was only one hundred yards away from my two rooms at 10 St Michael's Street, opposite the Oxford University Union. As a gesture of devotion to my mother I took communion early next morning in the Church of St Michael, seeking I knew not what, because the 'comforting words' Christ spoke to all believers meant nothing to me at that time. My mind, my heart, were on 'other things'. I was only twenty-three, and Dymphna just twenty-two.

George Kerferd, an old friend from Melbourne Grammar and Melbourne University days gave Dymphna away. We had had many talks about life, he always telling me he had abandoned the Christian view of life and replaced it with the Greek view. I always wanted something more than slogans such as 'Know thyself', 'Moderation in all things' – and the counsel of discipline, restraint, acceptance and resignation. My presence at the altar that day with my bride-to-be was not evidence of my submission to any deity, but of my wanting to do the right thing in the eyes of my mother. I wanted it both ways. I believed it was possible to keep alive the ideal of the Madonna in my heart while plunging heels up into the Dionysian frenzy.

Mervyn Austin was there, witnessing to the high solemnity of the occasion, while taking care no one should know what was going on in his mind. Mervyn was an Anglophile, a disciple of the Greeks, and an observer of the morals of Melbourne Grammar. Peter Lalor, the grandson of the Eureka hero, was also there. He was an enthusiast for many things, for T. S. Eliot, James Joyce, D. H. Lawrence, Baron Corvo, Mallarmé and Marcel Proust, and the liturgy of the Catholic Church. He was a playboy of the Melbourne world, who confessed late at night that he wanted to know what it was all about but no one so far had ever told him. He was a man who mocked at Father Murphy, the rector of Newman, in the bars around Melbourne University, knowing that within a week or so he would confess to a priest that he had sinned against God in thought, word and deed, and beg for forgiveness. He was a wit who adored his mother, he was a fossicker for 'precious metal in the dirt'. He was there dressed in the garments of conformism and respectability, his eyes at one time sparkling with gaiety, and then clouding over with the melancholy of a man who feared he had squandered his innocence in mad rushes down the 'primrose path of pleasure'.

Humphrey Sumner, my supervisor, sat in a pew, his face immobile, not even his eyes betraying whether he was at a charade of human folly or a ceremony which would live on in the minds of those who heard two human beings take the vows few have ever observed. Kenneth Bell, a history don at Balliol, the father of eight, a brilliant teacher, but author of no books, a man driven to behave in eccentric ways to ensure his prominence in the stories of Balliol men, lived up to his reputation. At the opening of the service he said in a stage whisper, 'Isn't she a corker?' To my later regret Fin Crisp was not there. We drew close to each other years later at Canberra, when the measurers put up their first take-over bid for the Australian National University. Other eyes and other ears also witnessed the moment when the young man with the capacious heart vowed to forsake all others from that day until death did them part.

Kenneth Bell invited us all to lunch at the Swan Inn, near Witney, on a day when, though there was not a cloud in the sky, the outside air was so cold that I wore woollen pyjama pants under my trousers to ensure my voice did not falter. Clergymen's sons and Melbourne Grammar boys must stand firm. There were no speeches. Dymphna was magnificent. I was like a telephone exchange in which if you were to plug in to all the voices you would have difficulty in making head or tail of what was being said. There was a happy man within: there was also the man who from childhood had heard his mother say, 'Just ask the others, Mann dear, and see what they think.'

My mother was generous. She and my father were then holidaying at Summerlands on Phillip Island. On receiving the telegram informing her we were married she did what no other event had ever persuaded her to do: she climbed down to the rocks on which my father was fishing, waved the telegram in her right hand, and called out, 'Charlie, Manning's married.' My father dropped all the fish he had caught into the sea. (That day must have reminded them of many things, but I never heard whether they were able to speak to each other about those events in Sydney and Kempsey which had cast a shadow over their lives.) My mother wrote a beautiful letter to both of us, welcoming Dymphna into her heart, telling her from that day on, that 31 January, she was also her daughter, and adding a coda for me, one of my mother's ways of displaying her concern for my morals: 'Morally, Mann dear', she wrote, 'we are all hoping everything is all right.' It was, but not for the reasons my mother would approve and sanction!

Dymphna's parents were displeased. Unwittingly I have cheated her father of what he had hoped would soothe the wounds he had endured as a non-Anglo-Celt, non-Protestant in Australia, the scars carried by every outsider in those days in Australia – his daughter would win the prize Melbourne University had declined to award to him, the prize of being a full Professor of Germanic languages. In the tumult of the moment he uttered words about the marriage of people too young to know their own minds, and other unfortunate reflections on the simple boy from the Australian bush.

These aspersions were promptly reported to me by those who must have known I could never abide an adverse character sketch. Perhaps Dymphna's father was so overwhelmed by loss that he could not resist the temptation to take vengeance on the young man who had inflicted such a wound. Once again there was a failure of my imagination. I concluded rashly that he believed I was unworthy of his daughter. Not so. I should have foreseen how deep his wound would be, and been understanding with him. That was my loss, as he had much to teach me. That was in time my pain, because Mr Passion had later to confess to himself that he had done an injury to another human being. That was one of the great follies of my life, one of those deeds for which there would always be regret but never a happy issue.

Dymphna's mother had her own private reasons for being sceptical, even cynical about the relations between men and women. Her own father had been a flogger, her brother a dominator, a thirster for success, a man for whom women were only vessels to relieve him of his lust, and not companions of the mind. Her husband was a man with whom it had all gone wrong, someone who had behaved in ways she could neither understand nor forgive. She wrote a letter which said many things, but not one word of approval. Probably she did not know what she was doing when she could not bring herself to write 'the one thing needful'. In the weeks that followed neither of them was able to say to my mother the words she wanted to hear: that however impulsive, or even foolhardy and precipitate, my action had been, they shared her belief in her 'Mann dear'. They were not prepared to say those words. They probably never knew, what my mother and 'Lofty' Franklin knew, of what lived in my heart. They only knew the young man who, by surrendering to his own passions, had exposed them to the Melbourne mockers – those frequenters of university drawing rooms who seemed more interested in watching the vulnerable squirm than in making 'the paths of true learning flourish and abound'.

Thanks to Dymphna my life began to flourish and to abound in the riches that mattered to me. The condescension of the English to all the people from 'out there' ceased to madden, and became a joke. They were to be pitied. Tocqueville was now my guide to the world. As early as 1836, in the first two volumes of *De la Démocratie en Amérique* he prophesied the two world powers in the twentieth century would be Russia and America. The English had already lost their material supremacy: they were gradually losing their moral authority. We Australians must also rethink our position in the world. We have always assumed the British navy was our umbrella. As Dick Casey put it: 'If we get into trouble in this part of the world the English will come to our aid.' But what if the British navy can no longer do that? What then? I did not put the question to myself in those months after the marriage when my private world at last knew some peace, some order, and the public world was collapsing into chaos. The English were on the way down. Then what of Australia? At that time this, for me, was a question which I could not answer simply because I knew so little about Australia. But English behaviour, English reluctance to acknowledge there was rotten timber in the ship on which they were sailing into the future, turned my mind more and more to Australia. To search for the river of life in England early in 1939 was like following a mirage in the desert.

Tocqueville turned my mind towards Australia. Tocqueville, like all men and women with the 'head piece clever' and the 'undisciplined heart' (Charles Dickens, *David Copperfield*) loved liberty, as he put it, to distraction. He was ill at ease and affronted if anyone presumed to tell him what he should think or how he should behave. But he had come to the conclusion that the great mass of mankind did not share his passion, that, in the words of the Grand Inquisitor in Dostoevsky's *The Brothers Karamazov*, the great mass of mankind did not want their liberty: they wanted their earthly bread, they wanted to find someone to worship. The great mass of mankind had what Tocqueville called '*un goût dépravé*' for equality. To satisfy their hunger for material well-being (their earthly not their heavenly bread) and this taste for equality, human beings would hand over their freedom to someone they loved to worship. Only the great and the strong loved and cherished liberty, the ones who hungered for 'heavenly bread'. The great mass of mankind hungered for their 'earthly bread' – or as T. S. Eliot put it much later than Tocqueville: they wanted 'their liquor and their women' – not liberty or a vision of God's throne.

The tendency of the age was towards the large state: large states led to centralisation of government, and that centralisation provided the institutional framework for the rule of the one or the few. So human nature and the tendencies of that nature were preparing the way for a Napoleon to destroy liberty. Again I began to think of Australia. My knowledge was slight. I knew about the centralisation of government in the capital cities of the States. I knew little of Australian intellectual history. Perhaps the history of Australia might explain why things are as they are.

Tocqueville was fearful of the tyranny of the majority. That was uncongenial to liberty: that was uncongenial to the creative spirit, uncongenial to the elite, the creators of the high culture of Europe:

that was fertile soil for mediocrity, conformism, for little souls, for devotees of cosiness – not for the *gens supérieurs*. Tocqueville was writing about America. But, like my Melbourne contemporaries, I did not know intellectual America – I knew only colonial British America: I did not know then that in the year in which Tocqueville published the first two volumes of *De la Démocratie en Amérique* (1836) Emerson was telling Americans they could not always 'be fed on the sere remains of foreign harvests'. Nor, I was to find, could we Australians. But not then, not then.

Tocqueville dealt with the question which has been with me ever since childhood. 'Liberty', he wrote in *De la Démocratie en Amérique*, was doing 'what is good and just'. Agreed. But what is the good? Answer: the teachings of religion. Yes – but belief was declining and would go on declining. What then? Tocqueville was not a ferocious man. Unlike Dostoevsky, Tocqueville did not suffer from the 'falling sickness'. Tocqueville had never spat at a man because he disagreed with his ideas, as Dostoevsky spat at Bakunin in Geneva. Tocqueville was not a 'great sinner': Tocqueville's past did not drive him, as Dostoevsky was driven all his life, to 'redeem the days' of which his madness and his folly had robbed him. Unlike Dostoevsky, Tocqueville made no extravagant prophecies, no prediction that without Christ men would kill each other down to the last two men on earth. He made no wild remarks. But he knew the dilemma of his day. Religious belief was the essential condition of goodness and liberty. But, alas, he himself did not and could not believe; he had lost his faith. Like Dostoevsky he had the thirst to believe. As a child he had heard from the members of his own family what the Jacobin atheists had done to bishops, priests and nobles. All his life he was tormented by the fear that he, too, might end his days on the scaffold rather than the pillow.

Others wrote of Tocqueville as an aloof man, a man who distanced himself from the common people, a man who disdained the vulgar, the coarse and the show-offs. Tocqueville, I already knew, had written of a French radical, Blanqui: 'It was then I saw for the first time a man the memory of whom has always filled me with disgust.' Blanqui wore a dirty collar: that was his offence against the *comme il faut* (establishment) lore of the salons of Paris, and the castles of the pre-1789 nobility. Tocqueville, unlike Dostoevsky, did not believe the peasants of Europe, the wretched and the poor, had kept alive the image of Christ in their hearts, that they would redeem Europe from the worship of the golden calf. Tocqueville was one of the elect. '*Ce que le vulgaire*', he told his contemporaries, '*appelle du temps perdu est bien souvent du temps gagné*' (What the common herd call time wasted, is very often time well spent). Tocqueville was no man of the people, no aristocrat seeking salvation in the labour of his hands. Tocqueville, I read, was not born a slave to sensual lust. But I suspected then that he had a 'capacious heart'. The sniffers for ancient indecency have lately produced the evidence that his passions were not, as he professed them to be, '*continuellement spirituelles*' (always for things of the spirit). His heart also was a battlefield between the ideal of the Madonna and the pursuit of Sodom. Working on Tocqueville became part of the quest for understanding.

In March in a crowded Cornmarket street in Oxford, while the clocks were striking midday, Dymphna told me she was going to have a child. I asked whether there was any way out of it. Her faith, her love, silenced the voice of the secular humanist and failed family planner. She knew 'the burden of the mystery'. We wrote to Melbourne. My mother rejoiced: a child was the wish of the Father. 'Thy will be done on earth.' My father was silent. My brother let me know he could not stand it if 'anything was wrong' – that I could not do *that* to him.

Others were not so warm, or so open. It seemed as though everything I did was wrong, that I only vexed them the more I tried. The administrators of the University of Melbourne, Tocqueville's 'men dressed in black', wanted their pound of flesh. In their eyes I was the villain who had seduced Dymphna from the path of duty, which was to write a thesis for her doctorate at the University of Bonn. The straiteners were teaching me what they lived by, what manner of men they were, just as my life with Dymphna was printing in my heart the hope, the promise, that work and love might give me the words with which to tell others what I have seen, what I have lived through during the quest for grace. It might cultivate in me the strength and confidence to report all the beauty and horror of what I had discovered and would go on discovering in the human heart. But, alas, it took me years, far too many years, to muster the strength to dispense with anodynes. It took me far too long to free myself from years in a vicarage, of governing behaviour, even peace of mind by asking what the others would think. Perhaps one never acquires the strength not to give a damn about what *they* say or what *they* do. Perhaps that ghost from the past never goes away – just as one never quite lives up to the advice, 'Judge not!'

In the spring we had a relief from one of our anxieties. At the time we were living on a diet of beans with bacon offcuts, mackerel (the cheapest fish you could buy in Oxford), bread and tea, all cooked or boiled on a spirit stove which cost ninepence, but which, being so cheap, often caught on fire and had to be thrown out of the window into the courtyard fronting the remains of Oxford's mediaeval wall – and another ninepence to replace it. Yet we continued to smoke, and have a weekly spree with a large bottle of beer – though unhappily not large enough for a man of my appetites.

The Director of the University Extension Board offered me the position of tutor or coach to a young man taking the university entrance examination in May or June. The salary was £5 a week. There was a cottage in the village, and £5 a week for expenses. We had been living on fifteen shillings a week for food. My pupil, Dick Turner, lived in a manor in Berkshire, near Newbury. His father had made a fortune out of ship-building, but had suffered some unspecified mental collapse. His mother belonged to the Buccleuch family. My pupil was a congenital diabetic who had never been to school. He needed no coaching or teaching, he being as well read and articulate as a final honours history student in Australia. He played the piano beautifully. So there I was, after the cheese-paring at Oxford, walking on the marble floors, gaping at the portraits on the walls of the landed magnificoes of the past and shipping magnates of the present on my way to a library, almost as extensive in its holdings in history, literature and politics as the library of a university college in Australia, and listening to Mrs Turner at morning and afternoon tea. I remember she said to us one morning in her beautiful English voice, as I risked lingering yet again over the sad eyes of a woman who had died years ago in the flesh, that Mussolini had made only two mistakes in policy since 1922, one being the attack on Abyssinia, and the other being the alliance with Hitler. I had never before heard a Fascist discussed as a rational human being.

The England of lord and master was still alive. The wife of the local vicar thanked Mrs Turner fulsomely for the pheasant they had so much enjoyed on Easter Sunday. The chauffeur stood to attention and doffed his cap when Mrs Turner came near. The vicar explained to us that matins on Sunday was for the gentry, and evensong for plough-boys, gardeners, gamekeepers and their families. At the one matins

I attended in search of what my children will later call 'Dad's atmosphere', the vicar preached a sermon on God's plan – how some were born to high estate and some to low, and how those who wanted to win the prize of eternal bliss would be wise not to 'kick against the pricks' in this life. I never found out what he told the ploughboys, though he did tell me he prepared a different sermon for them.

I wondered about a society in which a few had hand-cut chauffeur-driven Rolls Royces, and the rest sold their labour to produce such wealth, and country vicars and their wives ate their pheasants in return for a weekly correction of Christ's teaching in the village church – how long could this go on? I also wondered whether any social arrangements could ever remove the cause of Mrs Turner's sadness, whether any such change or any advance in self-knowledge could ever remove some 'primal fault' in all of us. Dicky Turner played a Chopin nocturne to me, and I looked out of the bay windows over the well-manicured grass, the flower beds with their edges cut so neatly that I wondered whether it was the work of a surgeon or an artist, rather than a village gardener. I had a vision then of those things in life which would never change.

Then the miracle occurred. We understood why Browning wrote the words: 'Oh to be in England, now that April's there'. The woods were carpeted with flowers. Wordsworth's daffodils were 'dancing and fluttering in the breeze'. Some of what I had learned in Australia was true. There was this yearly marvel: trees, shrubs, and flowers had each year a resurrection. England was William Blake's 'green and pleasant land'. We set off from our village near Newbury to cycle to Winchester, Salisbury and Stonehenge – both of us on bikes which would have been scorned by Hubert Opperman. But they became part of the fun, part of the journey of discovery – the discovery of two English Gothic cathedrals, one at Winchester and the other at Salisbury. We heard choirs of men and boys in bloodless singing of Evensong. We wondered why a country which had once produced men and women who had had the confidence and the faith to take their civilisation to almost every continent on the Earth were now singing like eunuchs. The statue of the Virgin and Child had been banished from the churches over four hundred years ago, as the ones with ink rather than blood in their veins took over.

And on to Stonehenge, not knowing much about that venerable stone arrangement which had survived from the centuries before Blake's fancy that 'those feet' had once trodden on English soil, that some ancestors of the English had seen the 'countenance divine'. I remembered Thomas Hardy's Tess had slept there the night before *they* took her away. I did not know then that Merlin visited Stonehenge – I had not read then that the sons of the devil and a pure woman sometimes have the gift of prophecy. At the time I was not ready for the idea that good and evil were a permanent part of the human condition. I believed naively that, if God were dead in men's minds, then there was no Devil, there was no evil, or what evil had survived from the Christian era would wither away. Enlightened souls would be tender and loving to each other. Or so I fondly hoped. The capitalist crisis might erupt into another destructive war between the nations. But the forces of good would win: a golden age for humanity would rise out of the ashes of the corrupt society in which we were all then living. Estates such as the Turners' at Newbury would be turned into parks and museums of rest and culture: cathedrals such as Winchester and Salisbury would be buildings in which people would be shown the statues, the stained glass windows, the engravings and the inscriptions as examples of human folly in the centuries when their sufferings caused by exploitation and domination drove them to such consolation and compensation, deluded by a hope of the life of the world to come.

Back in our cottage near the Turner estate the miracle of the English spring continued to delight us. Fin Crisp came for a weekend, during which all three of us took comfort from telling and listening to each other's stories about the foibles of the English. On a Lady Ryder course for colonials on how to behave in high society Fin had been embarrassed when the butler in his particular host's mansion removed his made-up dress tie, and laid out on his bed a black bow-tie which Fin could not tie. Australian resourcefulness came to his aid just in time, and he took his sherry while his host dropped some words of sympathy for the people who, he feared, would find themselves again in the trenches fairly soon.

Amidst all these signs of fruitfulness all around us, the sense of impending doom was always there as a relative minor to a major key of 'hope and triumph'. I remember reading in Gustave Flaubert's *De l'Education sentimentale* a remark by the hero, Frédéric: *'Si l'on avait de bonne foi, on pourrait s'entendre'* (With good will, we could agree). He was sitting in a park in Paris, listening with his lover to the sound of gun-fire in the streets of Paris during the June days of 1848. That was the point. What if one did not believe, what then? Well, rather like Scarlett O'Hara in *Gone with the Wind*, I kept telling myself I would think about that later on. For the moment there was my love, there was work, there was the whole of Europe to explore, there was the hope of better things for humanity, the hope that working for those better things, working until the past became my bible of knowledge and wisdom for the present (that would be my contribution) – all this would, as it were, 'stifle the sorrow' deep down in my heart.

Cricket in the summer term at Oxford led to more bizarre confrontations with Englishmen. The captain of the Oxford team and his advisers liked my performances with bat and wicket-keeping gloves in the freshmen's trials. Alas, they did not like my Melbourne University cap – that being, in their eyes, too large and sloppy. So they elected me at once to the Authentics, and presented me with a cap. I did not have the money to buy the essentials. Every gentleman owned his own kit – cricketing bag, bat, batting gloves and pads, and in my case wicket-keeping pads and gloves. Humphrey Sumner was so delighted a Balliol man had a chance to play for Oxford that he paid for my equipment – all save the bag. So my Gladstone bag branded me unmistakably as an Aussie. The equipment did not come before the next trial. So I innocently wore pads lying in the dressing-room and, on returning to the pavilion for the tea adjournment, was taken by the shoulders and given a good shaking and threatened with a 'good thrashing' by a young Englishman, a wearer of the right scarf, the right tweed coat, indeed everything very much *comme il faut*, whose gear I had unwittingly used. I was a usurper: I was again an outsider.

After a promising start against Gloucestershire, after which the *Times*, displaying their infuriating habit of assuming the English were the final arbiters in everything, gave me an approving verbal pat on the back, things did not go well. In the game against Yorkshire I decided rashly, and all too impulsively, to show my English colleagues that the way to play Hedley Verity, the English and Yorkshire slow left-arm bowler, was to use your feet – 'Don't bat as though you were chained to the popping crease. Launch out, take risks, dare and dare again.' Well, I danced down the pitch to the first ball, planning to take it on the full and drive it past mid-on for four. Alas, I took my two or three steps, only to find the ball was drifting away outside my legs. By some fluke I mishit the ball for four past square-leg. I heard from the pavilion the polite applause, the incredulous, 'Oh, well played, Clark'. I decided to do it again. But this time almost before

I lifted the bat, and danced down the pitch, the ball was in the wicket-keeper's gloves. There was a swift retribution for my *hubris*. After surviving all the wiles of Hedley Verity and the onslaughts of Bill Bowes, the Yorkshire captain called on Maurice Leyland to bowl. Rashly interpreting this move as a triumph, I became reckless. Leyland bowled me with a full-tosser. Exit Clark, the daring Australian, the man who believed he could play a few fancy strokes!

There was one memorable event in the game. Herbert Sutcliffe, a superb batsman on a sticky wicket, was still in when the last Yorkshireman, Bill Bowes, came to the crease. Knowing Bill Bowes was not likely to last for long Sutcliffe lashed out at the first ball he received. He mishit it. The ball flew straight up in the air. The Oxford captain did not call the name of the player to take the catch. The ball descended with a loud plop on to the centre of the wicket as the batsmen walked a leisurely single – so high had the ball climbed. Bowes looked back over his shoulder and asked Sutcliffe in a loud Yorkshire voice, 'Bert, have you ever tried walking on water?' Sutcliffe was not amused.

Years later when I told this story to Jack Fingleton in Canberra, Jack Fingleton said he had first sampled the laconic wit of Bowes on that memorable day at the Melbourne Cricket Ground in 1932 during the infamous bodyline series:

Manning, you'll remember the day when Bowes bowled Bradman for a duck? The Don, contrary to all his usual caution at the beginning of an innings tried to hook Bowes for four off the first ball he received. You remember the hush, Manning, which descended on the ground when the bails fell to the ground. What the crowd didn't know was that Bowes put his hands on his hips, turned to the umpire at the bowler's end and me, and said, 'Well, I'll be fooked'.

Bradman had his revenge on Bowes in England in 1934. It was always fatal for a bowler to rouse the wrath of the Don. He was merciless, he never having pity on those guilty of such folly.

Playing cricket for Oxford worked one miracle. The English began to speak to me. The head porter of Balliol lifted his hat and smiled as I passed through the entrance gate to Balliol in the Broad. Henry Whitehead, the nephew of A. N. Whitehead, and Professor of Mathematics at Oxford asked me in that picturesque language of his to join him in a 'controlled blind' at the Dew Drop Inn where the landlady served beer in pink pots so capacious not even serious drinkers needed a refill within the half-hour. Ted Heath, then an organ scholar at the college, gave me a smile – and that, for an Englishman at the time, said quite a lot. Roy Jenkins, who will later take the other side in politics, sought me out in the Junior Common Room after Hall and asked me, if I remember rightly, why Australian batsmen danced so far down the wicket to meet the ball. It was like asking why Australians were different from the English.

Tim Bligh, then a demon fast-bowler but somewhat erratic, made quite an intimate remark to me. He told me he did not need to go out with women, as he could enjoy it all in his dreams, in which, I gathered, each night he 'out-paramoured the Turk', adding, as a bonus, dreams were not followed by remorse. We laughed – and that was a change. Years later I was surprised to see a photograph of Sir Timothy Bligh in an English paper. He was wearing a pin-striped suit and a bowler hat. He had become principal private secretary to Lord Home, the Conservative Prime Minister, a man who, on his own confession, and on his appearance, did not look to me to be visited with such pictures even in dreams. But then, who can tell? After all, I never foresaw Tim Bligh in a bowler hat.

Humphrey Sumner invited Dymphna and me to tea to meet his friend Dr Julian Huxley. On meeting him I was so nervous I gave him a mini-lecture on the habits of the platypus, before realising I was speaking to a world authority. When I paused for breath he said one icy word: 'Quite.' I was silent for the rest of the afternoon. He told us why the novels of his brother Aldous were sprinkled with knowledge well off the beaten track. One winter the Huxley family holiday was spent high up on the Pyrenees. As the members of their party sipped their tea on the balcony he, Julian, noticed some mules struggling up the path to the chalet. He asked, 'What on earth is this?' Brother Aldous sheepishly confessed not to worry, it was his special rice paper edition of the *Encyclopaedia Britannica*. So no wonder the pages of his novels were sprinkled with the learning of the ages.

Oxford offered so much. We moved from 10 St Michael's Street to 13 Bradmore Road, to a one-room basement flat with a kitchen and bathroom and access to a spacious garden. Paupers though we were, somehow we bought a wireless and a gramophone. We were so happy that I was always singing, badly, but of course, with wild ecstasy the love songs from Schumann's *Dichterliebe*, with words by Heinrich Heine, songs such as 'Allnächtlich im Traume seh' ich dich'

(Every night I see you in my dreams). Dymphna was not quite so happy when I sang 'Ein Jüngling liebt' ein Mädchen' (A youth once loved a maiden); she was puzzled why that moved me so deeply. It was a time for singing, a time to tell the world, *'In diesen heiligen Hallen kennt man die Rache nicht'* (Within these sacred walls, / We know not vengeance), a time for the universal embrace; though one night, if I remember rightly, when the people in our little world were bubbling over with joy listening to the first movement of Bach's fifth *Brandenburg Concerto*, someone asked what it was all about, and I said it was about death, the death of all of us. There was silence for a while, till Dymphna told them not to take any notice, Manning was like that, he just said those things. I wound up the record, started the Adagio, and said, again if I remember rightly, this was a message about resignation and acceptance.

The mood of the time was one of gaiety. There was much laughter. George Kerferd visited us often. I told him this was the time in one's life for not being a Melbourne suburban coast-hugger. He laughed. He told me he believed in the Greek teaching about restraint and moderation. I told him I believed in moderation in all things, but not in moderation. He laughed again. Lloyd Austin, then a candidate for a doctorate at the University of Paris, and later a Professor of French at Cambridge, but never at Melbourne, because Melbourne has its special kind of envy about some of her gifted sons and daughters, spent a few days with us. He was then working on Paul Bourget. One or two of those pink pots in the Dew Drop Inn soon made it plain that Bourget was not his subject – that his subject was the whole of life, but he had to get on, and to get on he had to conform to what the passionless professors of the Sorbonne ordained a young man from 'out there' should be doing.

'Tokkers', as Dymphna and I called the work on Tocqueville, was feeding my heart. There were many delights. Humphrey Sumner advised me to read Balzac: 'I mean, Clark,' he said rather sternly, 'the political novels', adding with a twinkle in his eye and the smile of a man who had come to accept with regret that not all of his scholars were 'eunuchs of the kingdom' for Balliol's sake, his hope that I would not be sidetracked by the novels of passion. Well, I was. I devoured them. Sumner urged me to work on the Tocqueville papers in the château near Cosqueville during the summer vacation. He would write to M. le Comte. M. le Comte was gracious: he would be pleased to allow *'le jeune Anglais'* to read the papers. So, having practically no money, we planned a trip to Europe. My father-in-law was dumb-founded by such recklessness. In a letter he asked me, 'What are your prospects for the future?' I replied brazenly that my financial future was assured. That was also very cheeky. I meant it was certain to be disastrous, but that it did not matter. I was so happy at the time that I was even beginning to understand why Christ had told his followers that the body was more important than the raiment.

Like many of his colleagues in the Faculty of Arts at the University of Melbourne I have passed a false judgement on my father-in-law. He was, I realised later, offering to help me, but hiding his generous heart behind this bank-manager style interrogation of the finances of Mr Extravagant. Years later I discovered how generous he was, and how he had envisaged Dymphna achieving the prize the walnut-hearted men at Melbourne University were determined would never be his, and how much the marriage had hurt him because it had blighted the chance for at least that satisfaction. By then it was too late; he died in September 1964. His ashes were manuring a rose bush at Springvale Crematorium. My father's and my mother's bodies were lying side by side in Box Hill Cemetery. By then I had discovered what my father and my father-in-law had suffered, the one at the hands of the life-deniers of the Church of England in Sydney, and the other from the Dutch Reformed Church in Stellenbosch, South Africa. But it was too late to speak, too late to let them know someone had at least understood, and was sorry. When we are young we find fault: when we are old we view everyone, well almost everyone, with the eye of pity, and punish ourselves for being in the salad years like the eternal husband of the Russians – a man who does not notice such things.

We went first to Booischot, the village in Belgium near Aarschot where Dymphna's father had been a child prodigy in a large peasant family. The beginning was edgy. Dymphna's uncle, Louis Lodewyckx, and his wife lived in retirement in a villa on their farmlet. The family had come a long way since Dymphna's father turned the handle for churning the butter with one hand and held the book he was studying in the other. Alas, they all spoke to each other in a strange tongue – not Flemish (i.e. Dutch), but their dialect of Flemish. By then, thanks to Dymphna, and listening to much talk by her father in Flemish, I understood most of what was said in Flemish, but not this torrent which poured out of the mouths of her cousins, uncles and aunts. Her uncle Amandus bows to me and says, '*Zet je gat neer.*' I ask

Dymphna to translate for me. She tells me Amandus has invited me to 'Put your hole down'. I blush, and sit down. They all laugh.

They were not treating me as university anthropologists treat so-called primitive people – they were pleased to see me. The cousin who had married well, i.e. married a successful Walloon businessman, whispered to me in manageable Flemish that Belgian cooking was the best in the whole world. By then we were at the table, and I was trying to hide my inner recoil when food spiced by sour cream was fighting the uphill battle of feeding my hungers. By then I was yearning for roast lamb, roast potatoes, milky rice and tea, and a chance to meet people who understood the one language I knew well – Australian English.

That first afternoon Uncle Louis invited me to sit with him in the orchard. Uncle Louis had been drafted into the gendarmerie by the German army of occupation during the First World War. Uncle Louis not only spoke French: he spoke the French I could understand, employing none of those 'show off' Parisian 'r' sounds. Uncle Louis told me how at dawn every day for four years he watched the British climb out of their trenches. to be mown down by German machine-gun fire. In the late afternoon it was the Germans' turn to attack, and be cut down as a scythe cuts into young grass. As he spoke, the family inside opened the window so that we could both hear the choral movement from Beethoven's *Ninth Symphony*. Uncle Louis, he of the stooped back, but the warm, loving eyes, was saying his '*Figurez-vous, Manning, ce que j'ai vu . . .*' as the German tenor sang of the day when all men would be brothers, and the sopranos sang of that great human contradiction: 'Angels had a vision of God's throne. Insects had sensual lust.' Uncle Louis told me how the German army had entered Booischot in August 1914 and arrested all the men in the village, put them in the church, locked it up, and told the locals that for every German soldier wounded or killed by saboteurs one of the men would be taken out and shot, and how it was all too much for his older brother who went mad, and remained mad until the day he died.

Later that afternoon I went out with Uncle Louis and his son-in-law Georges Delespinette, an executive in Esso. For the younger members of Uncle Louis's family were already moving upwards to the life of what Barry Humphries will call the 'terribly comfortable'. We set out to sample Belgian beer in the local *estaminets*. The pots were of a generous size, the collar at the top was worthy of a Melbourne artist in pouring beer, and the colour of the liquid, not amber but a rose pink, so that the whole looked like a Hilliers' raspberry milk shake. By the time the second was put away my French had made a creative leap forward. We three began to giggle and gurgle. Alas, my French was not up to saying what I wanted to say, my French being literary; I did not have the vocabulary to talk about things that matter most to a man. I could not ask him in French how he had felt on first seeing the paintings by Rubens in the Rubens House in Antwerp, because to come near to a person, language must be the servant and not the master in the exchange.

I will never forget Uncle Louis's warmth in the *estaminet*, never forget that he always voted to have another one. I will never forget the faraway look in his eyes when he recalled the horrors of 1914–18. Uncle Louis had all the gifts of a historian: he could tell a story: he could see all the folly and the madness in the hearts of both sides of any struggle for power and supremacy. Uncle Louis had the eye of pity, the eye of a man who had seen so much he understood why for nearly two thousand years human beings had cried out to their God: 'Have pity on all of us for our great folly, for Thou only, O Lord . . .' But at that time my mind was not on such things as what it would be like to be a historian, let alone what it would be like to tell the story of human beings in Australia. At that time I was a victim of the delusion that such scenes, all the things that mattered, happened only in Europe. That was why I was in Europe.

I was also thinking how I could interest Uncle Louis in another visit to the *estaminets* of Booischot, or chewing over why Dymphna's aunts and cousins were so puzzled by the silence of this simple boy from the Australian bush. They kept asking her: 'Why can't he speak?' or 'Why doesn't he speak?' Rather like Rosa Dartle in *David Copperfield*, they were not imputing anything, they only wanted to know – or so they said. In particular they wanted to know whether I had any prospects, whether I would ever have a job, and, very important, how much I would earn. Dymphna, with that honesty which some will find difficult to believe – I mean that any human being could be so honest – told them she did not know. Nor, for that matter, did I then, except for a hope that one day I might have something to say as a teacher or a writer. They were peasants: they wanted to hear something they could understand – something about money or land or status. Dymphna was obviously expecting a child: that they noticed quick smart and got down to women's business about *that*. But how was this silent, melancholic young man with his head in the clouds, this sook who wept when listening to music, how in the name of fortune was he going to provide for a wife and a child?

So with a directness, a no-beating-about-the-bush approach which distinguished them from English hints, subtleties and nuances, one of her aunts said to her, 'Well, dear, at least you can go back to your family' – speaking in dialect to make sure Dymphna's companion did not understand. We both laughed. The fears they entertained were not my fears. I had my faith, or rather I was a man on a quest, a quest to find an order in the chaos. One day I would understand what it had all been for. One day I would know grace. Dymphna was my mate for the journey ahead. There was no need to worry about money, food, raiment, occupation; they would be found along the way; there was the assurance I had heard as a child that 'all these things shall be added unto you'. Well I was no longer a believer in that sense. I had a faith of my own – keep on the path; work hard; be single-minded like those mythical heroes who had searched for the Holy Grail; and all would be well. What mattered was what happened on the quest.

So off we went to Paris to collect material for the 'Tokkers' – or rather atmosphere. I say atmosphere because Thomas Babington Macaulay had taught me the historian must visit the scenes in his story. R. H. Tawney had put it even more picturesquely: a historian, he had written, needs a pair of good boots. So, in between the cheapest meals available at one of the many *prix fixe* restaurants near the Sorbonne, Dymphna and I walked to the main sites of the revolutions of 1789 and 1848. Carlyle was my guide for the former, and Tocqueville for the latter. We 'did' the Place de la Bastille, the Place de la Concorde where Danton, before placing his head in position for the head-chopper had said to himself in a stage whisper, 'Danton, no weakness', where Du Barry had lost her composure before losing her head, and where one of the modern world's first liberals, Camille Desmoulins, was tried in that fiery furnace and found wanting. We walked to the Champ de Mars where Tocqueville had taken fright on seeing the people in action. Marx had taught me that history is on the side of the people.

A visit to the house of Victor Hugo reminded me that I had other interests than the victory of the people. The man who had lived in that house had loved much. That, too, must be accepted and lived with, or anything one said or wrote would be a lie. The man in that house had wanted forgiveness both in this world and in the life of the world to come. The man in that house had been a lover and a believer – a lover of women, a man who had often been out of his wits for women, and a believer in the capacity of the people (not just the working class) to build a better world. I remembered my father's interest in the story of Jean Valjean and the bishop's candlesticks, and how forgivers lived in a state of grace. Again I began to play with an idea for some work in which I would tell some story from either the present or the past, either based on fiction or as fact (what difference was there *au fond*, as the French had taught me to say?), which would be both the history of a human heart, and the story of people. Wandering around the house of Victor Hugo should have warned me that unless I exercised discipline and restraint such a work would be all about the heart.

We went to the Louvre. Dymphna loved the works of Corot – an early intimation of what was to become one of the great passions in her life, the love of and nurture of trees. I stood in front of da Vinci's *Mona Lisa* for a long time, hearing at the back of my mind those words by Walter Pater, 'She is older than the rocks among which she sits'. I wondered about that smile, or whether there was a smile, or whether he (da Vinci) was the first modern human being – that is to say, the first who had the courage and the strength to peer into the heart of the darkness, to face the truth that here, as a poet put it later, 'we face each other alone'. Da Vinci knew what the author of Ecclesiastes knew. Those like da Vinci who have accepted how it is in the world can eye with tenderness and pity all other human beings. For me that will become clearer later. In the Louvre that afternoon there was a faint intimation of what one might want to write or say but not the faintest hint then that the setting would be in Australia, not even an acknowledgement that one can only write about what one knows.

There was one other impression. The French had no time for people who had no money. The French seemed to measure a man's worth by the amount of money he could spend on a meal. We had no money – and they made us suffer. The English were said to be both insular and imperialist. The French were cultural imperialists. Lloyd Austin had told us he had wanted to study English influences on Paul Bourget for his doctoral thesis. The professors at the Sorbonne told him firmly there was no such subject: the only subject in that field was the influence of Bourget on English writers. The French were impatient with, at times even rude to people like myself who made no attempt to master the Parisian 'r', people who spoke slowly, people who racked their memory for the right word and took time over it. Waiters, newspaper vendors, booksellers, library attendants, hectored me with the same words: '*Dépêchez-vous, Monsieur*' (Get on with it, Monsieur). 'Monsieur' had his own private reason for not being able to hurry when he walked or when he talked.

I had a letter of introduction to Monsieur Redier, the author of the witty book, *Comme disait M. de Tocqueville*. We met over coffee and, maybe (memory for these things is not always reliable) a glass or two of *eau de vie*. The French, I had noticed, often started the day with half a glass of that 'water of life', taken bottoms up – enough to last them till the carafe of *vin ordinaire* taken with the midday meal. M. Redier was lively, M. Redier did all the talking. Once when he paused to attend to his brandy, and take a deep puff at his Gauloise cigarette, I risked saying to him I had the impression, but he must correct me if I was wrong, that the present Comte de Tocqueville was a royalist. M. Redier rose to his feet, moved his moustache smartly left to right, then right to left, then back to centre, struck his breast with his clenched right fist, and shouted, '*Moi aussi. Je suis royaliste profondément convaincu*' ('I too am a profoundly convinced Royalist'). I did not know whether I was talking to a clown, or a prophet of what was to come. I wanted to laugh, but restrained myself. It was my first hint of what had happened to the French *haute-bourgeoisie*. They have abandoned hope in '*le jour de gloire*', they have begun to look backwards; they have begun to walk into the night.

Within a week Dymphna and I travelled to Cosqueville, some thirty kilometres along the Channel coast east of Cherbourg. We were paying guests of Mme la Baronne de Resbecq while we worked on the Tocqueville papers in the family château at Tocqueville. I knew the present Comte was a collateral descendant of Alexis de Tocqueville, the latter having no heirs. I knew too he was the head of the Department of Finance in Paris. Mme la Baronne de Resbecq was cordial. She liked to have guests from Oxford University. She knew, she said, they would be gentlemen, yes and gentlewomen too. Mme la Baronne had been honoured by the Pope for the stand she had taken against the anti-clerical legislation of that atheist and materialist, M. Combes.

Mme la Baronne had some of the qualities to make her a figure of fun in an *opéra bouffe*. She was always dressed in widow's weeds. Her bosom was massive. At the dining-table over which she presided with dignity and authority, she tucked an outsized serviette into the top of her dress, the bosom being so ample the serviette sometimes looked as though it were parallel with the floor. Mme la Baronne told us she loved reading history, that her library consisted mainly of history books, and that Monsieur must feel free to spend time there. When I did, I found that for Mme la Baronne history meant the lives of members of the European royal families. Mme la Baronne had a very special admiration for the British royal family because, 'Figurez-vous (Just imagine), Monsieur ... although they were regrettably Protestant they were all gentlemen.' Thinking she should not entertain such delusions (I was young at the time, no use to speak to me) and still being a good Melbourne man *au fond* (deep down), I told her the story of the death-bed scene of Edward VII, of how his wife Queen Alexandra had asked him whether he would like to speak to Mrs Wood. Mme la Baronne was so astounded she could not speak, though the heaving bosom told much about her shock and her dismay. Then she spoke: 'Figurez-vous (Just fancy!), *Monsieur*', she said, '*c'était sans doute l'action d'une grande reine*' (that was without doubt the act of a great queen). (English royalty always does the right thing.) '*Mais, quant à moi, Monsieur, je n'aurais pas pu, non jamais je n'aurais pu*' (But as for me, Monsieur, I could not have done it, I could never have done it). Then turning to Dymphna: '*Et vous, Madame?*' (And you, Madame?). But she did not want an answer. She fondly believed that, being from Oxford, we must have the right ideas on everything.

To Dymphna's amusement Madame la Baronne confided in her how much she, la Baronne, enjoyed her intimate conversations with Monsieur: '*Monsieur est si doux*' (Monsieur is so gentle). Madame la Baronne had not even caught a whiff of the ravening wolf beneath the melancholy mask. Madame la Baronne decided she could tell me everything: '*Monsieur comprend tout*' (Monsieur understands everything), she told Dymphna, who replied with a Mona Lisa smile – a hint that Madame la Baronne may one day learn what she knew. One day Madame la Baronne confided in me how anxious she was about her other two paying guests, two Swedish girls whose beauty of face and form I had already noted. Did I know they were going each night to the Café Oasis near Cherbourg? No, I didn't. Did I know there were French army officers there? No, I didn't. '*Figurez-vous, Monsieur*', she continued, 'I would not be worried if there were English army officers, because as you know, Monsieur, they are gentlemen! *Mais quant aux officiers français, Monsieur, ils sont un peu entreprenants!'* (But as for French officers, Monsieur, they are rather enterprising!). And she nodded sagely, knowing I would understand and agree. I never managed to witness these strange goings-on at the Oasis, or to discover whether those two Swedish girls supplemented the lessons in the French language with love lessons from French army officers.

Mme la Baronne held bizarre opinions on the world of 1939. In a burst of confidence she told me Karl Marx was the author of *Mein Kampf*. *'Mais, vraiment, Monsieur'* (Yes, truly, Monsieur), she added in an almost hurt voice, when I looked incredulous. As for M. Blum, he had offended in two ways: by birth he was a Jew, and by conviction a socialist. *'Ce Blum, Monsieur, vous comprenez, c'est une ordure'* (That Blum, Monsieur, you should be aware, he's a turd). She took Dymphna aside to say to her something she did not dare to mention to Monsieur, because Monsieur was not only *'si doux'* he was also *'Je crois, Madame, très, très sensible'* (I believe, Madame, he is very, very sensitive), but, Madame, when your husband waved to me with a newspaper yesterday morning, I could not help but notice, Madame, that it was *L'Humanité*, the newspaper of those immoral, godless communists.'

Mme la Baronne presented me with a problem. Here was a woman holding quite odious political opinions, and quite life-shrinking views on the relations between the sexes, and yet, as day followed day, I became very fond of her. She was so generous. We both enjoyed her *mousse au chocolat* and her pea soup so much that Dymphna asked her long-suffering cook, Palmyre, for the recipes. Mme la Baronne lives on in our home in Canberra, thanks to Dymphna. The Baroness served special afternoon tea for me because she knew the English loved their *goûter* – but, alas, the rusks on which she lavishly spread the home-made butter and jam had such hard crusts that the gums of Monsieur began to bleed, and not even all the training in discipline in a vicarage and at a boarding school could conceal from Mme la Baronne that the gums of Monsieur (*'le jeune monsieur anglais'*) (the young English gentleman) were bleeding. On every saint's day, and Mme la Baronne had a very long list of saints, she gave us all a special treat, a glass of *cassis* (blackcurrant liqueur) with our coffee, a glass you needed to drink quickly because the wasps also liked its sugary taste. Mme la Baronne looked pleased. Ah, she said, I am glad Monsieur has an appetite for my *cassis*. She was no fool. I adored her. Museum pieces from the past could have warm hearts.

Mme la Baronne gave shelter to those who could not manage the world. She heeded the divine command about 'the least of the little ones'.

When I returned to Cosqueville in May 1985 '*à la recherche du temps non perdu mais gagné*' (in search of time not lost but gained), I was pleased to hear from the local storekeeper and postmistress that the guardians of political virtue past and present who came to power immediately after the war did not punish Mme la Baronne for not being a friend of 1789.

By contrast, the reception at the Château de Tocqueville was bleak. Monsieur le Comte would love to invite us to dinner – in his eyes we were both '*gens supérieurs*' (superior people), though God knows why – but '*savez-vous, Monsieur, ma cuisinière est malade*' (you see, my cook is ill). She must have been a very sick lady, because we were not invited to dine during the three weeks we worked together on the Tocqueville papers. Monsieur le Comte knew how to wound a man, he having quite a woman's eye for a man's weak spot, and much experience and much pleasure in practising the art on those whose reactions he would enjoy. I spoke French in the Australian way, Dymphna spoke it in the French way. When Monsieur le Comte first met Dymphna he gallantly kissed her hand, exchanged a few pleasantries with her, and then turned to me, and said, 'Madame really speaks French.' From the beginning he expressed the hope that our stay would be short. I was foolish enough to appeal to his heart. The work would influence my chances in life back in Australia – and, supreme folly – 'as you will have noticed, Monsieur le Comte, my wife is expecting a child', hoping that would soften him. But, alas, '*Tiens, tiens*', Monsieur le Comte interjected, 'I did not notice your wife was *enceinte*' – pronounced with an exaggerated Parisian accent, the style and manner of a metropolitan addressing a provincial or a colonial.

The work on the Tocqueville papers proceeded slowly. His hand-writing, as everyone who had seen it had testified, was '*illisible*' – not that I was in any position to complain, or feel superior. The man himself eluded me. There was some mystery in his life-time which my youth, and possibly my lack of flair for such things, did not allow me to fathom. I was fascinated. There were so many Tocquevilles inside the one man. There was the man who wrote each morning in the room in which we were working – wrote those epigrams and generalisations about democratic societies, about the revolution of

1848 and the old regime and the revolution of 1789, and then worked in the fields with the peasants, without telling us a word about the man within. There were so many paradoxes. There was the man of letters who never referred to the work of his illustrious contemporaries such as the novelist Balzac, the poet Baudelaire (he was on the barricades in June 1848), Georges Sand, the historian Louis Michelet, the writer Ernest Renan, or the composer Frédéric Chopin. The observer of democracy, the prophet of the mass age seemed to take little interest in the intellectual and artistic circles of his day which fascinated me.

There was the man who, against the wishes of his family, had married outside his class and his country. He had married an English-woman, Mary Motley. Something had gone wrong: there were no children, and she gathered around her a large collection of cats of as many varieties as the colours in Joseph's coat. There were hints of excursions outside the marriage bed. He was a man of passion who was friendly with a man such as John Stuart Mill, the man who might have written the autobiography of a steam engine rather than the confessions of a passionate heart. I was fascinated, but the man himself always eluded me. Each evening on our way back to Cosqueville I stood in front of the stone bust of Tocqueville in the village square: each day in the castle at Tocqueville I peered at the portraits on the walls, but the man remained an enigma.

As we filled sheet after sheet with notes, the crisis over Danzig and the Polish corridor became graver and graver. Monsieur le Comte dropped the mask: we must stop working there forthwith. The French Army was mobilised on 28 August. We packed hastily, and said tender farewells to Mme la Baronne, who took Dymphna aside and requested her to protect Monsieur in the days to come. 'Figurez-vous, Madame, Monsieur n'appartient pas au monde de combat' (the world of military combat is not for Monsieur). We travelled to Cherbourg and scrambled on board the Cunard liner Queen Mary on 31 August for the crossing to Southampton, spending the time on board doing a nosey-parker on this museum piece of the years (soon gone forever) when there was meaning in the words, 'Britannia rules the waves'. War was imminent. I knew the French either did not want to fight again or could not. 1914–18 had cured them. I knew the French were deter-mined never again to pull chestnuts out of the fire for the English: to manure the soil of the patrie with the blood of French soldiers to save the skins of les Anglais. I knew the French bourgeoisie, the beneficiaries of the Third Republic, were more afraid of Bolshevism than of Nazism.

The English had their dangerous delusions. France, they kept telling us in the press that year, was safe behind the Maginot Line. Britannia still ruled the waves: so Britons never never would be slaves, because the British fleet, like Christ, was unsinkable: the Lord of Hosts was with them, the God of Jacob was their refuge. The left intellectuals were still playing the old record on their gramophones:

Look here, as we all know, old boy, the German tanks are made of cardboard, and, besides, as you know, old chap, they only have enough gasoline to power their Panzer divisions for two weeks, and, as you know, or should know by now, old boy, you've been here long enough, their leaders are stupid – Hitler is a failure in life, a clown, and a man who needs the psychiatrist's couch.

The British were still wallowing in their own virtues and their own moral superiority. Right, not might, they believed, must prevail. On Sunday morning, 3 September 1939, Neville Chamberlain told the British that as he had had no reply to his ultimatum, Great Britain and Germany were now at war. He spoke like a headmaster at an English public school. Hitler has told a lie: there was therefore no further place for him in the school of gentlemen. Hitler was a liar: he must be punished. It was evil things they would be fighting against, but he did not say what the British would be fighting *for*.

A few days later in Oxford I saw a poster issued by the Department of the Army: '*Your* courage, your co-operation will give *us* victory.' Was it still 'we' and 'they'? – the people fighting so that the members of the governing classes could preserve the right to return from lunch at 3 p.m.? That Sunday morning I saw the Tories of Oxford walking to church. Chamberlain stopped in time for them to get to Matins, where they asked their God to remain on their side. In their minds they were still God's chosen people. They did not recognise that Hitler's revolution was a revolution of destruction. They did not foresee that just as he had destroyed the old governing classes in Germany, he would bleed the English governing classes to death. He would so lay waste the old order that twenty years after the war 'grocerdom' would come into its own in England.

I remember also at the time noting the difference between Chamberlain's comments and Hitler's comments on the origins of the war. Chamberlain spoke like Dr Arnold of Rugby School: 'You lied to me, Flashman. There can be no further place for you at Rugby School.' Hitler at least was aware of the high solemnity of the moment. He wrote to the Premier of France, M. Daladier, about Fate: '*Wenn das Schicksaal entscheiden sollte, dass wir miteinander kämpfen müssen . . .*' (If fate should decree that, we must fight against each other . . .).

The question was: what to do? The shadow which fell across my life in 1929 excluded me from military service. There were problems on our doorstep. Our landlord, shrewdly anticipating that even a conservative government would soon have to peg rents, raised our rent to a sum well above our capacity to pay. The money I had earned coaching or tutoring students in need of such a booster disappeared as the young men dropped their academic gowns and put on the uniform of the King. What to do? Fin Crisp nobly helped us to move our worldly goods to the house of the chaplain of Balliol, the Reverend Malcolm Layng, and his wife Mabel. The English liked being Samaritans to colonials with overflowing hearts but empty pockets. It made them feel good, even eased their consciences about their own conspicuous consumption of wealth. So Fin and I pushed the Balliol handcart laden with Clark possessions along the footpath leading to 147 Banbury Road, where Mrs Layng was waiting to receive us. That began a friendship which lasted until her death in 1987 at the age of ninety-three.

But what to do? Dymphna was expecting a child in December, and we had no money. Humphrey Sumner came to the rescue. He told the headmaster of Blundells School to appoint me as senior history master. The headmaster, Neville Gorton, later Bishop of Coventry, was a man of vision. He had already begun to change Blundells from a school preparing young men to qualify for Sandhurst military academy and, after graduation there, for service in the British army in India, the West Indies, or one of the British colonies in Africa, into a school teaching boys the rudiments of Christian humanism. He was a missionary for the 'the wisest and the best', and a man who wanted his boys to love music, poetry and painting rather than learn how to maintain law and order in parts of the world where they would be oppressors and gaolers of the indigenous peoples.

Not long before I arrived at the beginning of November 1939 he had organised a working party of boys to knock down the insignia of Empire in the school chapel and to replace them with works of art which would arouse the interest of the boys in that man who had once walked beside the waters of Galilee. To help him, he had appointed Eric Gill as his artistic adviser. This was another declaration of war against the Philistines, for Gill was a convert to Rome, and, it was said, a man who had every reason to trust in Christ's promise of forgiveness to those who 'loved much'.

Gorton had already attracted into the school a number of boys who were, like himself, very gifted, but eccentric. Many of them were in the History Sixth, which was my main teaching assignment – that, and coaching the First Eleven in cricket.

There was Philip McNair, the son of a Plymouth Brother, who made his mark in the 1950s and 1960s as a scholar of the Italian Renaissance. Not long after I started teaching them, or, more correctly, after they started teaching me, McNair's father stormed into Gorton's office, and shouted at him:

Do you know there is an anti-Christ in the school? That young Australian taught my boy that the Old Testament was a history of the Jewish people – possibly the best history written so far, because it told us so much about the character of God and the Jews.

Gorton, defending me, replied to McNair senior, 'Well, thank God, the boys are being taught to think.' It was my first, but not my last, experience of what you must live through if you offend against or call in question the lore of the tribe.

Robert Sprigge was the son of Sylvia Sprigge, a novelist, and regular performer in the columns of the *New Statesman*; he was a delight to the Gorton men in the school, and evidence of all that was right with the school since Gorton led the philhellenes in a crusade against the Philistines. Sprigge was one of those human beings who were either greatly loved or greatly hated. There was Sam 'Hallelujah' Dewar, by day a model school prefect, and by night the self-appointed captain of an imitation Salvation Army band, the chief function being to salute their captain with the cry, 'Hallelujah Sam Dewar'.

There was John Fairhurst, a trier, a young man who wanted desperately to be judged by his peers as a 'Mary', the one who had the one thing 'needful', but feared he would be assessed by his examiners as a 'Martha', the one who was 'much cumbered'. Fairhurst was lucky: he was not envious of those in whom nature or the gods had planted just that little bit extra.

Philip Lawson was a young man who played with everything – with poetry, religion, music, accurate scholarship, and love – only to find it was all folly, but believed there must be someone, somewhere who could relieve him from the otherwise intolerable boredom. I often wondered later how long his search continued, and how desperate he became. I wonder now how he and many other kindred spirits came to terms with Thatcher's England.

There was Anthony Sedgwick, a young man so aware of all the beauty in the world, yet so puzzled by all the evil, all the abominations and all the horrors, that he had trouble in starting to speak. He was neither a stammerer, nor a stutterer: he was a non-starter. Later, he was exempted from military service as a pacifist, ordered to do civil work and pressed into the merchant service on a ship which was torpedoed in the Mediterranean. I wonder what the fish made of those pleading eyes, that dumb appeal to all of us to lighten his darkness, that appeal we either could not or would not answer. I wondered, too, whether he ever managed to say to his officers, 'Why did you do this to me?' There were others who live with me always.

They were a never-ending delight to be with. My task was to prepare them for the Oxford and Cambridge scholarship examinations in the following April or May. I was lucky. My predecessor as senior history master, C. Northcote Parkinson (later well known as the author of *Parkinson's Law* and other books to feed the English conviction that they knew what was what), let me know, when we were as it were changing the guard, that he was surprised Neville Gorton had replaced a man who had already made a name for himself with his books on British trade routes with a young man from 'out there'. He was easy to replace. The young men were ready for someone who did not put on side, someone who treated them as equals, someone who didn't know the answers, but was keen to join them in a hunt for such answers.

Gorton taught me much. In his first interview with me he asked, 'Do you think you have anything to give?' He answered the question for me: 'If you don't give yourself when you're teaching you'll never give yourself.' He took me and the members of the History Sixth into the library. He climbed a ladder, picked a book out of the second top shelf, threw it at Philip McNair, and said from the top of the ladder, 'That's your book, McNair – that will get you going.' Before McNair could say a word Gorton scampered down the ladder as quick as a cat, and shot out of the room. Later he told me the point of that exercise was to teach me first to find out what a boy was thinking about, and then to feed him with the books in his 'line of country'. Another day he told me boys should see history in the making: 'Why don't you take them once a week to Exeter to look at the city records?'

So a party of us travelled by train to Exeter each week. Fairhurst loved it, so did 'Hallelujah' Dewar. Lawson and Sprigge were bored, the latter taking it as a punishment on the imaginative by the latter-day Mr Gradgrinds. He later had his revenge on me. When Dymphna bought me on mail order a four-piece Harris tweed suit, with one pair of trousers and one pair of plus fours, I wore the latter at the annual cross-country race, thinking fondly that I was proclaiming my allegiance to the eccentrics, and the odd bods, the ones with whom I always seemed 'charmed to be'. Sprigge commented with disdain, accompanied by a brilliant performance of the special English art of running one eye down the left nostril, and the other down the right. 'You look like a bank manager at the annual staff picnic.' I never wore the plus fours again until I returned to Australia.

It was a flowering time in my life. I began to hope I had something to offer. There was to be another event which meant much. On 4 December Dymphna gave birth to a boy in the Radcliffe Infirmary in Oxford. Gorton generously allowed me to visit her for a few days. The child was part of those rapturous days, part of the challenge to bring 'other sons' to birth, different sorts of sons, the challenge to risk one day looking to see whether there was anything at all to come up from inside me – or to discover whether one was as arid in things of the mind as the deserts of Australia.

That would have to be faced, but not then, because just then there was this mystery of a new life. I remember after the excitement of being with Dymphna again, and seeing the child for the first time – he looked so skinny that I had told Dymphna to put him back and do some more work on him – we had laughed so loudly the English nurses looked startled, fearing such laughter might degenerate into hysteria. But we were so happy we did not mind their black looks and their conspiratorial whispering to each other, and their disapproving eyes. I remember walking back past Balliol and meeting Mrs Lindsay, the wife of the Master, and assuming, wrongly as it proved, I should speak of the event as an academic would speak of all events with detachment and a rigorous attention to detail. She interrupted me, and waved a reproving finger and said, 'Don't talk like that, Mr Clark. It's a mystery: it's one of the great mysteries.' She was right: the non-secular humanist in me wanted to give her a hug then and there, but one did not behave like that in England.

We told my mother by cable that a boy had been born. I teased her by adding, at huge expense, that we would call him Sebastian Wolfgang Amadeus – those two, Bach and Mozart, having eased Beethoven out of the place of supremacy in my heart. My mother was generous in her reply – and, for her, extravagant in the number of words put on the cable form. 'Reconsider', she said, 'the name beginning with W.' From others there was silence. The wound was still there, if anything it was deepening. What to do? A new life did not, alas, wipe clean one of the smudges on my heart.

During Christmas at Oxford the child was baptised by Ross Wilson in the Balliol chapel, while the organ scholar, Ted Heath, was practising on the organ. He was baptised John Sebastian Clark. Ross insisted that the water from the font should be sprinkled on the Earth, as a symbol of the mystical union between the child and the Earth. With the same religious fervour he insisted on taking me to the Dew Drop Inn after the service. He had taken off his clerical collar, which Dymphna insisted needed washing and ironing. Ross told me he was dying to tell me about his latest discovery at Cambridge – that I was not to laugh, that this was the real thing – 'Just you wait and see.' That made me feel sad and inadequate. Mrs Mabel Layng stood godmother, and her somewhat bleak view of the prospects of a lasting love between any human beings reminded me that my happiness, too, might disappear like the snowdrift. But not then, in the after-glow of one of the greatest mysteries of all. Sebastian was in some ways to be like me. He will want someone to tell him 'what it has all been for'. He will try mathematics: he will try history. He will find part of the answer in love.

In January Dymphna, Sebastian and I travelled to Tiverton. They were wondrous days together. The world there was full of delights. There was cycling together on the icy roads in Tiverton. There were walks along the canal in the early spring of 1940. There was music, Butterworth's 'Shropshire Lad', answering the gaiety, and the under-lying melancholy, an intimation of the end of an era. There were talks with the boys about history, about literature, about the existence of God, and the life of the world to come. I made no attempt to interest them in the history of Australia, or its literature. For me at that time they did not exist. I was an exile who had returned to the source of wisdom and understanding.

There was one shadow among all this light. In Melbourne it was being said that I preferred love to a degree. The wound inflicted on Dymphna's family showed no signs of healing. I could not understand how anyone could find fault in what had brought us such happiness. There was a failure of my imagination, a failure to understand that in the world one man's happiness might bring undying pain to others. I did not foresee then that the men in black in Melbourne would exact a price from this young Dionysian who had flouted the lore of his tribe.

The world kept intruding on the idyll of Blundells. On 9 April the German army invaded Norway and Denmark, and on 10 May Holland and Belgium. Within a few weeks all four had capitulated, as had been predicted in the German military periodicals. Chamberlain resigned, still talking to the English in the language of an English public-school boy, still professing what the English were fighting against and never risking any definition of what they were fighting for. Churchill replaced Chamberlain. In a stirring pot-pourri of the pep-talks by his ancestor, the first Duke of Marlborough, to his soldiers in the Low Countries, and the extravagances of Garibaldi during the invasion of Sicily, he brought heart to those who believed in Old England. Churchill spoke for an England which was a museum piece in the age of the masses. Like Chamberlain he had nothing to say about the future: like Chamberlain he made no serious analysis of the reasons for the crisis in Western society in 1940.

On 17 May the German army poured into France. The French High Command published military bulletins on the success of the French resistance to the onslaught, but they were vague on details. The *Times*, in one of their celebrated parentheses which conveyed the meat in the sandwich between the doughy bread, referred to 'the regrettable inaccuracy' of the French military communiqués. I knew The *Times* was right. Each night at 9 p.m. Dymphna and I had listened to the news bulletins in the German language from Cologne (or was it Berlin?). They began: '*Das Oberkommando der deutschen Wehrmacht gibt bekannt: Heute sind* (naming cities in the north-east of France) *fest in deutschen Händen*' (The High Command of the German Defence Forces has announced : the following cities ... are now firmly held by German troops). The German army was carrying out to perfection their revision of the Schlieffen Plan for the First World War. The agents of evil were not fools: nor were their tanks manufactured from cardboard.

111

On the night of 20 June I heard Marshal Pétain speak to the French: 'Français et Françaises,' he said in the voice of a tired old man, 'we must cease fighting. We have been defeated by a superior foe.' He went on to name the reasons for the military disaster. Very high on his list was 'l'alcoholisme'. As he gravely pronounced the word, stressing each syllable, the picture came into my mind of those office clerks in Paris putting down half a tumbler of brandy in a cafe on their way to the office. Pétain had a point. But, like Chamberlain and Churchill, he did not allow himself to ask the question, 'Why?' That night, after Pétain I switched to the short-wave broadcast from Moscow Radio, to their French program, and heard again their litany: 'La crise du capitalisme s'aggrave tous les jours' (The crisis of capitalism is worsening day by day). Was that true? But, if so, where did humanity's salvation lie, and who would be the saviour?

The following day I had to take the Blundells' First Eleven to Downside, the Benedictine public school near Bath. While watching the Blundells' team bat, and smiling inwardly at the English ways of showing approval (those restrained, 'Well done, Crosse-Crosse', 'Keep that left leg closer to the ball, Hotblack'), a priest began to speak to me about the debacle in France, and the possible fate of the British Expeditionary Force. God, he said, sometimes used evil to work an ultimate good: the French were paying for their hedonism, their pursuit of petty pleasures, their sensuality, and their godless materialism. I was not ready to see the disaster in France through God's eyes. Over lunch, ample, wholesome, and made even more pleasing by a bottle or so of vintage French wine, the priest said to me, 'The French, Clark, make a divine claret. Have some more.' I did: I needed the escape more than ever. Then the priest drew my attention to the portraits of William Bede Ullathorne and John Bede Polding which hung on the walls of the dining-hall. 'I believe, Clark,' he said, 'both of them were early Benedictine priests in Australia. But you would know more about them than I do.'

That was the whole point. At that time I did not even know who they were, so little did I, a member of the Protestant ascendancy in Australia, and an Austral-Briton, know about the history of the country in which I was born. But I like to think now that my eye lingered on the faces of these two men who carried the image of Christ *in partibus infidelium*, because within a week of that day at Downside I decided to return to Australia. The life of an exile was over. It was time for the native to return to where he belonged, to the one country where he could both understand and be understood.

That would turn out to be not just the return of the native, but a spiritual journey to discover Australia. I would start from scratch, or maybe ten yards behind scratch. Part of me was still 'over there'. That evening in Bath on my way back to Blundells it never occurred to me to see the church at Bathhampton in which Arthur Phillip was buried. For me, then, Bath was the glory of the English magnificoes of the eighteenth century. I did not think of the man who won the battle for survival in Australia. My mind was still on other things. I was about to learn that all those who live abroad are in a dream.

Mr Passion
on the Shores of Corio Bay

In early July 1940 Dymphna, Sebastian and I boarded the *Orcades* at Southampton for the return to Australia. For a while I was tormented by guilt, the guilt of escaping from danger into a funk hole in Australia. I believed then my one talent was as a teacher; Neville Gorton, the headmaster of Blundells, had told me I was 'a born teacher'. The years in England and Europe have given me something to say. My fear was that people in Melbourne would not want to hear it.

Fremantle was a shock. We no sooner had sat down in the bus for Perth than my eye noticed a poster of a soldier in uniform pointing an accusing finger at all of us in the bus. Above his head were the words in bold type, 'Shut up!', and below his head the words, 'That means you.' Were we as crude as that poster? Had I forgotten the contradiction about Australians, that we who boasted of ourselves as democratic and egalitarian accepted a tyranny of opinion? In the bus I had a vague foreboding about what James McAuley later identified in 'L'Envoi' as 'the faint sterility that disheartens and derides', that the people are 'hard-eyed, kindly, with nothing inside them'. I had already read the stronger comments by D. H. Lawrence that Australia was a country where 'souls, spirits and minds' had not grown at all, but reassured myself with the thought that Lawrence was already a sick man when he wrote those words. It could not be as bad as that.

I had my faith: I was going home. As the *Orcades* ploughed its way slowly through the blue waters of Port Phillip Bay, in a burst of enthusiasm I said to a refugee seeking a new life in Australia, '*Il y a un nouveau monde*' (There is a new world). He said, '*C'est fermé, Monsieur*' (It is closed). I did not believe him. My Australia was never closed to anyone. I was young and foolish. I was only twenty-five on that tenth day of August 1940 when the *Orcades* was finally moored to the Port Melbourne wharf, and Dymphna and I walked down the gangway carrying Sebastian in his basket, hoping our world was not closed.

Some things had not changed. My mother asked me, 'Are you all right, Mann dear?' My father and brother were telling jokes. My sister, still recovering from infantile paralysis, wanted to know how she could help.

Dymphna's father, to my surprise, lifted Sebastian out of his basket and embraced him warmly. One other thing surprised me: Dymphna's brother Axel was wearing the uniform of a sergeant in the Australian Imperial Force. Dymphna had told me how as a boy in Beatty Street, Mont Albert, her brother had written down in a notebook the name of the murderer who had chopped off the head of a bantam and the date of the execution, and how he had asked her to promise never again to pick a flower, because they had feelings too. He was to embark soon for the Middle East. He will come back and play a leading part in the creation of the Baillieu Library, an achievement those in high places at Melbourne University will be as reluctant to acknowledge as they had been to reward adequately the work of his father as a scholar in Germanic languages. Some things in Melbourne never change.

I was in for a greater shock. No one wanted to hear what I had to say. The indifference was so deep that I could not fathom it. No one was interested in the vision in my breast, conceived by the experience of seeing evil on the morning after 'Kristallnacht' in Germany, of standing in front of the Madonna in Cologne Cathedral, of seeing that the English were over the hill, and that the French were behaving like human beings with a creeping paralysis, the cause of which had not been identified but the symptoms plain to anyone with eyes to see. No one wanted to hear any of that message. The men in high places who decided who would draw a prize and who a blank in the lottery of being appointed a teacher at a university gave me the impression that what mattered to me held no interest for them. I was an outsider. I had offended against the lore of the tribe of intellectuals.

A great change had come over intellectual fashions, over who's in and who's out at the University of Melbourne. In 1934, under the brilliant teaching of A. R. Chisholm, French right-wing thought, French symbolism, were in the ascendancy. Mallarmé was the high priest,

115

and Chis his prophet in the antipodes. In 1937 Max Crawford made a successful takeover bid for the supremacy. History was humanity's bible of wisdom: history will teach students how and why things have been as they have been, and what might be. Those who know history can show humanity the field of the possible and how that can be achieved. History provides the blueprint for the future. History is for believers in humanity's powers. History provides the ammunition for those who believe they have something to say.

Now the scene was altered. There were new players in the centre of the stage. There was a new vocabulary. The first time I sat down to a meal in the 'caf' at Melbourne University I asked politely, 'Would you please pass the salt?' My neighbour, a gifted woman, looked at me with that eye of the saved for the damned, and said, 'I don't know what you mean.' I decided to listen to what was going on. In the ensuing weeks I picked up the new vocabulary. I often heard the word 'tautology': that, I gathered, was the sin against the Holy Ghost. I heard the phrase '*non sequitur*'. I was often asked: 'Is that a verifiable proposition?'

I noticed that the mighty men of renown were up for examination: the list of those deserving commendation had been revised. It was like a football team in which many changes have been made: there was new blood, some have been relegated to the seconds, and some put on the reserve bench. Plato, Hegel and company have been dropped; David Hume has been promoted; Newman, Carlyle, Rousseau, Tolstoy, Dostoevsky – all my heroes and teachers – have been sacked. Tolstoy was ridiculed. As for D. H. Lawrence, 'Well, I ask you, has he ever written anything meaningful? Listen to this passage carefully, and tell me what it means.' Teachers to whom I owed so much, such as MacMahon Ball, were put up for judgement and found wanting.

I was ill at ease in the company of the new men. At the time I did not know that the philosopher who had begun this revolution, Ludwig Wittgenstein, had spent much time reading Tolstoy on the Gospels. What irony! I had no idea of the mighty spirit behind his disciples in the antipodes. I noticed that these language rinsers imposed a silence whenever they were present. I did not know at the time that this was an idiosyncrasy of their founder, Ludwig Wittgenstein. Perhaps I would have listened more carefully to what they had to say if they had told me that after reading Tolstoy Wittgenstein had given away all he had, read the Gospels, and taught children in a primary school. The missionaries for Wittgenstein's philosophy had much to teach us all. They were like a bushfire consuming dead timber in the Australian bush.

I went silent. I yearned for the enlargers of life; I was tempted to think of these new missionaries as heart-dimmers, and straiteners, but that would have been unfair. Late at night I discovered that with them it was like peeling an onion. There was no more core in their thinking than in any other body of thought. I wanted to know what I would find when we all stopped speaking and writing tautologies, after the last *non sequitur* had been uttered, and when everyone was silent about those things of which he or she had no verifiable knowledge. What then? Pat Colebrook, the one with whom it was once possible to drop the mask, and who was now secretary of the Faculty of Arts, advised me to stay away. 'They're not your cup of tea', she told me.

These missionaries were not the only ones who claimed to have all the answers. There was a group of spiritual bullies – the ones who believed they were politically correct, indeed so politically correct that they were justified in first trying flattery and gentle persuasion, and if that failed then the tactics of the bully to force everyone to accept their view. They had one thing in common with the missionaries for correct thought: those who cannot or will not agree are condemned for their lack of virtue, or their lack of brain power. Those who disagree have been bought: they have sold out. There is neither truth nor virtue in them.

The missionaries for a new society had their own litany: the crisis of capitalism was becoming graver every day. This was an imported litany: it has not grown out of the mighty bush or the suburbs of Australia. We have borrowed the institutions to protect capitalist society: now these people wanted us to borrow ideas from Germany and Russia on how to start a revolution. They were still chanting the litany gleaned from the Left Book Club, the *Guardian*, the *Tribune*, the *Communist Review*, about the Nazis and the Fascists. The conservatives were still singing the old, old song, that the British navy will come to our rescue if we get into trouble in our part of the world. So stay under the umbrella; sing 'God Save the King'; trust in the 'land of hope and glory, mother of the free'.

I held my tongue, though it was grief and agony to me – or behaved like a buffoon, or chattered like a magpie. Sometimes late at night when alcohol convinced me there was no need to hold my tongue

I asked *them* a question which only tickled their animosity, or fuelled their malice: 'Where are the snows of yester-year?' *They* shook their heads, and warned me of what would happen if I did not mend my ways. I lapsed back into silence. I sensed there was no point in revealing to them the vision, or the faith, having at that time no clear picture of what it was I wanted to say or how I would say it – either in the lecture room or on paper, and if the latter whether in fiction or history. It never occurred to me then that the medium would be a history of Australia. I was like the narrator in Dostoevsky's *Notes from the Underground*. I was uneasy with all the prevailing orthodoxies: liberalism, secularism, humanism, social scientism, laws of history, and the lore of the bourgeois tribe in Melbourne. I believed in the role of Labour to change the world, but was often ill-at-ease in the company of revolutionaries.

One thing was clear. There would be no position for me at the University of Melbourne. Max Crawford was most understanding. He had lived through the same experience himself when he returned from Oxford. He wanted to help me. The problem was I had had no teaching experience at a university. Was I thereby forever excluded? No, not necessarily. Wait and see. Be patient. But how could I possibly get such a qualification? If Neville Gorton's words about being a 'born teacher . . . for school or university' were true, then the only thing to do was to seek a position in a school.

In a moment of despair I wrote a letter to James Darling, the headmaster of Geelong Grammar School, believing he was the Australian equivalent of Neville Gorton. He offered me a position as a middle-school teacher, and the possibility of taking over the History Sixth at the beginning of 1941, salary two hundred and fifty pounds a year, with an upstairs flat for Dymphna, Sebastian and myself. My fellow-drinkers at the bar of the Traveller's Arms (since demolished to make way for a Melbourne underground station) dropped dark hints that some people (always unnamed) were determined I should never lecture at Melbourne University. But if I could not tell left-wing drinkers what was going on in my mind, what I wanted to say maybe one day in a book, how could I ever say it in a lecture?

Perhaps I was not ready. Perhaps I needed to suffer far more to knock the mockery out of me. Mockers and destroyers, knock-down men, low-down men, might write a criticism of the work of others: those with a hell in the heart could never write a history. Besides I still had to find a subject. So, off to Corio Bay, off to discover what human beings do to each other in a dry year in a dry country – off on another stretch along the road in quest of grace, uncertain where salvation lay, but not ready then to understand why so many musicians have composed a *kyrie eleison*. I was not even hoping at that time that someone, somewhere, would take pity on all of us.

Mozart was my inspiration. The overture to *The Magic Flute*, and the flute obbligato after the lovers have passed through the rites of initiation and are vouchsafed a vision of a world free from ignorance and superstition, were part of what helped me to keep going. There were also the pleasures of mockery: mocking the pretentious, the pompous, the smugness of the inhabitants of Yarraside who sat in the pews of St John's, Toorak, and Christ Church, South Yarra, in sure and certain hope that there would be the same special things for special people in the life of the world to come as there were in SE1 and SE2. I was a wanderer on the face of the Earth. I had lost touch with the people, had turned my back on that mystical communion with the people I had known as a child and a boy on Phillip Island: I had turned my back on the world of Marge Thompson, Bella Green, Harry Williams, 'Plugger' Bennell, Bill Hayes and Noel Cleland. What had been lost must be found again. There must be a discovery of the Australian people. But not then.

My life at Geelong Grammar School reminded me of the description by Charles Dickens of David Copperfield's marriage to Dora. It was an act 'conceived in folly and endured in madness'. But that would be unfair, there being more to it than that. Perhaps no one was to blame. The boys welcomed me warmly, the masters with suspicion, fear, and at times secret and at other times open hostility. I was a challenge to their cosy little world, to their devotion to the education of young men to serve faithfully the class to which they belonged – the Australian bourgeoisie. To me, then and now, the bourgeoisie were not worthy of such devotion and service. My jokes to the boys about knee-benders and grovellers at the throne of grace alarmed them. I asked the boys to question the assumption that a God of love could view with favour the behaviour and values of the Melbourne version of Mr Money Bags. Did they, the boys, imagine for one moment that the man, whoever he was, who walked beside the waters of Galilee and asked his followers to consider the lilies of the field and advised his fellow fishermen to launch out into the deep, would approve of these puffed-up, pigeon-chested men dressed in khaki who barked out commands on the parade ground once a week? That angered most

119

of the other masters. They became hostile, began treating me as an enemy of the school.

That was not all. The people in charge often seemed to me to be more interested in stamping out any sexual behaviour by the boys than in causing the paths of true learning to flourish and abound. Those who were discovered were thrashed unmercifully, and then told to go and sin no more. I was appalled. Men, who on their own confession were plagued by what they called 'dark and monstrous thoughts', caned the bare behinds of young men until the blood flowed. But when the sons of the wealthy and powerful yielded to temptation the masters in charge forgave them. These lapses from their idea of grace were due, they explained, to the boy or the young man being so tired at the time that he did not know what he was doing. Not always so those whose fathers came from and would remain in the ruck. I did not know then, nor do I know now, a satisfactory response to adolescent sex. All I knew was that terror and physical pain were anathema to me. I befriended the victims of the savage punishments, offered them sympathy, and told them they were not the only ones who could not stop.

This maddened the self-appointed guardians of public and private morality. They pinned the labels of libertine, atheist and traitor on me. In their eyes I was a Judas in modern dress – a scholarship boy at Melbourne Grammar School, Trinity College and Oxford University, guilty of base ingratitude to his benefactors! They judged me hastily to be an atheist who was perverting the minds of the young, and inciting them to depravity, licentiousness and sedition.

My teaching methods scandalised them. I believed then, and believe now, that a joke is a good mood starter for a class. I also believed then, and do now, that the presentation should reflect what was going on in the mind of the teacher. Then, as ever for me, there were two questions: Did God exist, and if He did what was He like? Was humanity capable of achieving the aims of the French and the Russian revolutions? I wanted the boys in the History Sixth, they being between the ages of sixteen and eighteen, to think about the character of God. My way of doing this was to put to them the questions: Was God a cad? Was God a gentleman? They laughed. They took up the challenge. 'What do you mean, sir?' 'Well,' I replied, 'what do you think of a God who put a naked man and a naked woman in an enclosed garden and then expelled them for doing what no one could possibly avoid doing?' The results of the boys in the annual Leaving Honours examination seemed to vindicate these methods.

I asked them: Was God a sadist? I asked them if they had considered the behaviour of the Greek gods. Take Zeus, who disguised himself as a swan and then seduced Leda. There would obviously be no place for Jehovah or Zeus at any public school in England or Australia. They would 'have to go'. I never forgot the language of 'Lofty' Franklin at Melbourne Grammar School. The boys loved it. We were all trying to find out what life was all about. The defenders of the old order in the school were outraged. But at the time I did not ask myself what it would be like to be them. Nor was I bothered that I was upsetting the faith of the boys, and had no answers myself. I was driven to strip away all life-lies – and had not even asked then whether all human beings could live without a life-lie, or some great delusion about themselves or the past of the tribe to which they belonged.

I was never at ease with those who claimed to know all the answers about life. I was even less at ease with academics, school teachers and clergymen of the Church of England who told me with a pompous pout of the lips and a strut of the legs how busy they were and how important they were. Some of my teaching lapsed into buffoonery with bourgeois egotists as my prime target. I told the members of the History Sixth that there was a simple cure for all those driven to tell us how important they were. There should be a booth or a marquee in the back yard of all human beings, equipped with a microphone, an amplifier and a loudspeaker. When overwhelmed with a desire to pontificate, boasters should go into the booth and shout their 'I am's' into the microphone – 'I am the greatest thinker in Australia' – followed by applause from the loudspeaker. When properly purged they could then return to the bosom of suburban cosiness, freed temporarily from the power to give offence. I started my career as a teacher believing a joke could also be a parable or a metaphor for our times. Sarcasm and foolishness could be the prelude to an epiphany. Behind the mask of the fool there was a man searching for the answers. I was wearing the mask of a man who wanted to shout 'No' to much around him. In time I would discard the sarcasm. Why tear the flesh as the prologue to the truth?

There was a series of lectures at the school on the war and its meaning. I spoke at one of them in 1941 (I forget the month, except that it was after the German invasion of Russia in June of that year). I told the audience, composed of boys, masters, their wives, and maybe a few others, leaning heavily on Auden's poem (all historians are parasites feeding on the food of the genuine artists), that we had just lived through the 'low, dishonest decade' of the 1930s, and that we now found ourselves defending the bad (English and French society) against the worse. That seemed to me to be a statement of the obvious, although I suppose I was enjoying the role of teasing the bourgeoisie.

The boys loved it. They had not then taken one bite out of the apple of success. They wanted to find out why things were as they were. Not so some of the masters. One of them, who each Sunday wore a white surplice as a symbol of the mystical purity of Christ's Church, knocked on the door of the house to which we had moved in Biddlecombe Avenue, and handed me a note in which he informed me that if I did not desist from such outrageous and traitorous (yes, treason was mentioned) teaching it would be his Christian duty to report me to Army Intelligence in Melbourne.

That did not silence me. A few months later Colin Badger, the enterprising director of the Council of Adult Education, invited me to speak at a weekend school in Geelong. I made the same point, adding at the end, because no one would ever silence me or persuade me to grovel to the conformers of Corio, that maybe a victorious and purified Russia, a Russia which had rediscovered the humanism of Marx, would light a 'cleansing fire' in Australia. Later, yet another Church of England clergyman took me aside, and told me to curb my tongue forthwith or it would be his Christian duty to speak to people in Melbourne, and he dropped a hint that he was well known to the decision-makers at the top of Spring Street. So curb your tongue, old chap; bide your time. The defenders of the old order had their life-lie: what they were doing was a Christian duty, and not a defence of their right to live in affluence.

Hints were dropped at the school that if I did not keep my thoughts to myself I might be dismissed. Parents of boys wrote letters to the headmaster demanding that something should be done. It would have been hell, it would have been alarming, had it not been for the boys. They strengthened my faith: they gave me the courage to go on simply by letting me know they wanted me. They were my teachers. There was such a contrast between the chilly reception in the masters' common room and the greetings from the boys. They were hungry: I tried to feed them.

I remember still some faces in the first class I took – a class of gifted boys who were reading Tennyson's *Idylls of the King*. I told them, rashly, that Tennyson was a long-winded bore, taking shelter in the anachronisms of chivalry in a futile attempt to persuade himself and his readers that he had found an anodyne to deaden the undying pain in his life, his grief on the death of Hallam, the great love of his life. Some guffawed. I asked them whether they were feeling well, or perhaps needed help from the matron. There was laughter.

I noticed one face with pleading eyes. They belonged to Geoffrey Fairbairn, the son of J. V. Fairbairn, the Minister for Air, who had just been killed in the Canberra air disaster which had also taken the life of Henry Gullett. It was the look of a boy telling anyone with eyes to see: don't tell me there is any answer to my pain. He had an unerring eye for the pompous and the pretentious – and maybe (who can tell?) the insight to recognise immediately that my sarcasm and my jokes were a mask to protect the man within, to protect an innocent boy who had managed to survive all the descents into the gutter unstained. Geoffrey wanted something which no one could or would ever give him. We would all let him down. But on that morning in September when our eyes first met, and there was that moment of recognition, I did not foresee what we would do to him, or he would do to himself.

There was David Darling, a son of a director of BHP, who had the soul of an artist but was destined to spend his days in the counting-house. We have been told many mute inglorious Miltons feed the worms in England: in Australia many men of imagination became mute ministers to Mammon. Many of the boys I met on that first day would risk following Christ's advice to make 'friends of the Mammon of unrighteousness'. Many of them were already men of moral passion, young Prometheans who believed it was possible to steal fire from heaven. Three of them spoke to me outside the school dining-room.

One was carrying an armful of books, and wore the expression of a troubled man on his face, the fretful expression of a young man who wanted answers straight away, a young man with the energy and faith of a crusader for a better life for all of us. He was Stephen Murray-Smith. Another was carrying a black notebook in his hand. I was puzzled. He was a patrician who had adopted the stance and voca-bulary of the people. When he laughed the gurgle was an unmistakable pointer to what was driving him on. At that time he was singing in the choir, 'O love that wilt not let me go'. He was to become a great lover, and a distinguished poet. He was Frank Kellaway.

There was a tall young man who did not say very much but eyed me closely. When silent, and with lips firmly closed, he looked as if he might one day develop into a stern judge of all of us. But when I asked him if he was also a knee-bender before the throne of grace his face was transfigured. He laughed, and let me see the man who wanted to hold out his arms to everyone, but would need some sort of stimulus before he risked letting the ones in charge of the world perceive this other side of him. He was Don Baker. We began on that day a friendship which would deepen with the passage of time.

From 1940 to 30 April 1944, when I left the school, there were wonderful boys or young men to teach. They were not bothered by a young teacher who had doubts about all the School claimed to represent. There was Terence Fullerton, a scholar who was amused by my irreverence for the fence-sitters, the timid souls who sheltered behind the fig-leaf of 'objective history' or 'impartiality', the Gradgrinds and the dry-as-dusts pedalling away on the academic treadmill. Business will snatch Terry away from the path of true learning where he had all the gifts to flourish and abound. There was David Armstrong, later Professor of Philosophy at the University of Sydney, where he achieved international recognition in a field I am not competent to judge. I was not surprised to hear he threw overboard his schoolboy enthusiasms for the future of humanity. To remain a believer a man needs a different sort of heart from the one with which nature had endowed him. Sydneyside academics will say John Anderson knocked the socialist and logical-positivist nonsense out of his head, and made him into – well, what? – a defender of higher civilisation and a philosophical materialist? John Anderson had the power to move, David Armstrong the power to be moved.

There was Tom Potts, who talked like a buffoon, not as the overture to a parable about life but from an engaging uncertainty about how to behave. He expressed the sentiments of a Tory of the old school in those extravagant images over which Churchill was again throwing the mantle of respectability. It sounded like bluster or, to use a non-drawing-room expression, what Australians identify as 'all piss and wind'. There was much more to Tom than this verbal bragadaccio, this revelling in rodomontade, and catching out a sometimes reckless young teacher in one of his many contradictions, only to be set back on his heels by that young teacher's smart-alec reply:

Potts, how many times must I remind you that only small minds are bothered by contradictions? We are all the spouters of contradictions, Potts – and humiliating absurdity though it may be we have to live with what we are, not what we might be or should be.

The others laughed. Tom Potts had redeeming graces: he had the will to endure, and a loyalty to those whom he loved. He had a dogged determination to make the most effective use of his talents. If the parable of the talents is true, then Tom Potts should receive a rich reward.

The wit of a moment often lived on. One of the members of the class in 1943 was Bob Dalziel, a boy with an almost feminine grace of feature and movement, movements which he executed on the football field to the amusement of the footballers, but to no other purpose. He made sure he never got near the ball. In a rash moment I called him 'Footballer' Dalziel. The name stuck with him until he died twenty years later – that happening even before I had a chance to say 'Sorry' – although what could words do to soothe that wound? Alas, there were other lapses. One boy named Robin always blushed when spoken to. So I called him 'Rhubarb Robin'. To my shame, I enjoyed the laughter of the class, not foreseeing then the suffering he endured for this quirk of nature until drink desensitised him and painted a permanent red on his face. The news of his death added another item to my long list of self-lacerations in those nights when dreams project on to the private picture-screen of my mind the shameful moments in the past.

Many others live on in my mind. There was Tim Burstall, later a lively director of films in Australia, but then an unhappy boy, with an angelic face, a high-pitched giggle, and savage words about other boys and other masters. One side of him shook with laughter when listening to stories about his enemies, the other side scanned the face of everyone he spoke to in search of a sign that there was more to life than this world portrayed by the gossips. He had trouble with doing the right thing. I remember he told me once he had just been caned, and when I asked him why he replied, 'General attitude'. That inability to live with the moral policemen in our society enforcing right attitudes will be one of his problems in life. There was Ivor Bowden, graceful on the wing in football, and graceful with the pen. He laughed much, but never let anyone come near. Richard Woolcott, also a brilliant footballer, had the gift of understanding every point of view, and the more precious gift of liking other human beings. Those gifts made him a brilliant negotiator in Foreign Affairs, and ensured a distinguished career as a servant to governments of different persuasions in Australia. There was Peter Henderson, then a boy but later a man with a generous heart, and a degree of high-mindedness and fairness of mind for all to see in the government department which he served loyally. 'Jamie' Mackie was a young man with the industry and the drive to become later a world authority on Indonesia.

There was Rupert Murdoch. Years later the know-alls will spread a rumour that I radicalised him when he was in the first form in the senior school. Well, if so, my teaching was not destined to last! My memory is rather different. He was not in any of the classes to which I taught history. I remember him in a divinity class. He seemed fascinated by my talks to them based on Ernest Renan's *Vie de Jésus* – a prose poem of praise not to the man-God, or to the God-man, but to the man who spoke of love, compassion and forgiveness, the man who loved women, the fisherman, the man who had spoken to the woman taken in the act of adultery, the man who had uttered those words to Martha and Mary, and then made the disastrous journey to Jerusalem where, angered by the money-changers in the temple, and the letter-of-the-law men, and all the heart-dimmers amongst the Pharisees, he became very angry and made wild claims for himself and began to talk about a kingdom which was not of this world. Those in power in the school became very annoyed when they heard what was being said. I was never asked to teach divinity again.

My memory, and that may well be a memory of what I would like to be true about the past, is that there was one boy in the class who listened very attentively. He was Rupert Murdoch. I remember also that he was very helpful. He called at our house a few times to ask whether he could help. Later I heard that when another master was moving house he had volunteered to do a job no one else was prepared to do – to clean out the lavatory. I remember also many years later watching a television program on the ABC on the progress of Rupert Murdoch from proprietor of the *Evening News* in Adelaide to media tycoon. I scanned the face on the screen to see whether the boy who had listened with such ardour to the words of Christ was still there, or whether life and what was inside him had so engulfed him that that boy had disappeared without leaving a trace.

The classes with the sixth form were supposed to be in history, but they often wandered off into the fields I was exploring. I had started to read the philosophers. Being a historian I had started at the beginning with the pre-Socratics, then Socrates, Plato, Aristotle, Aquinas, Descartes, Locke, Hume, Kant, Schopenhauer, Moore, Russell, and Wittgenstein. At the end of it I understood why Omar Khayyám wrote the words:

> Myself when young did eagerly frequent
> Doctor and saint and heard great Argument.
> Around it and about: but evermore
> Came out by the same door as in I went.

I was interested in the other point made by Omar Khayyám in his address to the supreme being, namely, that for all the ills in the world 'man's forgiveness give and take.' Besides, listening to talk by philosophers I found my instincts were always on the wrong side. In the encounter between Hume and Rousseau, which the philosophers cited as evidence of the virtue of David Hume, I was on the side of Rousseau. In the encounter between Turgenev and Dostoevsky at Baden Baden my sympathies were all with Dostoevsky.

I also read the psychologists, beginning with Freud and moving on to Jung and Adler. Once again my sympathies were with the wrong man – with Jung and not with Freud. Years later I found out why. Freud had once said to Jung, 'Don't explore the darkness' or some such words, meaning 'Do not raise the question of religion. Concentrate on sexuality.' I found Freud most illuminating in his literary and general essays. *Civilisation and its Discontents* became for me as central as the remark by Dostoevsky about wanting to be there when everyone suddenly understands what it has all been for. Later I will discover his *Moses and Monotheism*, and that will teach me how to respond to the Dionysian frenzy. Freud taught me a lesson about discipline and restraint. Many years will pass before I will find the strength to follow Freud's advice. Rages and attacks of the 'sillies', drunkenness, the easy way out, will hang around for years. When they were finally conquered the memory of those past follies never grew dim.

For me Freud's wisdom was the principal thing. He had much in common with the prophets in the books of wisdom in the Old Testament. Wisdom, I learnt as a boy from Ecclesiastes, is the principal thing. Freud taught me one way to acquire wisdom. Freud also taught me never to reply to criticism, that the only reply to criticism is to write another work. But I was not ready then to receive his words of advice.

Freud and Jung mapped the part of the human heart which interested me. I knew then that every historian must read, mark, learn and inwardly digest that map. Acquiring that knowledge, both by observing others, glancing inward, and reading all the great map-makers of the human heart, was for a historian like pre-season training for a footballer. Just as the footballer prepares for the bounce of the ball so the historian prepares to tell the reader what he has discovered in the human heart. But I will never feel comfortable with Freud's elitism, with his view that only the great souls can achieve such restraint, and use the frenzy, or the madness, call it what you will, for creative purposes.

I talked in the classes about *Civilisation and its Discontents*. I invited university teachers to talk to the boys in the History Sixth after chapel on Sunday mornings. George Paul, who had introduced Wittgenstein to students and staff at Melbourne University in March 1939, was the first speaker. The boys were puzzled but delighted. He was followed by A. C. Jackson, a man with whom I could talk about everything, and later Professor of Philosophy at Monash University. He told them what philosophy was about. The boys were delighted to be given the knife of linguistic analysis to cut away the myths and ideologies with which masters and parents were encumbering them. George Paul told them with a twinkle in his eye there was just one chance in a million that the Church was right. The boys laughed the laughter of relief. George Paul looked at the palm of his hand, knitted his brow and said, 'No, there is one chance in a thousand million.' The boys liked that too.

At that time, as ever, I clung to Marmaledov's faith in Dostoevsky's *Crime and Punishment* that the drunkards would be understood and forgiven. So maybe it was more than coincidence that one Saturday afternoon in the winter of 1943 when, after a lunch at the Latin Café (then in Exhibition Street), which held out the promise that the afternoon would be full of many splendours, I decided it would be a good idea to stand in the outer at Princes Park to watch Carlton play football – I needed to be near people again after a surfeit of the company of the men and women with sharp minds, fine consciences, and disciplined appetites in everything except their hunger for approving words about their political and social virtues, the ones who complimented each other on not being like other people.

In the outer was a young man, dressed in a sergeant's uniform. With his craggy cheeks, and a face so ravaged by I knew not what, he looked quite old, though his body was young. He kept edging towards where I stood, and I kept edging away, fearing then, as always, that a drunk man in uniform might be looking for a fight. He was trying to say something to me, but the booze had deprived him of the power of intelligible speech. Suddenly words did begin to flow. I heard him say, 'I am a disappointed radical'. We began a friendship which was to last for nearly forty years. He told me his name was James McAuley.

He told me, in one of those moments when the crowd is silent as it waits to see which way the ball will bounce, that he was on a quest to find what holds the world together in its innermost parts. He had studied philosophy in Sydney under John Anderson; he wrote poetry; he had searched in vain for 'salvation in the muck'. I sensed beneath the appearance of degradation a mighty spirit. I invited him to speak to the History Sixth at Corio.

Late one Friday afternoon in the winter of 1943 there was a knock on our front door. I opened it to see Jim McAuley in sergeant's uniform with a toothbrush in the left breast pocket. He said, 'Here I am.' So he was. He accepted the little we had to offer. He smoked our cigarettes, drank our alcohol, enjoyed Dymphna's soups and continental fish dishes. He also gave much. Late on the Saturday night he asked whether anyone had a piano. Yes, two doors away. So off into the night to a house where there was a flagon of sherry and a piano, at which he sat, lifted the lid and, to his own improvised music, he sang a news commentary on the state of the world, with some Noel Coward 'Twentieth Century Blues' remarks slipped in for those whose minds had not been too blunted by alcohol. Then back to our house where he talked on into the small hours of the morning about the relations between the Papacy and Japan and Burma. Brilliant, brilliant. But how did he know all this? Was he making it up? He never paused long enough for me to get a word in, let alone ask questions. Again, there were hints that all this talk about politics was only a game: that it was not the real thing. There were other remarks to show what he was thinking about. He said he had started to read the Buddha.

On Sunday morning he enchanted the boys when he told them what it was like to be a poet, and why literature was central to life. Their approval did not seem to touch him at all. He was a candidate for a higher prize than the claps and smiles and flattery of gifted boys, school teachers and their wives. That afternoon we walked together along the north shore of Corio Bay. He told me he was disenchanted with the heaven-on-earth men and women in Australia – that they were shallow souls who glossed over the problem of evil. He asked me what I was thinking about. I told him we were living in the era of the double breakdown: the impending breakdown of capitalist society, and the breakdown of belief. He asked me whether I planned to write a book about that theme. I told him, yes I had, but a historian needed a subject, a carpet in which he could weave his pattern. I had no such carpet.

It never occurred to me then as we stood together gazing over the troubled waters of Corio Bay, listening to the slap of the waves on the sand, that the land on which we were standing was the setting for such a story, and that the ever-restless sea before our eyes was part of that sea over which the principal characters and the people in such a story had made the journey from a civilised country to a barbarous land they believed to be inhabited by savages. Perhaps he did not foresee then that one day he, too, would tell Australians that our concern is here and now.

At that time he was playing with the idea that the mass age in which we lived had been disastrous for high culture. He had absorbed Ortega y Gasset's *The Revolt of the Masses*, and O. Spengler's *The Decline of the West*. He knew what Tocqueville had written about democracy as a kindergarten training for the mediocre and the second-rate. We had begun an exchange of minds which would survive the Cold War, Korea and Vietnam – those events keeping people apart in the 1950s and 1960s. We knew where we were both flawed: we knew then the vision by which we hoped to guide our lives would be obscured all too often by our own follies, weaknesses, and madnesses – one of his being an obsession with conspiracy. We both raged far too often: we both still had far too strong an appetite for the affairs of the gutter. He was chasing the mirage of a society in Australia which tolerated and indeed provided incentives for an elite. I was chasing the mirage of living in Australia, while feeding my mind on what Emerson had called 'foreign harvests'.

My clowning with the boys went on and on. They loved it: they egged me on. One boy asked me why the few were rich and the many were poor. The rich, I replied, were those who wangled overdrafts and the poor those to whom the money-changers handed a rejection slip. They laughed. On another occasion I told them the squatters in the Western District owed their wealth to the sexual appetites of their rams and not to their own energies and talents. The more sheep there were, the more parents would put down the names of their sons for

Geelong Grammar School. Ha, ha, ha! Another day I put a question to Tom Potts: 'Tell me, Potts, which is the more difficult for humanity? Breaking brotheldom's domination, or breaking class domination? Cries from the class chorus of 'Oh, oh, oh!' But before Potts could get a word in edgeways I went on with mock sternness:

Remember, Potts brotheldom comes from the old English participle *brothen* meaning ruined. Don't forget, Potts, the brothels of the mind are the most pernicious of all, and the most difficult to destroy. So you may find brotheldom a more formidable foe to humanity than class domination.

Buffoonery was still the overture to the human tragedy.

Many years later there will be regrets about these vaudeville turns in the classrooms at Corio. There will be memories of puzzled faces looking at me as though I knew the answers. I will remember the face of the boy who gave me the smile of recognition. He was Trevor Seward. He wanted a new creation. He had the look in the eye of someone who believed sometime, somewhere, things could be different. He wanted it all to happen straight away. In May 1944 when British soldiers landed on the beaches in Normandy he jumped too early from his landing barge, sank into the depths, and was never seen again. In April 1985 I walked along the beach where he disappeared, and recalled his face at Corio looking to me for guidance. He was one of the many I had let down. I had given him hope, planted the daring in him at a time when deep down I had neither hope nor daring.

Jokes were also maybe the smoke screen, so opaque that no one would sight the anguish and the doubt behind all this tomfoolery. A young man tormented by doubt about everything, a young man who had nothing to say, had the impertinence to mock all beliefs and all believers. There was another life – the life of a man who wanted to say something in writing, but at that time did not know what it would be, or how to say it – a young man already tormented by doubt about his capacity to find the words. In April 1941 I began a diary in which I splashed on to the page night after night my alienation from the 'experts in ridicule' in the senior common-room, and my pain on once again knowing the failure of trying to write something, but lacking the words with which to express what was going on in my mind. The truth was that at that time I had no position, no point of view, no subject and no words. Nothing could come out of nothing.

No one wanted to hear about the experience in Germany. The universities presented an air of vast indifference to anything I might want to say. I was toying, as ever, with the billowing generalisations – with all the extravaganzas of the head and the heart. On 6 April 1941, according to my diary, though happily I have repressed all memory of this grandiose scheme, I was about to put pen to paper for an article on what Hippolyte Taine named 'le démembrement du monde civilisé' (the dismemberment of the civilised world). I thought of writing a story about life at the school, but that would have been a paper-thin disguise for settling scores with those with whom I never could, and never would, enjoy heart's ease. Perhaps the fear of showing the inner bankruptcy stopped me dipping my pen into the ink-well. Who can ever tell why we do not start, why we do not risk facing the blank sheet – because that would show quite quickly that we have nothing to say? But the desire was strong. On 10 September 1942, for example, I noted in my diary: 'I would like to be a writer!' And I went on to say that would require discipline, being an observer and not a participant, and not to be 'dependent on people' – to stand alone, a pace or two apart from the human uproar. But what would be the subject, what would it all be about?

I was still flirting with European subjects, still taking my food from 'over there'. That September I was intrigued with E. M. Forster's epigram: 'Our civilisation recommends ideals and practises brutality.' So what! There was one part of me which was still concerned with 'getting on' – a disease to which the sons of the clergy are so susceptible that the piece of folk wisdom which identifies success as a 'bitch goddess' might well be a fitting epigraph to the life story of many vicarage boys. I had begun to read Nietzsche, and had digested his words: 'God is dead. Mankind has killed him.' There was a theme, but where, as it were, was the clothing for that theme? I had come across the entry by Jules Michelet in his journal for 7 August 1831 about 'le Dieu qui nous échappe' (the God who eludes us), and how humanity would fill the 'immeasurable abyss which extinct Christianity has left them'. I agreed. But again where was the material with which to illustrate that theme?

At the time (1942–43) I was writing my thesis on Alexis de Tocqueville. That was part of 'getting on', whatever that might mean, and part of that quest to find out what it was all about. Like Michelet, Dostoevsky and Nietzsche, Tocqueville was concerned with the life of man without God. Like Nietzsche, Tocqueville was a prophet of

Manning Clark, Melbourne, 1938

Dymphna Lodewyckx, Mont Albert, Vic., 1936

Augustin Lodewyckx, Mont Albert, Vic., 1930

Anna Lodewyckx, Mont Albert, Vic., 1933

Manning Clark, Trinity College, Melbourne, 1938

Manning Clark, Tim Bligh and
Henry Whitehead, Oxford,
1939

Manning Clark, Oxford, 1939

Sunday *cassis* on the terrace, Château de Cosqueville,
Normandy, August 1939. *From left:* brother-in-law of Mme la
Baronne, Manning Clark, Mme la Baronne de Resbecq,
Dymphna Clark, Barbara Burton (from Melbourne), Yvan de
Resbecq, niece of Mme la Baronne, Alain, Baron de Resbecq

Margaret Kiddle, Melbourne, c. 1955

Geoffrey Fairbairn, Derrinallum, Vic., c. 1940

From left: Stephen Murray-Smith and Ian Turner, Erith Island, c. 1970

Geoffrey Serle, Melbourne, c. 1945

Geoffrey Blainey, Queen's College,
Melbourne, 1949

Ken Inglis, Queen's College,
Melbourne, 1950

Glen Tomasetti, Melbourne, c. 1960

From left: Axel, Katerina and Sebastian Clark, Croydon, Vic.,
1948

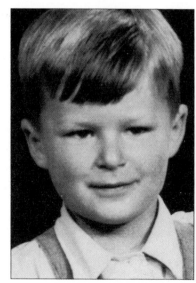

Andrew Clark, Canberra, 1954

From left: Manning, Sebastian, Andrew, Axel, Katerina and Dymphna Clark, in the study at Tasmania Circle, Canberra, 1955
(photograph courtesy of John Fairfax & Co.)

Rowland and Benedict Clark, Canberra, 1960

From left: Christopher, Bettina, Ruth, Nicholas and Heinz Arndt, Canberra, 1951

Don Baker, Melbourne, c. 1945

Helen Wighton and Fin Crisp, Oxford, 1939

Bill Gammage, Tumut, NSW, 1965

Noel Ebbels, Melbourne, c. 1950

Humphrey McQueen, Melbourne, c. 1965

Manning Clark at the tombstone of Thomas Carlyle, Ecclefechan, 1968

From left: Guy and Raina (née Campbell) Baring, David Campbell and Manning Clark, Canberra, 1976 (photograph courtesy of *Canberra Times*)

From left: Sebastian, Benedict, Axel, Dymphna, Manning, Rowland, Andrew and Katerina Clark, Canberra, 1962

Judah Waten, Manning Clark and James Devaney, Moscow, 1958

Dymphna and Manning Clark, Wapengo, NSW, 1988
(photograph: Heide Smith)

a mass age, a man with a great anxiety – democracy was the future of humanity, but democracy may be disastrous for higher civilisation. The work was finished in 1943, typed by Dymphna from my almost illegible hand-writing, and sent off for examination, in the hope that 'Tokkers' would rescue me from being a Mr Passion on the shores of Corio Bay.

A great change was coming over me. My eyes were ceasing to gaze with longing towards Europe and old civilisation. The beginning of that journey was like setting out from the centre of Sydney to drive to Canberra. There was much stopping and starting, much lane-changing before I got out on to the open road, out on to 'the Hume' – the human highway. Possibly Australian politics triggered me off. In August 1940, when we arrived back in Australia, it looked as though the dreary years of conservative rule were drawing to a close. After the election of 1940 the Menzies government had to rely on the support of two independents to survive. Labor had become more interesting. John Curtin, leader of the Australian Labor Party since 1935, had put new heart into its members. Labor could be pragmatic without losing its soul. Labor had something to say about the future of Australia. Dr Evatt had been elected as member for Barton to the House of Representatives, and had forged a link between intellectuals, artists and Labor. Dr Evatt was a child of the Enlightenment. Labor, under the leadership of men like Curtin, Chifley and Evatt would banish ignorance, superstition, poverty, drudgery and oppression. The years of unleavened bread under the conservatives were drawing to a close. They had no answers to the problems of the time. They were spitting at each other with all the fury of Kilkenny cats. Menzies, their leader, made enemies by indulging in his taste for mockery. A man guilty of *hubris*, of overweening pride and arrogance, was about to have a great fall.

The left-wing press in Australia became quite lively. Each week I went into Geelong to buy the *Workers' Weekly*, and the organ of the State Labor Party in New South Wales, led by Chandler and Hughes. The latter were not chanting a litany in the vocabulary which had come out of foreign lands. They wrote of 'Aussie' matters in 'Aussie' language. They held out a hope of a more exciting Australia. For me that weekly trip to Geelong was like taking communion ought to be, but isn't. It strengthened my faith: it was the booster I needed after a week of listening to and observing the men who had appointed themselves defenders of a doomed social order.

I had other things on my mind. On 20 June 1941 Katerina was born. She was so skinny my father likened her to 'a skun rabbit'. My mother, with her usual prescience, said she had the face of a 'little duchess'. Katerina later will write books on Russian intellectual history and become a successful teacher at Yale University. By an odd irony, the day after her birth the German army invaded Russia. So while the baby girl who was to grow into an analyst of the Russian mind was up for family judgement her father was quoting Dostoevsky to the boys at Corio: 'God will save Russia as He has saved her many times in her history.'

Late on Saturday nights when alcohol clothed even the bleak land-scape of Corio or the lifeless drawing-rooms of the Melbourne suburbs (especially of Toorak, where mothers of Corio boarders handed out free drinks to a penurious schoolteacher), I asked, 'Where are the snows of yester-year? Mother of God, thou canst not tell.' I could not tell them what was on my mind. I was troubled by the pictures of young Germans I had known in Bonn and Munich becoming the victims of the madness and the folly of the invasion of Russia. They deserved our pity. I also held a messianic view of the role of Russia in world history. Russia would save Europe from decadence and corruption. Russia would save Europe as she had saved it in 1812. The centre of power will shift from the British to the Russians and the Americans. Tocqueville was right. But how could I say that to the Anglophiles of Corio and Yarraside?

Events moved swiftly. In August 1941 United Australia Party and Country Party members of Cabinet forced Menzies to resign as Prime Minister. Arthur Fadden became Prime Minister. Some time later I heard what happened in Parliament House, Canberra, on the night Menzies resigned – how he had walked slowly from the Cabinet Room to the Prime Minister's office, fallen into the arms of the Cabinet Secretary, Cecil Looker, and had said through tears, 'Looker, I'm all in.' I noticed to my horror that some who shared my growing faith in the Australia that was coming to be, laughed the laughter of mockers when they heard this story. That gave me pause. I saw Menzies then as a big man, a giant in the land, brought to his ruin by little men and his own folly. I saw him as a tragic figure. That was the first time I had ever thought of an Australian as the subject for a tragedy. Previously for me they had been comic, never tragic figures. Tragedy was European: that belonged to the Old World. I recoiled when many secular humanists and advocates for a better society gloated over the fall of Menzies. I could not join in their glee, could not join with them in singing in triumph the song about 'the balls of Bob Menzies'. Secular humanists lacked the eye of pity, lacked the eye for the human tragedy. Perhaps I was perverse, but I could not share their lack of sympathy for an Australian Humpty Dumpty who had once sat on a high wall, and then had a great fall.

A time of danger was at hand for Australia. We were no longer safe. The Japanese were talking more and more menacing language: they wanted all the peoples of Asia and the south-west Pacific to be part of their co-prosperity sphere. The conservatives had soft-soaped Australians for years with their talk about the British navy. Thanks to the British navy, they kept repeating like a cocky in a cage, we were quite safe 'in case we got into trouble in our part of the world'. The British navy was the umbrella under which we would all be secure, yes, and go on being cosy for ever. John Curtin punctured this smugness, this complacency. Australia was vulnerable to attack by aircraft from aircraft carriers.

Events were now at the gallop. In October 1941 A. W. Coles and A. Wilson brought down the Fadden government. The Governor-General, Lord Gowrie, asked John Curtin to form a government. Labor members crowded into the party room in Parliament House to sing 'The Workers' Flag is deepest red'. Tears of hope flowed down my cheeks when I heard about this down on the plains of Corio. Maybe something beautiful was about to be born out of the Australian people. Maybe they were about to discover something about themselves. On 6 December the Japanese attacked Pearl Harbor.

Disaster followed disaster. On 9 December 1941 the Japanese sent two British battleships, the *Prince of Wales* and the *Repulse*, to the bottom of the sea. John Curtin did not lose heart. He had had his dream of the Australia that was coming to be. At the armistice day ceremony at the Australian War Memorial, Canberra, on 11 November, he had ordered the military band to play 'Advance Australia Fair'. Australia was on the move. Now after the disaster in the sea off Malaya he appealed to America, free, as he put it, from any compunction about our past relations with Britain. All through the dark days of early 1942 he spoke to Australians of his hope that Australia was about to build a nation which would be an example to all others. I did not know then that John Curtin believed in 'the Young Tree Green'. I did not know then the source of his ideas.

Finding out was one of the happy by-products of the spirit of the times. Reading radical papers had given me an appetite for things Australian. I must find out more. The only Australian literature I had read so far had been *Robbery Under Arms* by 'Rolf Boldrewood' (a good yarn), and Marcus Clarke's *For the Term of His Natural Life* (gothic), but my mind was intrigued by the character of the Reverend North, Dostoevsky having taught me what I already vaguely knew, that a man's heart may be on fire with both the ideal of the Madonna and the ideal of Sodom. They both lived together in the human heart. Here was an Australian author making the same point, though not in such memorable words.

John Curtin and his colleagues wanted Australians to read their own literature. In 1943 the Australian Pocket Library series of books was announced. So, on one of my weekly excursions to Geelong to the Left Wing bookshop to buy the *Workers' Weekly*, I bought W. K. Hancock's *Australia*. I had met Hancock with his father, Archdeacon W. Hancock, and had put on the granite face for him because his father was one of those off-putting jolly parsons who, despite the teaching of his religion on good and evil, had time only for the 'solid mandalas', those who were solid as a rock or white as the driven snow. He was yet another of those virtuous men with whom I can never be at ease. Hancock himself was an Austral-Briton, a very brilliant and persuasive representative of the position from which I was moving away, not of the position I was groping towards. He was still a romantic about England's 'green and pleasant land', and deep in a love–hate relationship with the 'wide brown land', the 'haggard continent'. He taught me much. One moment he talked like a fellow of All Souls, the next moment he told stories about fishing for yabbies in the Mitchell River at Bairnsdale. Keith Hancock knew the tug between the country in which he was born, and the country in which his mind flowered.

I also bought in 1943 the Australian Pocket Library edition of the poetry and prose of Henry Lawson. I had only vaguely heard of Lawson before reading him. It was one of those moments in life when one is lifted up. Here was an Australian putting into memorable words a criticism of a society based on encouragement to greed, a society which identified material well-being with happiness, a society of worshippers of Mammon. I became a Lawson man for life. Years later I read more in 'Freedom on the Wallaby':

> But now that we have made the land
> A garden full of promise,
> Old greed must crook his dirty hand
> And come and take it from us.

It went on:

> But Freedom's on the Wallaby,
> She'll knock the tyrants silly,
> She's going to light another fire
> And boil another billy.
> We'll make the tyrants feel the sting
> Of those that they would throttle;
> They needn't say the fault is ours
> If blood should stain the wattle.

There was more. Poverty, oppression, exploitation and the misery of the people, were not things that happened 'over there': they were here in our midst:

> They lie, the men who tell us, for reasons of their own
> That want is here a stranger, and that misery's unknown . . .

('Faces in the Street')

Faces of misery drifted past in the street. What was to be done? Words were not enough:

> The warning pen shall write in vain, the warning voice grow hoarse,
> But not until a city feels Red Revolution's feet
> Shall its sad people miss awhile the terrors of the street . . .

We Australians were not condemned to being second-rate Europeans forever – Australians had a destiny. In his poem, 'A Song of the Republic', Lawson called on Australians to

> Banish from under your bonny skies
> Those old-world errors and wrongs and lies
> Making a hell in a Paradise
> That belongs to your sons and you.

137

Australians must choose:

> *Sons of the South, make choice between*
> *(Sons of the South, choose true)*
> *The Land of Morn and the Land of E'en,*
> *The Old Dead Tree and the Young Tree Green,*
> *The Land that belongs to the lord and Queen,*
> *And the Land that belongs to you.*

I had no knowledge at the time of the man who had written those words. I did not even know how old he was, or where he was born, let alone the events in his life which had planted these ideas in his head. In the stories I read there were hints that all was not well with the author, that he was a man who knew he should stop drinking but found he could·not, that he was a man who wanted to love and be loved by a woman but things had gone wrong. I had a suspicion that once again I had fallen in love with a person with a fatal flaw in his clay. I will find out much about Lawson the man later on, and my account of what I found will provoke some to mock and vilify me.

I did not notice at the time that Lawson was preaching mainly to men, that like his contemporaries he either excluded one half of humanity, women, or praised them too fulsomely. I did not notice that he sometimes excluded Englishmen, Americans, Europeans, Jews, Chinese, Japanese, Aborigines, and all other coloured people. His generation's mateship was for an all-white, all-male cast. That too will come later, when I was ready to see that mateship belonged to the dead hand of the past in Australia, when I began to think about a mythology for the suburbs. I had alighted again on a Merlin, a devil, and at the same time an innocent boy from the bush.

In between clowning with the boys of the History Sixth, I moved on from Henry Lawson to Joseph Furphy. In comparison with Lawson, Furphy was a dull dog, a preacher who took a long time to deliver his message. I kept going, and received a modest reward. I enjoyed his wit – especially these thoughts of Dixon the bullocky in *Rigby's Romance* on first reading the Old Testament:

'Samson, he was the strongest (individual) ever lived', he [i.e. Dixon] remarked in a careless tone; 'an' Solomon he was the wisest – an' who do you think was the foolishest?' 'The man who built his house on the sand',

I suggested. 'Ain't come to that bloke yet', replied Dixon, 'but I'm thinkin' Moses could give him about half-ways an' lick him (adv.) bad. Yes, Moses was the foolishest (person) ever lived. Bible cracks him up, mind you, because he was a decent feller in his own sort o' soft-headed way. But he didn't know his road roun'. Cripes, if I got slants like him I'd shift things a bit! my (adj.) oath!'

Furphy was unmistakably Australian. He had Australians speaking the way they do, their drawl and their rich language. Furphy believed in Australia. He had a simple motto, a motto I was not ready for at that time: 'Aut Australia, aut nihil.' (Australia or nothing). There was the rub – I was not prepared, never will be prepared, to discard Europe.

Furphy was one of the good-time-coming boys. Furphy saw the Englishman as the corrupter, and the Australian bushman as the innocent one. That was his subject in *The Buln Buln and the Brolga*. That appealed to me, I always cherished the belief that there was an innocent person inside me, a person who could not be corrupted by wallowing in the mire. Well, I only escaped in time – but that is to anticipate. A weekly dip in the gutter at that time was the only escape from the straiteners of Corio.

Mocking the pompous and the pretentious was a balm for all the common-room and Biddlecombe Avenue gossip. I have never understood why in denominational colleges and schools men and women who go down on their knees each Sunday, and hear the chaplain exhort all those who are 'in love and charity with their neighbour' and intend to lead a new life following the commandments of God, should spend the other six days of the week practising the art of the character assassin. As a vicarage child at Cowes, and a vicarage boy at Belgrave, such behaviour had been one of the puzzles of my childhood. Now here at Corio I was both the observer and the victim of such attacks. In time I will learn that the only response to a character sketch is to get on with one's work, and not to consume one's energies conceiving wounding replies. But then, alas, mockery was the one weapon in my armoury, the one weapon with which to soothe my wounds. It did not occur to me that by indulging in such satisfactions I might be hurting other people. There would be many years of remorse and regret for having been both a corrupter and one of the corrupted.

It never occurred to me at the time that such venom reflected the hollowness of Corio life. They were apologists for an anachronism, apologists for Englishmanism in Australia. The forces of history had driven them from their one-time position of prominence in Australian life. They were a group of people who had lost their way. They were like a boat which had once ridden proudly on the bosom of the great river of life but had drifted into a billabong. They were living proof of what the young Henry Lawson had labelled as 'The Old Dead Tree'. But my 'muddy vesture' at the time did not permit me to see clearly what was going on. Both literally and metaphorically I was looking 'through a glass darkly'.

There were moments when I did see things 'face to face'. There was that time when some of the masters, to my surprise, invited me to join them on a drinking spree in Geelong. The beer was on in Geelong, I was told, and we drinkers must drink it while we could – beer in any quantity by then being almost as rare as hen's teeth. When the time came to return we were friendlier with each other than on the trip into Geelong. One of the rather crabby masters said to me as we drove along the Melbourne road, 'You know, Clark, you're a much nicer chap when you've had a few beers: I have never seen you smile before.' Confidences were exchanged. He had never been made a house-master. He was a pathetic figure: he was like the narrator in Gogol's *Diary of a Madman*. He wanted to know, 'Why have I always been a clerk?' Sober, he was submissive, deferential, a toucher of the cap to those in high places. Elevated, he was ready to settle scores with those who had always spoken to him with that English air of the 'tranquil consciousness of an effortless superiority'.

After the bus stopped outside the headmaster's house, looking as it did rather Edgar Allan Poeish in the light of a full moon – a dark presence in that eerie landscape – my temporary friend (I knew the drawing together would not last for long after the effect of the booze wore off) jumped out of the bus, shook his fist at the headmaster's house, and shouted in rage, 'There's too much slapping the mutton in this school, and that fucking Pommy's responsible for it.' All the others agreed. 'Good on you ——,' they said, 'you're on to something there.'

The little stage on which the lives of the teachers were being played would shrink and shrink and shrink. The stage for the audience of the world was now on the battlefields of Russia and on the islands of the south-west Pacific. The people were winning their war against Fascism. The German army, under the command of General von Paulus, surrendered at Stalingrad in January 1943. For those who believed, as I did at the time, that the people were the origin of all just power, the future held out the promise of a day not too far distant when the people would prove their 'capacity for better things'.

Australia, too, was on the march. Australia has a destiny: Australia will shed the 'old-world errors and wrongs and lies'. I set out on a journey to discover Australia. I read Martin Boyd, *The Montforts*, and find much in it to delight me. Here is a man who knows all about the pull in two different directions – the pull to Australia for human warmth, the pull to Europe for 'older civilisation'. I begin to believe it is possible to be magnificently alive in Australia. I notice, too, that Martin Boyd is on the same journey – he too is a seeker after grace.

I read Henry Handel Richardson, *The Fortunes of Richard Mahony*, and standing beside the waters of Corio Bay I think much about us all as exiles here, and wonder for the first time whether we belong here, whether, in the words of the Psalmist we are just sojourners here. I notice that the author wants to know what I want to know – why we suffer as we do, and what it has all been for? She has taken me up into a high mountain and shown me all the kingdoms of this world; she has lifted me up; she has put a magnifying glass in front of my eyes which enables me to see the tragic grandeur and the high solemnity of life.

That did not last for long. The wild life was resumed. Dymphna read the *Mahony*, and told me the principal character was the man she knew as her husband, that she, too, was married to 'a wayward, vagrant spirit'. That gave me pause, but not for long. There had to be suffering before I was ready to say anything on paper.

In the afternoon of 31 March 1943 I was coaching the First Eleven at cricket, when a boy ran on to the field to tell me I was wanted on the telephone in the headmaster's study. It was the Reverend Roy Tunks. 'Mr Clark,' he said, 'your mother passed away peacefully this afternoon.' I begin to shake: something deep down is struggling for a place in my mind.

I set off for Melbourne in the train. Dymphna is already in Melbourne awaiting the birth of our third child. She holds out the hand of sympathy and understanding, because the sun of love will never be extinguished in her heart. But I cannot stay with her, the members of her family having no sympathy with my mother and her world. They belong to Europe, my mother to Old Australia. They know nothing of what she has lived through, I only know what I can guess from her cries out of the deep about 'things in my life, Mann dear'. They do not know of my loss, my grief, my pain.

I go to the vicarage at Mentone where my mother lies on one of the beds in a front room. My brother seizes me by the shoulders, shakes me and says to me, through tears, 'Promise me faithfully, Mann, you won't look at her.' I cannot give such a promise. I open the door, and walk towards the body, and again begin to shake. I try to speak, but no sound comes out of my mouth. I try again, but the tumult within still deprives me of the power of speech. I rush out of the room on to the side lawn, hoping the darkness will hide my grief. Death has altered all. No one must know how great my grief, how great my loss.

Two days later there was a funeral service in the church of St Augustine at Mentone. The church was packed, for my mother had been and always would be much loved. My brother asked me to put on a 'Christian witness' in the church. He asks me with a wild look of anxiety in his eye, 'You do believe, Mann, we will see her again?' I do not say a word. What could be said? A clergyman recited the comfortable words: that as in Adam all died, even so in Christ shall all be made alive, but this meant nothing to me. Why not face the truth? Death was the end, or as Philip Larkin put it later, the anaesthetic from which no one wakes up. Death should not exist: but it did. Nothing could help.

Comedy provided a diversion. Archdeacon Hancock (the father of the historian), by then an old man with a florid face, closed his eyes, gripped the rails of the pulpit, opened his eyes and gazed upwards as though there were someone above us all who would listen to what he had to say. He told the congregation he loved to visit the vicarage at Belgrave, because the family there always reminded him of the family of Jesus in Nazareth. I remembered the last time the Archdeacon visited us my brother, in anger, tried to shoot me. The Archdeacon spoke of my mother as a paragon of the Christian virtues. The cong- regation sang the hymn, 'On the resurrection morning / Soul and body meet once more.' They all looked so smug that for a moment anger supplanted my grief. Their faith in the resurrection morning, their confidence that they would all see one another again, seemed to me to be a licence to keep on doing what they were doing, a divine authority for not examining their own lives. They would still be smug on the resurrection morning.

At the grave site at Box Hill cemetery the Archbishop of Melbourne, the Very Reverend J. Booth, also eulogised the Christian virtues of my mother. He was right. She was one of the riders in God's chariot. But, as he spoke I kept hearing her say to me what she had first said to me in childhood, and kept on saying until she 'walked into the night': 'There are things in my life, Mann dear, I hope you will never know anything about.' No one else seemed aware of the tragic grandeur of the occasion, or to ask why for her it had all gone wrong. There was a story there, but I was not ready to tell it. My mother belonged to Old Australia. One day I would tell the story of Old Australia, or try to, but not then. All I knew at the time was a regret that now we would never speak again.

I knew one other thing: that Christian cheerfulness, Church of England fashion, was not for me. Yes, and there was one other bitter lesson, one other disenchantment which will live with me forever: the inadequacy of the secular humanists on death, an inadequacy they attempted to cover up beneath a surface arrogance, a certainty that they knew, that was just as off-putting, just as offensive as the hospital cheerfulness and the Kolynos smiles of the Christians. In their presence I always wanted to put to them the question in Job: What knowest thou which is not in us? They were just as off-putting in their response to the miracle of life. Our son Axel was born on the day after the funeral.

There was much to discover. There was so much to be said as a teacher or a writer, which could not be said at Geelong Grammar School. The fact was, I did not understand them, and they did not understand me. Full stop. It was like standing on one side of a thick plate glass window: I knew *they* were talking, because I could see their lips were moving, but I did not know what those words were. There must be someone, somewhere, to whom one could speak. At Corio, apart from John Barber, Margaret and Kay Masterman, the kind Marge Tunbridge, and the understanding Ted Pinner, there was no one to whom I could speak, except in the language and gestures of buffoonery and mockery. One cannot be a clown in the classroom forever, or a jester in the drawing-rooms of Yarraside.

John Barber spun the most delightful fantasies. They generally began with someone asking him, 'Are you thirsty, Barber?' I remember one which began with the conductor on the transcontinental train from Adelaide asking John on a day in January when the temperature was over 100°F, 'Are you thirsty, Barber?' John was always thirsty. The conductor produced a dozen bottles of ice-cold beer; after drinking which, in John's words, 'I kind of staggered out and saw a naked woman in the corridor, who asked me "Are you hungry, Barber?" No, Manning, fair dinkum, she did.' Such fantasies made the world of

Corio bearable for John. The longer he stayed there, the wilder, the weirder they became. I remember one night in Toorak when he asked the taxi-driver to drive carefully because he had just that day been discharged from hospital where he had lain in an iron lung for six months. John was so afraid the conformers of Corio might discover his secret that he served in the cadet corps as a lieutenant. He also voted for the conservatives in an effort to be accepted. But *they* were not deceived. And John's fantasies became more and more bizarre.

I must not lapse into fantasy. I must face the blank page to see whether I have anything to say. I had written some articles in the *Melburnian* in my last years at school. In 1931 I had told my fellow-Melburnians that the Australian Aborigine was not the 'idiot and brainless man that some historians have made him out to be'. In 1933 in the *Melburnian* I adopted, rather brashly, the language of prophecy. The stage was set, I wrote, for 'the outbreak of a war of the first magnitude'. War would be waged, I told them all, both in the west and in the east. In the same year I arrogantly announced that human nature was 'the spanner in the works', that it was what came up from inside us all which was leading us all on to destruction.

Ten years later, in the shadow of my mother's death, I put pen to paper again to write 'A Letter to Tom Collins'. It was published in *Meanjin* (Autumn 1943, vol. 2, no. 1). I was beginning to think about some of the themes which will be developed later in *A History of Australia*. I posed the question: Do we belong here?

I told 'Tom Collins' (Joseph Furphy) that the Lawson–Furphy version of 'mateyness' was not enough: we wanted something more. We needed either 'a prophet to preach a new myth or a sage to convince us it is better to accept things as they are, better to forget the something more.' For just as Mrs Warren, then aged sixty-five, once said to Mabel Taylor (another tutor in philosophy) in the old Melbourne University cafeteria, on seeing a beautiful young man walk through the door, 'It never leaves us, does it Mabel?', so those themes will never leave me. The question then, in 1943, was: could this grain of mustard seed grow into a stately tree, or would it also look like Marcus Clarke's Australia, inscribed with 'the weird scribblings of nature'?

Melbourne University was my goal. I clung to the hope that there was a place where it would be possible to develop these ideas at a university. But the universities did not want what I had to offer. They were polite: they would love to have me, but, alas, I had no university

144

teaching experience. There must be a way over this brick wall. In 1944 I volunteered to take two tutorials a week in political science at the university (the historians were still on the other side of the brick wall). Ian Milner, the acting head of the Department of Political Science, was enthusiastic. A lectureship in political science was advertised. I applied. Some counselled Ian Milner to play safe. He stood firm, and persuaded the electoral committee to recommend my appointment. I had climbed over the wall.

So, on 1 May 1944 I left Geelong Grammar School to take up the lectureship at the University of Melbourne. There were many voices inside me. There was a clown who put on a show for the misfits of Melbourne suburbia; there was a young man driven by ambition to rise out of the society of the genteel poor; there was a pilgrim for the means of grace; there was a young man who had already decided the measurers, the social scientists and the spiritual bullies were disastrously wrong, but who did not know what was right, or what he had to offer. Within two years I would be given a chance to begin the discovery of Australia. But as the train rocked over the Werribee plains on the way to Melbourne I enjoyed the exaltation of escape. I did not foresee the journey I had begun. I was still one of those travellers who wanted their liquor, their women, and their mockery. A time would come when I would set out on 'such a long journey'. But not then.

The Discovery
of Australia Begins

On 1 May 1944 I gave my first lecture at the University of Melbourne. It looked then as though humanity were about to display that capacity for better things which Immanuel Kant had identified as the central lesson of the French Revolution. The people were winning the war against Fascism. The Soviet army was slowly expelling the Germans from the territory they had occupied in eastern Europe and the Soviet Union, and the Allies were about to start a second front in western Europe. The Japanese thrust into south-east Asia had come to a full-stop: the Japanese were on the retreat. The Australian Labor government has committed itself to work for a world in which there was peace, freedom from hunger, freedom from want, and equality of opportunity for all. The years of drudgery were coming to an end. Soon, very soon, the whole of humanity would sing and dance and shout for joy. One young woman told me: evil conditions have made men evil; good conditions will make them good. They were heady times. The great dreams of humanity were about to come true.

I shared the hopes and enthusiasms of the time. I was in part a believer in the coming great good time. I believed there was only one criterion by which all of us, save those with walnut hearts, should judge political institutions: did they promote the principle that all power resided in the people? The university lectern was not for dry-as-dust scholars or sneerers: it was the secular pulpit for future-of-humanity men. Objectivity, impartiality, detachment, cool reason, well, they were all part of the mythologising with which previous paid hirelings of the bourgeoisie had shielded a doomed and corrupt society from judgement. They were part of a confidence trick to stop people asking such questions as: Why are the many so poor? Why is there domination of class over class, of man over woman, of white man over coloured man, and, though this came later, of professors over students? I had no body of theory. I believed then, as I believe now, with Mephistopheles in Goethe's *Faust*: 'Grey is all theory, my friend, / But green is the golden tree of life.' I did not stand on any 'entrenched ground'. I was in that blessed state of those that have not seen but still believe. If pressed I could not have put into intelligible words what I believed. I could only quote others – such as William Lane's 'the Australia that is coming to be', or Henry Lawson's faith that Australians would banish from under their bonny skies those old-world errors, wrongs and lies, or those words by John Ruskin which had inspired my mother from his 'Unto This Last'. I was an apostle of the Enlightenment.

There was also that other person inside me warning me not to expect too much from human endeavour. One side of me was still sceptical when anyone told me the heart was a 'jewel of perfection'. For me the heart was always a battlefield between good and evil. As a boy at Melbourne Grammar School I had learned the tormented had no choice but to betray those who had betrayed them, and that betrayers must live with their guilt. I had seen it again on a much larger scale at Geelong Grammar School. The experience there convinced me that betrayal was one of the principal manifestations of human evil. There I understood for the first time why Judas was central to the Christ story. The innocent must be betrayed, because the dominators, the power men and women in any society, cannot tolerate goodness. They must destroy it. The great mass of humanity cannot live with good or innocent people.

The future-of-humanity men and women I met at Melbourne University reminded me of the men and women in the church at Belgrave. They complimented themselves on their political virtue with the same enthusiasm with which the parishioners at Belgrave congratulated themselves on their religious virtue. They thanked Karl Marx they were not as stupid or immoral as those who had not seen the light: the parishioners at Belgrave thanked their God they were not like the other people in the mountain district – adulterers and liars and drunkards. Yet these men and women at the University of Melbourne who claimed they knew how to prepare humanity to take a seat at the great banquet of life often spoke as though they were taking part in a procession round the secular stations of the double-cross.

The minds of the students illustrated the point Tolstoy made about love in *Anna Karenin*: 'there are as many kinds of love as there are hearts'. There were many kinds of students. There was Frank Crean, then a member of the Taxation Office in Melbourne, and later Treasurer in the second Whitlam government. He believed Labor would gradually create a society in which human beings would be kind and tender to each other. Unlike me he knew his economics and so had empirical foundations for his faith, not just those messages from the human heart which were all I had to offer. Frank Crean was already an expert in Commonwealth–State financial relations, and that will give him the air of quiet authority which later pervaded his speeches in the House of Representatives in Canberra.

There was Anna Wittner, a member of the family which owned the chain of Wittner's shoe stores. Her hopes for humanity were as beautiful as the features of her face and body. I remember the light in her eyes as she told her fellow classmates that what this country needed was not less, but more, democracy. She pronounced the word 'democracy' with all the fervour of a neophyte. Her eyes often looked as though they were moistening at the sheer pleasure of being alive. They will moisten more when she meets the man she was to marry. His name was Zelman Cowen.

Anna was one of those enthusiasts at the end of the war who believed knowledge would increase virtue and happiness. She was as thirsty for knowledge as she was for life. At parties she would ask Zelman, 'What are the reserve powers of the Crown, Zelman?' – not knowing then of the storm to come in November 1975. She, the innocent pilgrim, wanted to know so desperately that the light in her eyes never faded during the learned but somewhat lengthy reply by the man who was to make a distinguished career as a teacher of constitutional law. Other eyes faded, or looked longingly at the drinks tray, as they muttered to themselves, 'How long, O Lord, how long?' The warmth in her will not grow cold: success in the world will not exact its usual terrible price.

There was Carlotta Ellis, a niece of Ulrich Ellis (the historian of the Country Party), and of Malcolm Ellis, the biographer of Macarthur, Greenway and Macquarie, and the author of articles signed *Ek Dum* in the *Bulletin* which lined him up with the extreme right in politics, to the considerable embarrassment of his niece Carlotta. At that time, though not later, she accepted the Marx–Lenin diagnosis and prophecy on the past, present and future of capitalist society. Carlotta was an enigma. She was a gentle spirit who recited the Marxist-Leninist teaching that communists should be hostile in the presence of the class enemy. Carlotta was not a hater, or one of those revolutionaries who taught the doctrine that the blood of the bourgeoisie would be good manure to fertilise the earth for some future human harmony. Carlotta was not a spiritual bully: she always looked as though she were the sort of woman bullies pick on for their own subterranean satisfactions. Human beings may express token sympathy with victims, but their interest is in the hunter rather than his prey. Carlotta had by nature too much of the eye of pity for all human beings to last for long with a team of people who were the Pharisees of the secular humanist persuasion.

There was Geoffrey Serle, the son of Percival Serle the writer and Dora Serle the painter. Geoffrey puffed on his pipe and looked at the ground when fellow-students or lecturers ran the risk of taking sides on any question of the day. When their confidence was sapped by Geoffrey's silence and his expressionless face, he would slowly take the pipe out of his mouth, puff out a smoke screen, catch briefly the eye of the speaker and pronounce a middle-of-the-road position. I was already toying with the generalisation that all pipe-smokers occupied the middle position between the Dionysians (the men of passion) and the Apollonians (the eunuchs of the classroom). But one night at a students' hostel in Fitzroy I had the good fortune to see Geoffrey dancing with Amirah Gust (later Amirah Inglis), a history student through whom the gale of life blew very high. I was astonished. He looked so happy, so teeming with life that I had difficulty reconciling him with the man who was so sensible in class and elsewhere. This combination of head-piece cool and warm heart would have a flowering time later. The pipe-smoker and the dancer combined to write the fair-minded, judicious biography of Monash, and to be a most meticulous general editor of volumes in the *Australian Dictionary of Biography*.

Sol Encel was also a member of the class. From him, and later from Geoffrey Blainey and Ken Inglis – all students who rarely said a word – I learnt a lesson: the silent ones are often the best performers on paper. I could see then that Sol was one of the deeper sort, that underneath the cool smile with which he regarded the performances of others there lived a man who wanted to find out what held the world together in its innermost parts. Sol was both a fine flower of the Enlightenment, and a man who had learnt from his fathers that there was madness in men's hearts. He was a young man who had already learnt not to expect too much from all human striving, a man

149

who knew all about the 'field of the possible'. In time he will put down on paper the fruits of his knowledge and his wisdom.

There were some comical moments. I had never taught a class before in which there were both men and women. In one of the tutorials there was a Miss Chesterman. In 1944 there was none of the current familiarity and mateyness between student and teacher. Men were Mr and women Mrs or Miss, and that was that. Like my father too, I liked conventions which checked breezy familiarity. There was also a Miss ——, who must remain anonymous. Nature had endowed her with a bosom as large as Abraham's. Well in my first or second class with this tutorial I called her of the bosom 'Miss Chesterman'. She blushed. Others giggled. Miss Chesterman and The Bosom waited behind after the class to point out my error. I was embarrassed. From that day I rarely risked identifying a woman by her name in a class, preferring the coward's solution of calling them 'Er', just as later I will always call a Governor-General 'Er', not being prepared to call any man 'Your Excellency'. One has to take a stand on some things. Even clergymen's sons can sometimes take a stand on principle in fields of life which do not matter very much.

The majority seemed to accept the superficial assumption of the day that a change in the ownership of the means of production, distribution and exchange would be followed by a change in human behaviour. Pauline Grutzner did not share that hope. She had a beautiful face, which in repose wore an expression of tender melancholy, as though she already had intimations her soul would not be happy until she was united with God. At the time she seemed to be planning to be united with a student from Newman College, a young man as handsome as she was beautiful. But she had her eye on a greater prize. As soon as she graduated she entered a religious order, took the vows of poverty, chastity and obedience, and after finishing an arduous course of prayer, fasting and study she left Australia to win souls for Christ by her example in India. We wrote to each other from time to time. Perhaps she guessed there was a man within me who understood, and possibly even shared, her longing.

Three years ago she invited me to a mass in St Christopher's pro-cathedral in Canberra to wish her well for another mission. When the priest invited members of the congregation to make to each other the sign of peace, she shook me warmly by the hand. It was as though she knew about the man within. I could not speak. She was always well ahead of all of us in the quest for the means of grace. Perhaps

150

God puts women like Pauline Grutzner in the world to show there is an alternative to the academic world of back-biting, character assassination, and that oppressive tyranny of opinion. Who can tell?

The members of the teaching staff in the Faculty of Arts were just as varied as the students. The take-over bid by the disciples of Wittgenstein for Intellectual Enterprises Proprietary Limited in the Faculty of Arts had been accepted. If anyone risked betraying an enthusiasm for Tolstoy, Dostoevsky, Hardy, Carlyle, Newman, Melville, Hawthorne, Thucydides, Macaulay, and company, they were asked with a glance of scorn and a curl of the lip had they not noticed that the pages of these works were littered with tautologies, *non sequiturs*, meaningless propositions, and other errors too egregious to mention. There was a debate going on between the social scientists and the Wittgensteiners in which the latter wrote on the blackboard: Laws of history = 0. So no history! Ha, ha, ha! Cop that, and shut up, or better still read the *Tractatus*, and you will learn that on all questions on which you cannot speak with certainty you should be silent. Melbourne always had two Beatitudes: blessed are the pure in morals; blessed are the pure in politics. Now it had a third: blessed are the pure in language. I was always uncomfortable in the presence of improvers. Perhaps that was why I had to become an exile from Melbourne.

The ridiculing of the laws-of-history men did not bother me. I believed that only one kind of history was open to me. That was the history which told a story about the past to entertain and instruct the living, to make them more aware of 'the field of the possible' for human beings. At that time telling a story was out of fashion. The historians at the university, alas, had no place for me as a teacher.

My colleague in the Department of Political Science, Ian Milner, was very understanding with me. In 1944 Ian Milner was acting head of the Department. His story was a parable of the times. A chance event in Oxford had converted Ian the poet into Ian the Marxist. I liked and still like the poet who has survived all the years with the engineers of the human soul. He was the son of a prominent high-school head-master in New Zealand. He had studied English literature in New Zealand, was friendly with and admired by the small groups of New Zealanders who had fought for years the good fight against the giant of British Philistinism. He knew Dan Davin, Vincent O'Sullivan, and James Baxter. He had won a Rhodes Scholarship to Oxford.

At that time he held no political opinions, except some sympathy with Heine's fear that the self-appointed improvers of humanity might condemn all human beings to a spiritual diet of 'Spartan black soup', rather than a walk in the paradise gardens. The political creeds which moved men's hearts were vain. Or so he believed until a night in Oxford in the early 1930s when he attended a meeting of the British Union of Fascists addressed by Oswald Mosley. There he saw thugs beat protesters with sticks. He was horrified. He decided to find out why people behaved in that way. He began to study politics. He found the answer he was looking for in the works of Marx, Engels and Lenin. From that time he devoted his talents to what he believed to be the noblest cause of all – the liberation of all human beings from their gaolers and their oppressors.

He had one of the distinguishing characteristics of a true believer: he never put pressure on other men and women to accept his opinions. Like all true believers he was so convinced he had discovered the truth about history and the future of human society that, to my knowledge, he never descended to the tactics of the bully-boys and the bully-girls of the Left. Nothing ever shook his loyalty to the revolution of 1917. For him the salvation of that revolution against its enemies both within and without the Soviet Union became the greatest good. He defended the treason trials of 1936–38, and the death penalty for the guilty. Such loyalty pushed him into situations where, to an outsider, he seemed like a man defending the indefensible. Early in 1945 the Soviet government ordered the execution of two Polish social democrats. Colleagues asked Ian to tell them why. Ian stood firm. The 'Ruskies', he said, must have had a good reason.

When he lectured to the students he observed so strictly the bourgeois principle of impartiality and detachment that the poet became a bit of a bore. I remember attending one of his lectures on the High Court of Australia, at which, after fifty minutes of what must have been for him the most agonising fence-sitting, he blushed a deep scarlet, fiddled with his gown, and declared with great passion that the High Court was an arm of conservatism in Australia. He then smiled, looked very embarrassed, rather like a naughty boy who knew he had just said the wrong thing, and apologised for speaking like that. He knew that was not done in Melbourne. The professors who wanted the university to be a citadel of British philistine and bourgeois culture would not like it if he went on like that.

As we walked back to his room, Ian muttered, 'I should not have let myself go'. He had so much to say which could not be said in a capitalist university. He would have to wait for the revolution. Well, he did not wait in Melbourne. He became a Professor of English at the Charles University in Prague. There, once again, he had to curb his tongue. The things unsaid would stay unsaid. I wonder if, given the chance to speak, he would have cried out in anguish, 'It's gone wrong, it's all gone wrong.'

Dick Downing was one man who would never want to utter such a cry of anguish. I had known him first when he was a student at Ormond College. He was then friendly with Ross Wilson and Dorian Le Gallienne, the composer, another man who knew all about 'Grammar and that sort of thing'. Dick was a brilliant economist who had worked with Professor Copland in government services and at the International Labour Office in Geneva before returning to Melbourne to take up the Ritchie Chair in Economic Research. There were many Dick Downings. He had a chest-of-drawers mind, that is, a mind which pulls out the drawer relevant to his company and leaves the others tightly shut. There was the public finance expert; there was the academic gossip, the man with the *mauvaise langue* (malicious tongue) for the pompous and the pretentious; there was the man who liked to reminisce about Ross Wilson and allied subjects; there was the man whose idea of heaven was to return to his room in Ormond, fill a tumbler with sherry, turn on the wireless and sip at his sherry while listening to an instalment of Gwen Meredith's 'Blue Hills'.

There was one drawer, I suspect, which he never opened when others were present. That was the drawer which contained the real Dick Downing. But if there is an art which allows us to read 'the mind's construction in the face', then Dick Downing always seemed very determined no one would ever practise the art on him. Yet behind the tobacco screen, behind the mask of the wit, and the dropper of outrageous remarks, the man whose eyes sparkled when he mentioned one of the many Melbourne unmentionables, the man who enjoyed the latest gossip on who were sharing beds in Melbourne, there lived a melancholy man who knew that what he wanted most in life would never be, a man who had sampled all the 'goodies' of the flesh and the spirit, and still enjoyed life with great gusto. He was very tender and loving to those who could not manage the world. He enjoyed making digs at MacMahon Ball, Gordon Wood and Wilfred Prest. He loved dinners at the Latin, listening to music, talking about the painting of Arthur Boyd, solving a problem in public finance, and later, as the Chairman of the Australian Broadcasting

Commission, voting with gusto for the right of announcers and performers to use four-letter words. He was a man for the gaiety of the moment. It was all great fun. But he remained an enigma to all who knew him. He was probably an enigma to himself, a man not haunted or troubled by the past, the present or the future. The melancholy eyes spoke of one man: the laughing mouth of another.

Jim Cairns had a room on the floor on which the staff members in the Department of Political Science were housed in the Commerce Building in 1945. He was then a lecturer in economic history. We ate our sandwiches together almost every day of the week during term, and went for walks around the university and Carlton before returning to our rooms. There, at two in the afternoon, I was often still finding out what to say in a lecture at five-fifteen that evening.

Jim Cairns was a stranger to the pleasure-loving Dick Downing. He puzzled me. He was a late starter in the academic race who looked as though he would take the lead when the horses turned into the straight. Rumour had it that Jim and Ian Turner were the only two students who had ever received a mark above ninety per cent in a history examination, Jim's performance being in economic history. The unkind said this was an estimate of their memory rather than their talent. Jim had been a policeman. He told me many stories about his life in the police force. The stories reminded me of my father's stories of his experiences with the criminals in Long Bay and Darlinghurst gaols. But there was a difference. For my father men and women in gaol were both figures of fun, and objects of compassion. He knew they were his *alter ego*, his double. He had deep sympathy with all those who could not stop, all those who were, as the Prayer Book put it, 'in any way afflicted or distressed in mind, body, or estate'. He cared. He wanted to 'comfort and relieve them, according to their several necessities'.

Jim Cairns cared, but not in that open, warm-hearted way which came naturally to my father. Jim was another Melbourne child of the Enlightenment. Religion for him, as for so many other Melbourne intellectuals at the time, was medieval dirt. The Christian teaching on innate depravity was an insult to humanity, and the man who originated such a story a monster. Jim had his faith. He believed in the preamble to the American Declaration of Independence that all men were born equal, that they all had a right to life, liberty and the pursuit of happiness. Yet most of the time Jim looked desperately unhappy. He stared into space. I had the impression that there was a part of him

154

which he did not want anyone to see. He never spoke about his early life, or about his family. I suspect Jim was often in groups whose talk caused him great pain. But the 'Ha! ha!' men of Melbourne were not distinguished then for their sensitivity to another man's pain.

Jim was a Labor man, a man with political ambitions. But again I did not know where he stood. He had read Karl Marx, but was not, I gathered, a total convert. He was then, like so many others, an eclectic Marxist. Besides he was such a loner, such an individualist, that it was not open to him to submit himself to the discipline of the Communist Party leadership. He was not a Christian Socialist. I never heard him mention either the name or the words of the founder of Christianity. The man who spoke of coming to the aid of 'the least of the little ones', the man who spoke about life as a banquet, made no appeal to him. Jim, I suspect, was a Labor man partly because Labor held out the promise that the society which had turned him into a long distance starer would disappear off the face of the earth. He was a wrongs righter – a man who had been the victim of a great wrong, who elevated the curing of his own wound into a national cause. But I never knew what that wound was. I still ponder whether perhaps he did not know, or, if he did, that it was too painful for him to talk about to anyone.

In 1946 I met another tragi-comic public figure who had already written one half of his letter of introduction to posterity – Robert Gordon Menzies. I say tragi-comic because Menzies at that time was one of the whipping boys for the mockers of radical Melbourne. He was the boy from the bush, the scholarship boy, who had prostituted his great gifts to the service of a corrupt and doomed society. The humiliation of August 1941 when his colleagues called on him to resign from the prime ministership was a terrible price he had to pay for his *hubris*, his overweening pride and arrogance. At the time, August 1941, the radicals of Melbourne had no eye of pity for the sufferings of Bob Menzies. At drunken parties they gloated, they gave the screw another turn, they sang with gusto the ribald songs about the boy from Jeparit. There was one for mixed company:

Verse:
Menzies loves us, this we know,
For the 'Argus' tells us so.
The unemployed to him belong,
They are weak but Bob is strong

Chorus:
Yes, Menzies loves us,
Yes, Menzies loves us, [*crescendo*]
Yes, Menzies loves us,
The 'Argus' tells us so. [*rallentando*]

There was another, the ballad of big business:

There'll always be a Menzies
While there's a BHP,
If Menzies means the same to you
As Menzies means to me.

There was another for men only – a song about what my mother would have called 'Down there, Mann dear'. It was sung to the tune of 'The Bells of St Clements'. We all called him 'Pig Iron Bob' or 'Bob Superming'.

His son Ken Menzies, who had been a trier in Political Institutions A the previous year, introduced me to him outside the Melbourne Cricket Ground in 1946. The conversation lasted only a few minutes. Expecting disapproval, or even jokes at my expense, I had put on the 'do not come near' look. But that was not necessary. He charmed me. He put his arms round me, looked me in the eye for a moment and said, 'I should have been a teacher too. Give them all you have.' And he passed through the turnstiles before I had a chance to reply.

That day I sensed the man wanted something no one ever could or would give him. The man in front of me was not the man portrayed by the press, or by the wintry sneerers of Melbourne. Later I will watch him ride on to glory in the service of an anachronism. That brief encounter outside the entrance to the Members' Stand at the Melbourne Cricket Ground taught me a lesson: the low-down version of a man is not the man at all, but a caricature or a grotesque. Man is broad, far broader than his portrait, as painted by the self-appointed improvers of humanity. A historian or a teller of a story must look on all human beings with the eye of pity – or so I dimly realised that morning, when for me 'Bob Superming' became a human being. The memory of the moment lived on, even though in the years that were to come I was often a backslider, often found myself in the company of the muddiers of the waters, often found myself repeating their stories.

156

There was a change in our lives. We became property-owners. We bought an acre and a half of land on the golf-links estate in Croydon, fenced it (weekend labour, with help from obliging students), and built a house on it. All in all, it was a revealing experience. I learned many things. Estate agents I found reminded me of a phrase in the Book of Common Prayer, 'and the Truth is not in them'. Architects and builders were like housemasters at a boarding-school: they knew what was good for you. Bank managers were like the founder of the Christian religion: they knew what was in man. The frowners pursed their lips and dropped unkind remarks about wild young men wasting their substance, using money they had not earned, at the end of a suburban railway line. My father was as generous as ever to those who dared to 'have a go'. Life had helped him to understand that most difficult advice by Christ, 'Judge not'. Like his prodigal son, he was never at ease in the company of that vast army of disapprovers and self-appointed judges in Melbourne.

Our neighbours on the golf-links estate reminded me of the families at Geelong Grammar School. Between me and them there was a great gulf set. Like their counterparts at Corio they were the guardians of a life-denying respectability cult. They had their own commandments, their own list of 'Thou shalt nots'. Their idea of pleasure was a game of solo played in the afternoon, at which the only permitted excess was character assassination of those who erred and strayed from the lore of their tribe. They ostracised all non-conformers. Jack and Thelma Emerton were different: their warmth and kindness made up for much.

I remember one scene in our living-room in Croydon. The *comme il faut* men and women were being very frosty to Denis O'Brien – a young man of Irish-Catholic descent who had lost his faith temporarily in the brothels of the Middle East as a member of the Second Australian Imperial Force, had then fought in New Guinea, and returned to Australia a missionary for Catholic Christendom. He also found another kind of salvation in the bottom of a beer pot. The golf-links army of the righteous put on black looks whenever he came near. That evening in our house Denis was well on the way to seeing the world as the world is not – in fact so far that he had sought the comfort of the floor, doubting, as he did, whether he could stand upright.

Incensed by the empty prattle all round him, he rose with difficulty to his feet, pushed his sandy hair away from his troubled eyes and sang: 'Hail Queen of Heaven . . .' One of our neighbours said in a stage whisper that she always suspected Manning Clark had unsavoury friends: now she knew. Years later when the world gave me some sort of recognition she shook my hand and told me she always knew I was something special. I went very silent.

On 6 August 1945 I was standing with our son Sebastian (then aged five), and our daughter Katerina (then aged four), in the shopping street of Croydon when I read in the *Age* that the Americans had dropped an atomic bomb on Hiroshima. I put my arms around Sebastian and Katerina, and tried to explain to them why I looked so sad. Surely, I thought, human beings will huddle together, will speak to each other in the presence of this threat to all of us, and talk about things that matter most. But no – after the one-and-a-half-mile walk back to the golf links estate I found that not even the dropping of the atomic bomb had brushed aside the causes of division on that lovely hillside, and all those things that kept human beings apart. Things were still the same as ever. Our houses were all like burrows in which we sheltered from other people. We were all alone.

The same year Dymphna and I cycled into Croydon one night to see the film *The Man Within*, based on the novel by Graham Greene, with Michael Redgrave, Richard Attenborough and Joan Greenwood in the leading roles. On the surface it was a story about cowardice. I saw in it a truth which had lived inside me ever since the years as a boarder at Melbourne Grammar School. We are all betrayers and betrayed. The betrayed are so hurt by their betrayers that the only satisfaction open to them is to take their revenge against their betrayers by betraying them. After this they must live with the horror of what they have done, knowing there is no forgiveness, walking in terror of what will happen to them if they are found out, and never able to forgive themselves.

The film reminded me of a moment of terror I experienced on first seeing *The Informer*, based on the novel by Sean O'Faolain, with Victor McLaglen playing the role of the informer. Then there had been forgiveness. The mother of the betrayer had said to the betrayer, 'I forgive you, Gyppo, you didn't know what you were doing.' There had been a suggestion that God would forgive, that God's mercy was more generous than man's justice. But what if there were no God? What if someone had done something for which human beings would never forgive him, and he would never forgive himself? That, perhaps, was an odd obsession, an odd private ache in the heart for a man who was telling students he looked forward to the day when

158

knowledge won the final victory against ignorance and superstition.

There had been nibbles at writing. In 1945 Station 3XY invited me to write and present some talks on contemporary politics. Some of the experiences in Germany sneaked past the censor. No one was encouraged to speak or write then of the Germans as subjects for a tragedy, to see them with the eye of pity. Oh dear me, no! There were talks on 3LO in Melbourne. Clem Christesen, the editor of *Meanjin*, kindly asked me to write some of the trailers he was publishing each quarter. That gave me a chance to 'have a go', because the trailer article was unsigned. Well, I did just that in a piece on the public schools, and that provoked an uproar. That was possibly the first warning that my voice would tickle the madness in the blood of those who, as it were, were still fighting the Spanish Civil War. These occasional pieces were no more than snippets. I was experiencing all the frustrations of a film projectionist who was striving for continuity but was only putting snatches up on the screen.

Then at the end of 1945 there was a quite unexpected turn in fortune's wheel. Max Crawford, the Professor of History, gave me a chance to discover whether I had anything to say. He asked me whether I would like to teach Australian history, adding he knew I had always been interested in it. He told me he had been delighted, but not surprised, by my reputation as a teacher. He knew history was my true love, and the department needed a teacher to give his or her all to the teaching of Australian history. He did not seem to be bothered by my ignorance, or by my doubt whether I had anything to say.

Luck was with me. The war had turned the minds of many Australians towards the question of who we are. The myths which had sustained previous generations were being discarded. Australians were looking less and less on Europe as a land of holy wonders. Australians were about to become Australian-centred. Our history was not a branch of British colonial history, or the story of the beginning of British civilisation in the ancient continent of Australia. Our history was not as boring or second-hand or mediocre as previous generations had grown up to believe. We need not always be a people who lived in Australia but drew their knowledge and wisdom from overseas. We knew the historical map of England, Ireland, Scotland and Europe. The historical map of Australia was almost a blank: I must set out on a journey without maps.

Well, almost, but not quite. Men of present or future renown have already planted ideas in my head. Ten years earlier in 1936 I had bought P. R. Stephensen, *The Foundations of Culture in Australia*. I noted the sentence: 'We inherit all that Britain has inherited, and from that point we go on – to what? . . . our Australian culture will evolve distinctively.' The passion of Stephensen lived on in my mind. Teaching Australian politics had reintroduced me to Keith Hancock's *Australia*. Were we Austral-Britons, were we an Australian version of British civilisation, or was that already a museum piece? Had history moved on? The experience in England in 1938–40 pushed me more towards the Inky Stephensen position, minus his extravaganzas and his passions. I was already ill-at-ease with the Keith Hancock compromise of combining the values of a boy from the bush with the culture chat of members of an Oxford high-table. Keith loved to cast a fly on the lovely waters of the Goodradigbee. He also loved to stroll along the bird walk at Magdalen College on a summer's evening.

There was Eris O'Brien's monumental work on *The Foundation of Australia*. I had noted especially his remark about my old *bête noire*, the Church of England: that the Reverend Samuel Marsden had brought to Australia 'the scanty virtues of the Church of England'. Such an aside set me thinking. What did they bring with them in those convict fleets? I had read as a child the question, 'Is not the body more than raiment?' Eris O'Brien told me about the raiment of the foundation years, and Brian Fitzpatrick in his pioneer works, *British Imperialism and Australia* (1938) and *The British Empire in Australia* (1940), had taught about the backdrop to the story. From my mother I had heard stories of the fret and fever of the early days. I wanted to know of the dreams, the visions of the men and women who had made the long journey over the ocean. I wanted to know what went on in their minds and their hearts, mindful though I was of the question about the heart: 'Who can know it?'

Some memorable experiences helped me. In 1944 in the Union Theatre at Melbourne University I had seen the Dolia Ribush production of the verse play *Ned Kelly* by Douglas Stewart, and had been strangely moved. Some of the words of Joe Byrne lived on in my mind, namely, that Australia was a country where 'only eagles are fit to travel the skies'.

In April 1946, a few weeks after I started lecturing in Australian history, by chance I heard Henry Handel Richardson read on Radio 3LO (Melbourne) the passage from *The Way Home* in which Mahony meditates on again seeing England's 'green and pleasant land', after his years of exile in Australia. I looked again at the passage of Horace, part of which she had chosen as the epigraph to the work: 'Those who cross the sea' ('*Qui trans mare currunt . . .*'). There again was the question: what did they bring with them in their minds, and what did the ancient continent of Australia and its original inhabitants do to that intellectual and spiritual baggage?

Years later I will go many times a year, almost as a pilgrim, to the entrance to Sydney Harbour at South Head, and gaze over that vast sea, and try to think my way into the minds of those who arrived on the ships, and then turn round to face the land, and ask the questions: What did the 'haggard continent' do to them, and what did they do to the 'ancient, barbaric continent' of Australia? But that was in the future. That night in Croydon I heard this fragile voice exploring a subject almost as vast as the seas the migrants, both bond and free, were to cross.

That same year, or maybe early in 1947, I turned on the wireless and heard the voice of the sailor–narrator in Laurie Lee's radio play, *The Voyage of Magellan*. I was so moved I could not sit down. There were magical moments, such as that moment when the narrator told of how the sailors informed the Captain-General (Magellan) that they had found a way into what was to be called the Pacific Ocean. The narrator continued: 'and how his black eyes wept'.

There was the shock of discovering a harsh inhospitable land. I had read D. H. Lawrence in *Kangaroo* on the spirit of the place. In the words of the catechism I had digested many passages in that work and in the letters published in the Aldous Huxley edition of 1932, my copy being a present to me by Tampion Daglish. Lawrence liked the look of the country – 'wonderful sky and sun and air', 'the endless hoary bush', and Sydney Harbour, which was 'quite one of the sights of the world'. But he was troubled by the people who had a 'rather fascinating indifference' to what people of the Old World called 'soul or spirit'. He felt, he wrote to a friend, as though he were being 'resolved back almost to the plant kingdom before souls, spirits and minds were being grown at all'. Australia left him with a great yearning for 'old civilisation'. But that was the response of a European, not the response of an Australian.

For that I had to thank Eleanor Dark. In the week in which I gave the first lecture in Australian history I read *The Timeless Land*. Unlike Henry Handel Richardson or Martin Boyd, Eleanor Dark was no spiritual exile, no gifted sensitive soul living physically in Australia, but spiritually in England, no delicate flower agonising over whether he or she belonged in England or Australia. Here was no angry woman shouting that the whole bloody trouble was that she was born here. She belonged. She told the story of the two 'characters' who were here from the beginning, the land and the Aborigines. Here was someone looking out, not looking in, and not recoiling from much that she noticed. She began her story with the land: she began the human story with the Aborigine Wunbula and his son Bennilong seeing a huge 'winged bird' moving on the waters of that 'very vast sea'.

For someone seeking a sign, the fates had been very kind and generous. One day in 1943, angered by the pompous pronouncements of Justus Jörgensen, the artist, to his followers in a room at the Mitre Tavern in Melbourne I had sought instant relief at the bar. Two other refugees from 'the Master' were there before me. They were Arthur Boyd and John Perceval. We began to talk. We understood each other. Arthur was a communist – on the surface. Deep down he had already seen that the world is not divided into classes but into those who mock and those who mourn. He had also intuited the role of art in driving out evil spirits, and bringing comfort to a man. He had been given a vision of the Australian landscape, of trees, of plains of desolation, of a vast sky in which there lived a fragile beauty. He had seen the mighty bush as the cradle of the one myth created by the white man here: he was groping towards a myth for a nation of suburban dwellers. Our talks will go on. Arthur had begun a journey to discover Australia. Arthur is the fool in Christ. The face will live always in my mind – the face of a man who has seen not so much into the heart of a great darkness, but has seen something about Australia and Australians. He will devote his life to putting that vision on canvas, in ceramics and painted tiles.

The painters were on the move. Sidney Nolan was already at work on his first Ned Kelly series. Russell Drysdale was putting on to canvas the truth about life in our country towns, the life of the men and women of the outback. I had not seen much of his work at that time. The inspiration from him will come later. Nor have I read the poetry of David Campbell. That will come later. We will get to know each other, and he will give me much.

The novelists, the poets, the playwrights and the painters, had sensed the tragic grandeur in the story of Australia. A historian must tell the story. He must evoke the spirit of the place, he must portray the Aborigines, he must create characters and scenes in the drama, not in the manner of a Gibbon as another tale of the follies and passions of human beings, nor as an Old Testament prophet who had taken up residence in the Antipodes and was chastening a wicked and an adulterous generation, but to evoke pity for all men and women – yes, and a little love for all of them.

A Man Has a
Duty to Save his Dream

In Dostoevsky's *The Brothers Karamazov* Alyosha (the spiritual one) asks his brother Ivan (the intellectual) the question: 'But the little sticky leaves, and the precious tombs, and the blue sky, and the woman you love! How will you live, how will you love them? With such a hell in your heart and your head ... you will kill yourself, you can't endure it!' Well, at the beginning of 1946 I was not suffering from a 'hell in the heart': I was suffering from confusion in the head. I had to begin the lectures in Australian history in March 1946 and I did not know what to say.

From my diary I gather all sorts of ideas and dreams lived side by side in my mind. I was going to write a book on democracy in Australia, to be an *ersatz* Tocqueville in the antipodes. I was going to write a book on how to make the Australian bourgeoisie human. I was going to write short stories, the first one of which was to be called 'The Rebuff'. Yes, I wanted to let the world know I was a sensitive flower. I could not make up my mind whether Marx was right, or whether Freud or Jung or Adler was right, or whether Wittgenstein was right or whether I should just look into the pewter pot 'to see the world / As the world is not'.

There were still many persons inside me. There was a Mr Passion who wept when the tenor sang the words in Beethoven's 'Hymn to Joy', 'All men will be brothers'. There was Mr Sad who needed to hear prelude number 24 in B Minor from Book One of Bach's 'Forty-eight Preludes and Fugues'. There was Mr Spirituality who wanted to believe there was someone, somewhere, who would take pity on all of us, and forgive us all for our great folly. There was Mr Storyteller who wanted to tell a story about the past to say something to those then living, but had no idea then of what the story would be about or how to tell it.

In March 1946 I invited the thirty-six students in Australian history who gathered in the English classroom to join me on a journey of discovery. I do not know whether they knew that the captain of the ship seting out to explore Australian history had no map and no navigation instruments.

I was lucky. My travelling companions were a constant delight. Don Baker had a stern countenance, but the beautiful smile of a man who was full of sympathy and understanding. Tom Truman was as consumed by doubt as I was – and that was saying quite a bit. Peter Ryan, fresh from the jungles of New Guinea, was a great wit, who enjoyed jokes about the morals or the politics of the bourgeoisie. His eyes glistened when 'country matters' were touched on obliquely in the classroom and explicitly around the communion rail in the bar. Peter Ryan wanted middle-class Caulfield to be exposed as a hypocrisy and a sham. There was Geoffrey Serle, a dinky-di straight-down-the-centre social democrat, a sweetness-and-light man, who wanted middle-class Hawthorn to spread its beneficent influence over the whole world. Sam Goldberg, who will make an international reputation with his books on James Joyce and William Shakespeare, looked full of knowledge, wisdom and understanding. Noel McLachlan wore an expression of expectancy on his face, as though soon everything would be made plain. Mick Williams, later my colleague at the Australian National University, offered to help me collect material in the Public Library. He was one of the affirming angels. (I will see him years later in his room at the Canberra Hospital on the day before his fatal operation. Typically he had converted the sick-room into an office in which he was still helping others.) Hugh Stretton was one of the silent ones who conveyed the message that in his presence trivial things were out of place. He was like Tolstoy. He encouraged others to talk about things that really mattered.

Women tended to speak only when called on to do so. It was assumed at the time that the men were the heroes, and the women their servers. The women were the quiet ones who often had most to say on paper. The men turned every tutorial into an aria for unaccompanied males, but often lacked confidence when it came to filling the blank sheet. A bemused smile spread over the face of Althea Stretton when the teacher said something stupid. Rosemary McGowan had the talents and the interests of a bibliographer. It was perhaps typical of the spirit of the times that a woman of her great gifts should be cast so early in the role of a server.

I still succumbed to the temptation to play the clown and the buffoon. In a lecture on the squatters I told them the Reverend Samuel Marsden had put a interesting interpretation on Christ's words: 'Feed my lambs. Feed my sheep.' The students laughed. So I told them the sheep of Australia had multiplied to the great delight of the Councils of Melbourne Grammar and Geelong Grammar. I told them many of the gentry of the Western District were descendants of Scottish ploughboys. They laughed again.

Sceptics asked what we expected to find in the 'deserts' of Australia. We, the captain and his crew, took no notice. We were bubbling with enthusiasm. We had discovered no deserts: we had discovered a land flowing with milk and honey. There were perils in our path. To change the image the captain and his band were like explorers trying to cross a river just above the rapids by leaping from stone to stone. There were helpful stones to stand on.

There were the reports on the convict system. There was the Report of the Committee of 1812, the Committee of 1836–37 (the celebrated Molesworth Committee) and the Committee of 1846. These were all supplemented with literary material. There was Marcus Clarke's *For the Term of His Natural Life* (and I note at the time the character of the Reverend Mr North, the man with a fatal flaw, and store that up for the time when I will have the confidence to write the story of Australia). I also draw on the stories of 'Price Warung' (William Astley) of the convicts because he knows that the heart is a battlefield between good and evil. He tells me about the convicts' creed: 'I believe in the Devil ... the lord and giver of life'. That, too, will be stored away for the time when I am ready to write the story.

The next leap was to the stone marked 'Immigration'. Scotty had told me about E. G. Wakefield's *A Letter from Sydney*. Scotty had told me about Wakefield's attempts to explain things to his grandmother, ha, ha, ha!, and what fools we all were, ha, ha, ha! Karl Marx had told me about Wakefield and Mr Money Bags in London, but he had not introduced me to a human being. The annual reports of the Legislative Council of New South Wales on Immigration gave me the facts. But again literature came to my aid. I came across Alexander Harris's *Settlers and Convicts* (1847) in the Melbourne Public Library; later I bought a second-hand copy for one shilling. He kindled my imagination. The bush was the cradle of mateship: the bush was the nursery of much that was different from other lands. I began to think more about who we are and how we came to be. I was beginning to see the mantle with which to clothe the story of Australia. I was becoming more and more impatient with the social science historians with their picture of humanity moving towards perfection, and their simplistic accounts of human behaviour. Their world was divided into 'goodies' and 'baddies', with the 'baddies' opposed to and the 'goodies' in favour of progress towards the great far-off event.

To write such a story I needed to find out a lot more about human beings. I needed to find out a lot more about what had happened in Australia since the beginning of time. Professor Crawford, with his genius for managing university committees, persuaded the Melbourne University to pay for second-class return rail tickets for Dymphna and me to collect such material in the Mitchell Library in the spring of 1947. That was another stroke of good fortune, for in Sydney I met Ida Leeson, the Mitchell Librarian. She was probably the only librarian at the Mitchell who had a photographic memory of the contents of its vast collection of manuscripts. You could say to her you had some idea that (I am making this up) James Macarthur had written to William Charles Wentworth at some time during 1842. And she would say, her eyes blinking with excitement, 'Yes, Macarthur Papers, vol. 73, pp. 600-1.' Within five minutes she would bring the volume to you, open it at the page, and say triumphantly, 'There it is', and blink and blink and blink. We became close friends. She visited us at Croydon, where she delighted our children by playing cricket with them on the pitch I had made, and entertained us over tea (it was always strictly tea with Ida) with stories of the men and women she had known.

She was a genuine eccentric. She wore bloomers which reached down below the knees where they were kept in place by coloured garters, tied in a most becoming and dignified bow. I know this because one of the competitions the young readers had each day was who would first see Ida's garters. That was easy. You asked her for a book so high on the shelves in the reading room that she needed to climb up a ladder to fetch it. During the climb the hem of the tweed skirt she wore slid high enough for the garter of the day to be visible.

She had a long list of Australian literary drunks, whom she never could or would forgive. But she had a most delightful list of exceptions. Christopher Brennan was forgiven because he always put a flower on her table after one of his many bibulous lunches. Henry Lawson was forgiven because he had such beautiful eyes. She forgave Brian Fitzpatrick because he had such charming manners when he was sober. Dowell O'Reilly was never forgiven. I wondered why, because everyone I had read was very fond of him. Florence Birch, Ida's companion, let me know why. One night when Ida was delivering her anathemas with great ferocity Florence whispered to me, 'Ida can never forgive Dowell O'Reilly. He once made improper suggestions to her on the front seat of the old Bondi cable tram!'

For much of their lives Ida and Florence searched for a mystical experience. Ida was slightly amused by the intensity of Florence's pursuit. One night Florence told me that when a mystic came to Sydney in the 1920s she had joined a group which had participated in all the exercises recommended by this 'guru':

The other women began to see all sorts of people in the room, dead friends, saints of the church – all sorts – but no matter what I did I saw nothing, nothing . . . [long pause, expression of disappointment on the face, replaced by a beatific smile] but once I saw Christ in San Francisco Cathedral.

Again, much blinking by Ida, and questions about whether I would like some more tea, or some more of Florence's cream cake, more blinks, because she knew I had a sweet tooth.

I was drawn to Florence because she had a thirst to believe. I was drawn to Ida because she was tormented by doubt about everything. At the time I did not see anything odd in a young man with great hopes for humanity knowing a rare moment of heart's ease in the company of two eccentrics who spoke eloquently about spirituality, who disdained all those who equated material well-being with virtue and happiness. They taught me something about love. Years later Ida was so overwhelmed with grief when Florence died that she lost her appetite for life. She even lost her appetite for food. Friends – she had many, for she was greatly loved – and doctors tried to persuade her to take just enough to remain alive. But that was what she did not want. She was found one night lying dead in a street in North Sydney.

I met again my three cousins on my mother's side: Bob, 'Bill' and Jeffrey Hope. With Bob I began to talk about my mother's and his father's family – the Hopes. There was much laughter at their expense, as both of us had scores to settle with the bullies of patrician Sydney masquerading as paragons of gentility and sweet reason. In between the laughter and the search for some other certainty than the lore of the tribe of country gentry now resident in the great city of Sydney, Bob and I began a conversation about the history of our family, the ghosts in our past. This took us back to 1794, the year in which Samuel and Eliza Marsden, and their daughter, born at sea, arrived in Sydney, and to 1797, the year when Rowland Hassall, his wife Elizabeth and his son Thomas, arrived in Tahiti on the mission ship, the *Duff*. During those talks some of the puzzles of childhood began to be solved. I was discovering a story, and finding myself more interested in the story of the past than any theorising about the laws of history.

I met Ann Hurley in the Mitchell Library. We will meet again in Canberra in the late 1950s when she, by then Ann Mozely, was one of the unsung heroines in the turbulent early years of the *Australian Dictionary of Biography*. We found we could talk to each other. We were both then (1947) enthusiasts without a cause. She was a woman driven to taste all the world had to offer, a woman driven to mix in the world, and yet very vulnerable to slights which her sensitive soul could not abide. She had the strength and the will to endure to the end, never to let *them* crush her spirit.

In the Mitchell Library I also met Noel Ebbels, a Melbourne student. He too was collecting material in the Mitchell Library. Noel was an ex-serviceman studying history and political science in Melbourne as a preliminary to a law degree. He was then an intellectual in the Australian Communist Party. I had wondered what drew me to him, because all the communist intellectuals I knew seemed more concerned with displays of political virtue, and raging against those who were not 'correct' than with being open-minded, or having the grace to confess they did not know. Noel was different. He told me he had intended to become a clergyman in the Presbyterian Church, but had lost his faith, and become a convert to Marxism. Noel knew about the man who had spoken to those who loved him beside the waters of the sea of Galilee. Noel was a gentle spirit who believed that the communists would build a society in which all human beings would experience the truth of Christ's remark that there is a kingdom inside everyone – a kingdom of man, if not a kingdom of God. In this brave new world human beings would be loving and tender to each other as he, Noel, was to all with whom he felt at ease.

I was so elated to be sharing minds with another human being that on one of those magical spring days in Sydney when the golden fireballs from the sun sparkle in the waters of Sydney Harbour, I rolled a penny down the footpath of Macquarie Street. Noel told me gently I was not to do that. But Noel was soon to die – and that loss, maybe, will strengthen my tragic vision of life, my ever-growing fear that what mattered most in life could never be.

So back to Melbourne for more wondrous moments with the students. What riches there were! In 1948, to play leap-frog with the calendar, one young man was so silent all through the first term in an honours tutorial that I did not know his name, even though from my farcical early teacher-training I had learnt that every good teacher gets ninety per cent participation from the members of his class. In the lively exchanges in that tiny room on the first floor of the Old Arts building there was never silence. Yet this young man never said a word. He rarely smiled: he seemed lost in all the hubbub, all the clashes between the giants in the room. At the end of the term one of the students whose name I had never heard before submitted a brilliant essay. I asked the class, 'Is Mr Geoffrey Blainey here?' The silent one smiled, and reached out for the essay.

Years later at one of those public occasions when Geoffrey Blainey was the chairman, he read out some of my comments on this first essay. Modestly skipping over all my enthusiasm he concentrated on the one rebuke. I had drawn attention to one of his errors of fact: he had put Broken Hill in South Australia. Odd irony! My critics will accuse me of the very fault I was correcting in Geoffry Blainey. Perhaps in those early days when the vision of what could be put down on paper was taking shape in my mind, I might have been wise to take note of the divine command: physician, heal thyself. But perhaps it was significant that those words had always passed me by.

Ken Inglis was also evidence for the adage that still waters run deep. He was then an enjoyer; he laughed generously at the jokes and wisecracks of others, he looked grave when the mood of the class changed from the laughter of fools to the sighs appropriate to matters of high solemnity. He had no body of doctrine save for a general sympathy with Labor and the Student Christian Movement, while distancing himself by his example from the men and women who had perverted Labor into 'a vast machine for the capture of political power' and the unctuous superficiality of those who seemed to believe that being a Christian was just being 'matey' during a weekend at Chum Creek near Healesville, where practitioners of Christian cheerfulness smiled many empty smiles.

170

Like Geoffrey Serle he was a middle-of-the-road man, with an insatiable curiosity, a taste for the quaint and the bizarre, and an eye and an ear for anyone who spoke or wrote lively, elegant English. He was an Erasmus in groups where the Savonarolas of Rome or Moscow were making feverish takeover bids for the minds of all members of the class. He had the gift to understand every point of view, but the Savonarolas wanted much more than understanding: they wanted total obedience. Ken had the strength to hold the middle ground without giving offence to the would-be engineers of the human soul, and without losing their respect. He was lucky. Nature can be kind to some.

Nature had been more than kind to Ian Turner, being quite wanton with the gifts she planted in him. His mother had singled him out at birth for higher things: she had given him the names Alexander Hamilton after a founding father of the United States of America. Her boy, she knew, was someone very special. Everything he did at Geelong College and at the university confirmed her faith. He was the first Communist Party member to become president of the Students' Representative Council. He was a brilliant debater. He performed with distinction in the annual examinations. It seemed there was nothing he could not do. Women adored him: men respected him. 'Ask Turner' was the catch-cry of the time. Yet there was another man behind the Dionysian exterior he presented to the world. There was a man within with intimations that one day it might all go wrong – a man giving simple answers when he knew of another world in which life was a 'vaudeville of devils'. In time he will grow quite sad – but not then, for then he was a Moses leading his followers to a promised land, a Moses not fearful lest his people deserted him for the Golden Calf but fearful of what might come up from inside himself.

Kit McMahon knew no such fears. Nature had been quite wanton in endowing him with gifts. He had a huge capacity for both work and pleasure. He walked and talked, not with a swagger but with the inner confidence of a man who knew much had been given to him. He was not a prey to Hamlet-like doubts. He was probably ill at ease with Melbourne conformism. He will leave for England, where he will rise high in the British Treasury, become Deputy Governor of the Bank of England and a fellow of Magdalen College, Oxford. So a man with the imagination of a poet served the measurers. That was Melbourne's loss and London's gain. Melbourne was then no place for a Renaissance man.

Creighton Burns was then a young man of many gifts. Like Kit McMahon he was a great lover of life. He had a lively wit, a lively pen, and a very lively interest in human behaviour. He had the capacity to understand every point of view and a charming uncertainty about who was right and who was wrong. These qualities will stand him in good stead later as the editor of the Melbourne *Age* newspaper, one representative of the best in the Melbourne liberal tradition.

Though the conventions of the times dictated that women should also be the silent members of a class, the listeners to male knowledge and wisdom, the war had given women a voice – though not as yet a voice equal with the men. Even Helen Ginz, who will become quite chatty later in public as Helen Hughes, chose to smile when the men spoke in ways pleasing to her, or frowned if a reactionary opened his mouth in such a future-of-humanity atmosphere. Glen Tomasetti, pianist, folk-singer and future novelist, seemed an enthusiastic supporter for the men who were swimming with the tide. I say 'seemed', because our not perceiving Glen as a special human being was one of many examples of male blindness at that time. Women were servants: women were adorers: women were *claqueuses* (applauders). They were muses, sources of inspiration to the men of imagination, but not at that time persons who stood alone. In time I will learn how wrong we all were. But not then.

In time these women will make their mark. The eighteen- to twenty-year-olds of those years will have their own pulpits in the 1960s. Then we accepted their service, we thought of them as aids to getting on, wound-bathers for those maimed in the male bear-pit, muses who, like music, persuaded them to put pen to paper rather than boast about how one day they would write a great book. Glen Tomasetti and Helen Hughes will say the angry words twenty years later. Then the men of the 1940s will learn what women really thought of them, learn what swine they had been and were. But not then, for then women's eyes looked up in adoration and men's eyes looked down with longing and hope for what would probably never be.

Some women will go into exile. Judith Attiwill (later Egerton) was then a silent achiever: she came top in the final honours examination in 1948. She sat silent in the class in 1947, sometimes indulging in a smile not at what was being said but rather at the arrogance of the men, their assumption that they knew what women did not and could not know. She will find satisfaction abroad. She will prove Dostoevsky to be wrong when he wrote that all those who lived abroad were in a dream. In London she will make a reputation as one of the curators in the Tate Gallery. There she will find men such as Philip Larkin, Kingsley Amis, Arthur Crook (editor of the *Times Literary Supplement*), and others who spoke to her about the things she wanted to talk about in Melbourne in 1946–49, only to find that was not what men wanted from women. In those years she gave the discerning a peep at what was going on inside her in her portrayal of Joan of Arc on the stage. But, in the eyes of many men, that was only make-believe: that was not real life.

Pat Ingham (who later married the historian Tim Suttor) had the Mona Lisa face, the face of a woman who from either observation or intuition knows how it is in the world, but has decided not to make an angry protest, but to adopt an air of acceptance and resignation, lest her last fate be worse than her first. Pat rarely said a word in class, but when it came to writing an essay it was clear there was much inside her waiting to come out. The atmosphere in Melbourne in the mid-1940s not being conducive to that, she and her husband Tim Suttor will go into exile in Canada, only to discover that, for her, suffering is the well-spring of wisdom. I like to think that even in those early years in Melbourne I saw in her the will to endure the blows with which fate would smite her. But then her silence was an enigma, a response imposed on her by the Melbourne variety of male domination.

Joan Thwaites (later Joan Anderson, and still later Joan Crawcour) laughed a lot, not because she thought the world was a joke but because she had a faith. God would not, or could not, change the world, but human beings could. The years of drudgery were coming to an end: soon, very soon, the whole of humanity would sing and dance and shout for joy. The world was about to be changed: the Earth would no longer be soaked from its crust to its core with the blood and tears of humanity. I remember Miriam Dixson, later a much praised writer of books on the role of women in Australian history, was just as enthusiastic. I remember one day in the reading room of the Public Library she told me with tears of joy in her eyes the world would soon be 'beaut'.

We had all taken a seat in the carriage of Historical Enterprises Proprietary Limited, a carriage which of course carried no gamblers or midnight ramblers – dear me, no, what's the world coming to? It was of course an express train, travelling non-stop to a station marked 'The Great Good Time'. Some believed Uncle Joe would do it all for us, and some believed Labor in Australia was the hope of the world. Solidarity was the thing. So Solidarity forever for union makes us strong, and be on guard for the Judases in our midst, because we who had all grown up with a knowledge of the Galilean fisherman expected to meet Judas in every classroom, every sporting team, every committee, or leaning on the rail in every public bar within walking distance of the university. I remember John O'Brien, the senior lecturer in ancient history, reminding me of the Greek precept of moderation in all things. He was a restraining influence on my tendency to go in for everything 'heels up'. He 'meant more to me than suits a man to say'. But by the time I was ready to tell him that, he had died. Such is life!

There was so much to discover, so much to explore. The glow of those years was like the effect of music on the mind: it made me believe I was capable of things I was not really capable of. In that glow I wrote to Eleanor Dark, the author of *The Timeless Land*, one of my teachers on the influence of the spirit of the place on all those who live in Australia, the creator of Wunbula and the image of the 'winged bird' sailing on the bosom of the 'very vast sea'. I asked her to speak to the honours class in Australian history. She came. She was shy with the class until David Bennet, the grandson of John Monash, but as different from his illustrious grandparent as Melbourne is from Sydney, asked her to tell us why she wrote such beautiful prose poetry about the Australian landscape. Words gushed out of her, her eyes, hitherto dim, lit up as though the woman within had switched on a light. The discussion became lively.

She invited Dymphna and me to visit her at Katoomba. There it was like resuming a conversation which could never have an end. After tea, and that exchange of those special looks which acknowledge a bond, and the inner confidence nourished by such an awareness, she took us for a walk to a place in the Blue Mountains where we could see not a mark of man's presence or interference, but only the gaunt rocks, the steep valleys, the ridges clothed with trees which did not move, one of those views in Australia which seem to me to convey a message of vast indifference to all human striving, all human hopes. She sat on a rock, her face as much a riddle as that universe down below us. She quoted from one of the diaries she had read for *No Barrier*: 'The country ahead appears to be not easy of access.' I got the message that the human heart was even less easy of access. That was something I then wanted to hear from someone of her stature, because, unlike the dominant secular humanist spirit of the times, for her the human heart was the stuff of history. We should have spoken more. That is 'the whole bloody trouble' – when two people meet who might say much to each other they rarely risk exposing what the heart doth say even though they know they are with someone who would understand everything.

There was the rich experience of meeting Eris Michael O'Brien, the author of *The Foundation of Australia*, then a Monsignor and priest in a parish in Sydney, and later Archbishop of Canberra and Goulburn. He did not need to tell me about himself. Perhaps he never spoke to anyone about himself because he told everything to God. The reticence surrounded him with an air of mystery, an air intensified by the craggy cheeks and the sorrowful eyes. It was as though he had lived through a sadness so deep that he dared not speak about it to anyone except when alone on his knees at the prie-dieu, where he hoped that the Virgin, Christ and God would have pity on him, would so strengthen him that he could endure the pangs of loneliness.

In his youth, he told me, he had wanted to gain recognition as a writer. He had written a play on Macquarie. He had all the prejudices of his generation towards the members of the Protestant ascendancy. He had the habit of catching with his eye those on his side. When I introduced him to the class in 1946 his eye lit up when the eyes of the priests, the brothers and the nuns met his, but I noticed that when a well-known Protestant clergyman made frantic attempts for an eye-catch, Eris passed him by. Yet with me, an outsider, possibly then still a mocker, he was very warm.

As we got to know each other later he dropped hints which seemed intended to help me fit together the pieces in the jigsaw puzzle which was his life. Once he told me the Pope's encyclical on evolution had been a green light for him. Another time he told me, with one of those sideway glances he employed whenever he was close to uncovering the man within, that he understood W. A. Bland, a middle-class con- vict with intellectual interests, had joined the church shortly before his death. I added that it was widely believed at the time that Bland was impotent, that this incapacity had caused him much humiliation, especially from women. A quizzical smile spread over his face, as he said to me I was becoming quite a philosopher. I wondered whether that was intended as a rebuke or just a signal not to raise painful subjects, any of those subjects which seemed to have cast a permanent shadow over his face. He always looked as though he might even have

175

regretted a decision a long time ago to spend his whole life out of the bright light of the sun. It was as though he were longing for the life promised to all who believed in Christ and truly turned to Him.

Brian Fitzpatrick was different. Just as Eris O'Brien came close to losing his composure in the presence of the more smug members of the Protestant ascendancy, so Brian lapsed into gentle sarcasm when speaking to young university teachers. I did not know the reason for that at the time. Outwardly he was the man of achievement. He won the Harrison–Higinbotham prize for his book, *British Imperialism and Australia*. His next book, *The British Empire in Australia* (published in 1940), became a mine out of which many university essays, many lectures, and many books were quarried by those who, in their own words, were 'far too busy' or 'too important' to sink a mine of their own. Yet they always seemed to have plenty of time to niggle away at the errors of Fitzpatrick. Indeed there was a most insidious idea in currency amongst those who ran the show in Melbourne that Fitzpatrick was brilliant but wayward. He was, it was said, not really Melbourne 'professorial timber' – Oh dear me, no! Don't you know . . .?'

As an example of that I remember years later, at the history section of the ANZAAS conference in Canberra in 1954, Malcolm Ellis, a stout defender of capitalist society against its would-be destroyers, feared what Brian Fitzpatrick might say to Eris O'Brien. He was anxious that they should not meet – or, if meet they must, then it should be very early in the day, please, please, please. Well, I introduced the Archbishop to Brian in my room at the old University College in Childers Street. I have never forgotten that moment. Brian bowed and said, with eyes dropped in reverence, 'Your Grace'. Eris O'Brien shook him warmly by the hand, and said, 'Mr Fitzpatrick'. So much for the fears of Malcolm Ellis.

Brian was a bundle of contradictions. He was a prominent member of the Rationalist Society: he wrote the poem 'Cenotaph'. He wasted his substance drinking with the bar-room wits and evoked gales of laughter from his cronies in the Mitre Tavern and later in the Swanston Family Hotel, and still later in the evening around a table at the Latin Café, then in Exhibition Street. In 1953 he appealed to Dr Mannix to plead with General Eisenhower, the American President, to show mercy to the Rosenbergs, because we must all expect mercy. Together with Ralph Gibson, Lloyd Ross, W. MacMahon Ball, Kathleen Pitt (later Fitzpatrick), he had founded the Melbourne University Labor Club.

He believed that the unity of Labor was the hope of the world, he believed that Labor in Australia would one day 'make and unmake social conditions'. He agreed with Emily Brontë that the creeds which moved humanity were vain.

I doubt whether anyone ever got close to Brian Fitzpatrick. Even when lapsing into unconsciousness, he preserved the Old World courtesies which were designed to check anyone who tried to pluck at the heart of his mystery. The brilliant verbal clowning was a part of his outer defences, the ramparts which no one must be allowed to cross. It is possible that he lowered the drawbridge to allow some women to speak with him. It was perhaps both funny and tragic that often late at night he would sway on his heels, and say to any others who had lasted the distance with him, 'If you have the slightest trouble, send for me', and then fall flat on his face. He would be up again by five the following morning, start typing by five-thirty, and finish three thousand words by noon, that moment when the sun passed over the yard-arm, when he could leave for the city and join again the world of Bohemia. He spoke and behaved like the member of some aristocratic club. Yet he pushed out his bum with the cheek of a man who enjoyed taking the mighty down from their seat. He was no crusader for a new creation: he had seen no rainbow. Like many middle-class intellectuals in the Labor movement he consumed much of his energy in a love–hate relationship with the world he professed to despise.

I remember one night in his flat at 22A Clendon Road, Toorak, praising warmly his chapter on the economic consequences of the gold discoveries in his monumental work, *The British Empire in Australia*. He lowered his eyes during my aria, and then slipped out of the room. He returned with a black notebook in his right hand. 'Manning,' he said with one of his majestic bows, ' a word with you.' He took me into another room, opened the black book and showed me the first draft in his own hand of the chapter I had praised so highly. We were both too moved to speak. We embraced in silence, and returned to join the revellers. That was the closest I got to the man within.

The next time we met his defences were again in place. I also remember that when volume one of *A History of Australia* was published in September 1962 he shook me warmly by the hand, bowed, blushed, and asked permission to say something to me. Leave was granted. 'I think I know', he said, 'the direction in which you are going.' I remember, too, at the launching of that volume in the old upstairs dining-room of the Melbourne University Union he came back into the room after all the others had left, looking for someone, looking for something. Who knows? He wore on his face the expression of a man who feared life was all slipping away.

Not long after that encounter I lunched with him and some members of the Rationalist Society at the Italian Society Restaurant. At three or three-thirty some of his fellow-diners made a move to return to their offices. Brian rebuked them: 'Face reality,' he said, 'the drink's here.' We all laughed. Perhaps we should have cried. By then he had a ravaged face. I was not certain then, and I am not certain now, whether Yarraside had cut those ravines in his cheeks, or whether what came up from inside him led him on to his destruction. A man of talent, a man of lasting achievements, had become a heap of ruins. Maybe the city of moral rectitude had again destroyed one of its gifted sons, as earlier it had destroyed Marcus Clarke and Adam Lindsay Gordon.

I remember also that the Brian Fitzpatrick circle at the Mitre Tavern, and later at the Swanston Family Hotel, was suffering from the same hysteria which swept America in the McCarthy period. In left-wing groups at the university there was much talk about the Australian security service. Take care, it was said, their agents were everywhere; their agents were snooping on all radicals. So beware, your best friend might be in their pay. Students, and even members of the teaching staff, it was said, were earning a few extra quid a week reporting on friends and colleagues. Melbourne was a society divided between the 'buggers' and the 'bugged': Melbourne was becoming a surveillance society.

I was told in the strictest confidence, and of course only for my own good (Melburnians have this habit of appointing themselves guardians of the behaviour and morals of others), that I had a Security file. That did not bother me at all. I was determined not to fall into the pit into which I noticed some people had already tumbled – namely, to blame Security for their failure to be appointed to positions to which they believed their talents and their industry entitled them. Some were already pointing the accusing finger at Security, and not asking themselves whether the fault lay not in Security but in themselves. Security was not the reason why some spent their afternoons on a stool in a bar rather than at a desk in a library.

The fear of Security unsettled the weak: Security, and those behind them, the apologists for and the defenders of Yarraside, were good 'pickers': they knew what was in a man: they knew those whom nature and circumstance had fashioned to be victims. Catholics and Communists did not lose their composure through fear of the Security snoopers. Those troubled by doubt, nihilists sheltering behind the mask of vague radical sentiments, panicked and became so obsessed with Security that they saw spooks everywhere. Security had its greatest successes with the men and women of little or no faith.

The Security gentlemen were not the only guardians of political virtue. I remember once in 1946 enthusing to a woman in the Communist Party about William Dobell's portrait of Joshua Smith. She was enraged. The work, she said, was an insult to humanity. I pressed on. I praised William Dobell's *Billy Boy*. Putting on the looks of a Grand Inquisitor about to send a heretic to the flames, she said, 'The work is a gross libel on the Australian working class.' It was not easy to stand alone at that time. There was always the temptation to wallow in debauchery. There was the never-ending obsession with death. I knew of the warning by Baudelaire in his poem, 'Les Deux Bonnes Sœurs', that death and debauchery were the two amiable whores who have never borne a child. Debauchery offered 'terrible pleasures, horrible delights'. But midnight revels only led to remorse and shame.

There was to be a child of the heart. Teaching Australian history has borne a great dream about Australia. There were many components in that dream. There was some of Ned Kelly's mad dream of Australia as the big country where only eagles fly in the sky, of Australia as the country for the fearless, the free and the bold. There was some of 'The Banjo' in it, some of the 'vision splendid on the sunlit plains extended', some of the exaltation when 'down Kosciusko way' where the air is 'clear as crystal'. There was much of Henry Lawson in it, of his message in the poem, 'Freedom on the Wallaby':

> . . . *we must fly a rebel flag*
> *As others did before us.*
> *And we must sing a rebel song*
> *And join in rebel chorus.*

> . . .

> *They needn't say the fault is ours*
> *If blood should stain the wattle.*

There was some of the Henry Lawson call to all of us in his poem 'A Song of the Republic', to

> Banish from under our bonny skies
> Those old-world errors and wrongs and lies
> Making a hell in a Paradise
> That belongs to your sons and you.

There was a vision of an Australia that was coming to be, a vision of an Australia which had made the choice between 'The Old Dead Tree and the Young Tree Green'. There was some of the Victor Daley vision: 'And my true name is Labour, though priests call me Christ.'

There was a dream that we Australians were about to make a contribution to the conversation of humanity – towards humanity's search for a society in which there was equality without any restraints on liberty, without mediocrity, without conformism or spiritual bullying. There was that surge of hope, that moment of exaltation when listening to Bach's *Magnificat*. The time had come to put the dream down on paper.

Life has already interested me in many things. Life has interested me in the problem of desert, in who drew the blanks and who drew the prizes in the human lottery, and in the delusions we concoct to enable us to live with our lies about ourselves. Life has taught me the human heart was the battlefield for the conflict between good and evil. Life has interested me in the difference between man's ideas of justice and God's idea of justice, in the life of man without God, in human behaviour in an age of unbelief. The knowledge of failure was my finishing school in the getting of wisdom. In things trivial, I have known failure on the cricket field. In deeper things I have known failure as a writer, the failure of trying but never succeeding in bridging the gap between the desire to say something and the capacity to say it. I have known the failure of wanting but not being able to say something to another human being. Failure teaches a person what they can and they cannot do. Failure can feed the vice of envy. But failure, the knowledge of what stands between all of us and what we want can nourish a sympathy with everyone. Or so I found.

I was beginning to see the history of Australia as a story of a people who had come here with Great Expectations – either in the life of the world to come, or the capacity of human beings for better things, and of how events had robbed them of those hopes and left them all as citizens in the Kingdom of Nothingness. I was beginning to see the coming of the white man to Australia as a story of tragic grandeur. It would take me many years to learn how to tell that story. I still feared I may not be able to tell it as I wanted to tell it.

On 19 March 1948 another child, Andrew, was born. Sebastian said, 'Axel-lil [as he called his brother], we've got a wicket-keeper!' Katerina wept. I said to her, 'You will still be Grandpa's only granddaughter', and she stopped crying. Andrew was to be more than a backstop in life. He moved in the fast lane. He became for newspaper readers a source of information on and interpreter of the upheavals in the communist societies in 1989 and 1990 – possibly the greatest event in human history since the Russian revolution of 1917 and the dropping of the atomic bomb in 1945.

It was perhaps another stroke of good fortune that while I was musing over these things I should meet one of Australia's great story-tellers. He was Martin Boyd. My friend Patrick Ryan, whom I had taught at Geelong Grammar School and Melbourne University, drove him over from Harkaway to our house in Croydon one day in 1948. As our eyes met over the tops of the tea-cups there was a moment of recognition between two people who could share many things. He was a man of achievement: he had proved he had something to say. I had not even dared to face the blank sheet. I had enjoyed *The Montforts* and *Lucinda Brayford*. His family, both on the Boyd and the à Beckett side, reminded me of members of my mother's family – the spiritual exiles in the drawing-rooms of the patricians and country gentry of New South Wales and Victoria.

I enjoyed his wit. He told me that he would like all the young men of Australia to wear pantaloons and hose so that we could all enjoy the beauty of their legs. I asked him what he would do with the bandy-legged. He replied, 'I would make them wear cassocks.' He asked to see my collection of books, adding he would tell my character from the books I bought. While he read the titles on the spines I kept talking, and he sensed that character sketches were not my favourite subject. I was to meet him again. He told me to have a shot at doing in history what he had done in fiction. But in 1948 I was not ready.

I was still collecting material. I had a plan to select some of the documents I had found useful for teaching and put them into a book. By a strange coincidence a lecturer at the Teachers' College, Len Pryor, had the same idea. We decided to collaborate. He was a most con-genial man to work with, and, happily, exercised a kindly restraint on my undisciplined imagination. We decided to call the book *Select Documents in Australian History*. We sent off the manuscript to Angus & Robertson early in 1949. The collection betrayed not a hint of the dream about Australia which was to become the great passion of my life.

By the beginning of 1949 the Melbourne experience was coming to an end. The enthusiasm of the first two years of teaching Australian history was waning. I needed a change. Dymphna understood. The stereotype in which my colleagues in Melbourne had cast me no longer corresponded with the man within. Ambition was another nagger: get on, climb higher, create something of your own: stop being a member of the choir in the Melbourne History Department: sing a solo of your own composition.

I read an advertisement for a Chair of History at the Canberra University College. I really had little to say for myself – no publications, no Ph.D., none of the without-which-nots of today. There was much against me: there was the rumour that I was 'difficult', that I was 'erratic', that in moments when inflated by strong drink I said 'the wrong thing', and took perverse pleasure in mocking the pompous. Was I also perhaps known to Security? If so that must be a laugh: how could I threaten anyone?

Luck was with me. Max Crawford and Alexander Boyce Gibson told the selection committee about my teaching. The council of the College, I found out later, asked Security whether I was a risk. They answered that I was a socialist, and not a communist: Security knew more about what I believed than I did. The council did not pry into my temperament, or the great liberties I sometimes took with the lore of bourgeois Australia. One night in May 1949 Joe Burton, the principal of the college, rang one of our neighbours, who ran down the hill for me. Joe said, 'Congratulations, Professor.' I could not speak. Another journey was about to begin. I was about to go into exile from the world which had made me, and which I must outgrow if I was ever to tell the story of Australia.

Becoming a
Historian of Australia

At the interview for the Chair of History at the Canberra University College one of the members of the council, Dr Bertram Dixon, asked me whether I wanted to come to Canberra to have more leisure to write a history of Australia. I replied, yes, I did. But there was more to it than that. Exile from the world of the Melbourne intellectuals was essential if I were to write a history of Australia. Melbourne made me: there had to be another me, a me which had broken with Melbourne mockery and nihilism: there had to be a lot more suffering: there had to be discipline and single-mindedness: the days of being a buffoon around the communion rail in the bars of Carlton must come to an end.

Canberra had much to offer. There was the beauty of the place, the valley of the Molonglo, Black Mountain, Mount Ainslie with its flashing beacon at night, like 'Airlie Beacon' lighting the way to I knew not what at the time, only hoping there was a beacon somewhere. There was the Goodradigbee River, in which a man, maybe, could be washed clean, and in the distance the Australian Alps, with their message to all who had eyes to see that some things were from eternity and would not change.

The human scene in 1949 was just as inviting as the other scene. On 1 October Chairman Mao had proclaimed the People's Republic of China in Tiananmen Square in Peking (Beijing): maybe there could be socialism with a human face, maybe a socialist society need not be run by spiritual bullies, maybe there could be equality without restraints on liberty, maybe dullness, greyness of spirit, conformism and mediocrity were not permanent features of socialist societies.

In communist Russia Anna Akhmatova, the poet, had thought of her fellow-writers as 'My companions on the way through Hell'. She summed up her life after November 1917 as 'Thirty long years have I lived / Beneath disaster's wing.' In the nightmare years of her son Yezhov's terror she spent seventeen months queuing daily outside a prison hoping to catch a glimpse of her son. In 1937 she said she had been crying for two years. As she put it later about the years of terror:

> It's all mixed up – can't understand
> What's happening on this earth,
> Who is an animal, who's man.

China might be quite different from Stalinist Russia.

There was still a Labor government in Canberra. True, it had degenerated into a government of men who seemed to have lost their way, but, whatever filth the communists might pour over the character of the Labor leaders, for me, then as now, it was still true: better a Labor government than a non-Labor government. There was hope for them: there was no hope for conservatives, even when they wore the mask of liberals and spoke of themselves as servants of the forgotten people of Australia – the middle classes.

I asked at the time: Why save the bourgeoisie of Australia? Why make Australia safe for the members of the Melbourne Club, for Bob Menzies, for the dwellers in South Yarra, Malvern, Toorak, Kew and Kooyong, and all those of like mind? I had a fantasy at the time of a boat leaving Port Melbourne for Heard Island, having on board the last defenders of bourgeois society. I found it satisfying to draw up a list of the people at the rails waving farewell to Melbourne as the tugs nudged their boat away from the wharf. I even invented last messages – Bob Menzies doing a General Douglas Macarthur, assuring the Melbourne Club, Malvern and Kooyong, 'I will return.'

Canberra held out the promise of relief from such Melbourne smugness. There were some with whom I soon knew heart's ease – something quite rare for me. Among them was Don Baker, one of the lecturers in history. I had first met him at Geelong Grammar School in October 1940, not foreseeing then the bond which would unite us so firmly later in Canberra. I had taught him again at the University of Melbourne, and during weekend visits to our place on the golf-links estate in Croydon I caught glimpses of the man within, and began to think maybe he was someone to whom I could speak, maybe even risk letting him see what went on behind the buffoonery, the showing-off, and the Friday-night descent into hell. Well, we did begin to talk, to my lasting delight. Don was a server who never became servile, a man reaching out to others, but a jealous guardian against any who presumed to 'pluck at the heart' of his 'mystery'. He had liberated himself from his low-church Anglican background. On the surface it looked as though as though he were also rebelling against bourgeois tidiness. That was misleading. Don was a tidy man, an orderly man in things of the mind, and in his daily life. His heart knew no bounds. He chafed then and ever against the restraints his tribe wanted to impose on him. He would do anything for those he liked: he was generous with his time and his labour. His students adored him, they having the grace to perceive that he had that rare combination of a brilliant mind and a warm and loving heart.

Laurie Gardiner, his colleague, was different. He was an honours graduate in history from the University of Bristol. He saw no reason to abandon the faith into which he was born. He was a fine representative of Catholic Christendom. His faith conferred a grandeur on the lectures he gave to the tiny band of students at the Canberra University College. Faith and temperament were so blended in him that his lectures were free from any vulgar scoring of points at the expense of the heretical or schismatic churches. By his example he strengthened my conviction that true believers did not torment or cajole those of little or no or wrong faith. The example of these two – Don Baker the stern, uncompromising son of the Enlightenment, the man who could see no good in any of the Christian churches, and Laurie Gardiner, the fine flower of Catholic Christendom – sowed in my mind the germ of the idea that when the time came for the College to break away from Melbourne University and for us to prescribe our own syllabuses, our department should have lecturers who would represent the different points of view on history – a Marxist, a Catholic, a secular humanist, and a scholar.

Perhaps the two of them, by their example, turned my mind and my heart towards what was important in the history of Australia. Who can tell? I was assuming then, rather naively, that in such a department all the members would be as tolerant of those with whom they disagreed as Don Baker and Laurie Gardiner – that they would not shout, or behave like bullies when a colleague said or wrote words which were displeasing to them. Many years later, to my dark, undying pain, I would say to myself, 'How wrong can you be?' I was to learn that there were historians who, given the chance, would have rewritten the first of the Ten Commandments this way: 'For I, the Lord thy Marxist historian, am a jealous historian. Thou shalt have no other historians but me.' But not then: Don and Laurie made me feel glad to be alive. I had read many books, but they taught me how to live.

So did many other colleagues in the College. Fin Crisp was the Professor of Political Science. I had first met him at Belgrave as long ago as the late 1920s. I had met him again at Oxford in the winter of 1938–39, and had danced with his wife Helen (who was from Adelaide), at the Balliol ball in June 1939. The memory of that never left me, nor the wonder that someone so beautiful could move so gracefully on the dance floor. We will all speak later in the season of the sere, the yellow leaf, driving me again to put the Hardy question: 'Why then did we not speak earlier?' There will be many such regrets, many times when I will ask: Why did we not say more to each other? Whose strange laws kept us apart?

At first Fin Crisp was not easy to get to know. One man inside him wanted to draw all manner of men and women unto him. That was the Fin of the universal embrace. There was another man inside him who often, I suspect, was tempted to recite the words 'I wish I loved the human race'. The sight of some men and women released a rush of blood into Fin's head. He flushed scarlet, his chin dropped almost on to his chest, his eyes, which some could cause to sparkle with ecstasy, clouded over. He had never been able to make up his mind whether to be a scholar, a public servant or a Labor leader. Fin always needed someone to worship. Some of his idols let him down, but not Ben Chifley. Fin's tragedy was that he had the gifts to succeed, the industry, the drive, and the absence of any distractions, he never being tempted by the Hindu aphorism that the roots of the lotus flower feed on the slime. Fin was never one to believe a man could find precious metal by rooting around in the dirt. He had a prodigious memory: he was widely read in politics, economics and history, though not in the literature of the non-English-speaking world. He was a persuasive speaker and a lively lecturer. He told me often, and I imagine he told many people, that religion was a man's private business.

He accepted without question the myth about British political institutions. In politics he was an Australian Labor Party man, not an ideologue, not a man of abstract political principle, but a pragmatist. He was a numbers man. Elections were his great political passion. He was as excited about the election of members of a university committee as about an election for the Commonwealth parliament. I remember once overhearing him reciting numbers on the telephone. He sounded as though he were talking to a starting-price bookmaker. He told me later over a cup of tea that he was instructing a group how to vote in a forthcoming election for the Superannuation Board in Canberra.

Many things delighted him – a victory for Collingwood in a football game, a victory for Australia in a test cricket game, a Labor victory. Yet, despite all the arrogance and condescension to which he had been subjected by the English both before and after the war, he spoke of them with affection, even nostalgia. He was never free of the Australian vice of 'Englishmanism'. He accepted the lore of an Oxford senior common-room as rules for the conduct of his own life. He loved to do things for other people, to help them with their careers, to help them get what they wanted. He was at his happiest washing up with a bunch of students or members of his local Labor Party branch at the end of a long party, or taking the tea-towel from his hostess at the end of a dinner party. There he bubbled over with warmth and affection for those he liked. But I still remember that even in such moments of gaiety a scowl would suddenly appear on his face, the chin would drop, the cheeks flush red, and the eyes rivet on to the water in the washing-up basin if one of his great hates came into view or spoke.

He told me of his hopes to win pre-selection for a Labor seat in the House of Representatives. Not standing for the pre-selection ballot for the seat of Canberra had been a blow. Yet as a key to the degree of self-knowledge he possessed at the time, he did not attribute his failure to his feud with Dr John Burton, then head of the Department of External Affairs.

In time he will drop hints to me that he paid a high price for the luxury of indulging his hatreds. That was his fatal flaw, the point at which the hand of the potter had faltered in shaping his clay. Yet, as far as I could tell, he never cursed the potter for playing such a trick on him, of planting in him the spur of fame and ambition, but also planting inside him a temperament which would cheat him of the prize he coveted.

Getting to know Fin well, winning his confidence, was not easy. But it had one rich prize for me. Earlier I had been tempted to laugh at those who, through their own folly, found the prize they desired forever out of reach. I began to see Fin with the eye of pity – and in time will believe that a historian must view all the characters in his story with the eye of pity. That will come slowly: there will be many backslidings, many lapses into mockery and buffoonery.

Getting to know Heinz Arndt was also not easy, but in the end just as rewarding as getting to know Fin Crisp. Heinz was elected to the first Chair of Economics at the Canberra University College in 1951. I had known him in Oxford in 1938–39 when he lived in a room above mine at 10 St Michael's Street. At that time he was a bachelor, a refugee from Nazi Germany, a socialist on fire with righteous anger against the crimes and follies of the British governing classes. He approached life with a German deadly seriousness. His first question to me at that time was often put with brow furrowed, and eyes darkened with rage and indignation, as he asked me, 'Did you read the leader in the *Times* today?' Of course, my mind being at that time on 'other things', I had to tell him no, I had not read the *Times*, I was reading Flaubert's *L'Education sentimentale*. Heinz made me feel that was not good enough, that was too frivolous.

He arrived in Canberra with his wife Ruth, also a refugee from Nazi Germany, and their three children in January 1951. In one way, and one way only they resembled Jack Sprat and his wife. Heinz was an encyclopedia of information on public life, Ruth on private life. Beneath Heinz's forbidding exterior and Ruth's insatiable curiosity, there were two people who really cared, two most lovable human beings. There was another man behind Heinz Arndt, the man who argued with or corrected anyone who ever dared to open his mouth in his presence. Heinz reminded me of the remark by Dostoevsky: 'Man is broad, too broad. I'd have him narrower.' There was Heinz the economist, the expert on public finance and the banks; there was Heinz the chess player; there was Heinz the pianist (as a boy he had heard Arthur Schnabel play the piano in his parents' home in Germany); there was Heinz the Labor Party member; there was Heinz the university politician, the man who would debate with anyone, anytime, and for any length of time; there was Heinz the friend of Dick Downing and Dorian Le Gallienne, the man of sympathy, the man who understood but was no secret sharer; there was the gregarious Heinz, the man who loved to join a gathering, but had disqualified himself from the one favourite meeting place of Australian men – the bar – because his German upbringing had taught him the bar was a place for those who were not serious about life.

Heinz had a horror of all displays of excess. He was a German humanist, a believer in restraint, in discipline, in moderation in all things, not those vulgar excesses at the bar of which some of his colleagues boasted. So Heinz sentenced himself or limited himself to being a guru of the Canberra classrooms, common-rooms, and drawing-rooms. Yet although he had never been tempted himself to wallow in the gutter, and in speech was often censorious of all wallowers he was kind and helpful to the victims of the gutter. Heinz was a disapprover, but not a punisher. I learned a lot from listening to him, having decided a dialogue was not in the field of the possible with Heinz. I enjoyed him as a fine representative of the German belief in higher civilisation, of the point made by Goethe, by Thomas Mann and by Sigmund Freud, that the 'great souls' must achieve a harmony between passion and reason, that they are the guardians of culture and must preserve it from being debased by the rabble or the masses. Heinz was a German patrician who, by an accident of history, was temporarily in the Australian Labor Party.

In time he will see that between him and Australian Labor, with their mythology of mateship and equality there was a great gulf set. Heinz will find his natural spiritual home with the founders of *Quadrant* and the Council for Cultural Freedom in Australia. For him religion was an illusion. He agreed with Freud's thesis in his *Civilisation and its Discontents*. I never heard him say a word which betrayed any interest in or sympathy with the idea of the god in Christ, or any interest in who had kept alive the image of Christ. I suspect that, like Freud and Nietzsche, he judged all those who were drawn to such a view of the world to be guilty of weakness, and that for a man or a woman who had the talents to be a servant of 'higher civilisation' to draw inspiration from the Don Quixotes, the Myshkins, the Alyosha Karamazovs or the Miss Hares of the world, was the worst betrayal of all.

Alec Hope probably held a similar view, though he would be a bold man who claimed to know what Alec believed, or what he stood for. He came to the Canberra University College as the first Professor of English in January 1951 – the same time as Heinz Arndt. I had known Alec – that is if anyone ever was allowed to know him – for a brief period in Melbourne in 1948 and 1949. During that time he had given a lecture to the students in the English Department on *Crime and Punishment* by Dostoevsky. He was then interested in the 'great souls' who were beyond good and evil, the ones to whom the moral law of transgression and punishment did not apply – the ones who were

'East of Eden'. He had told the students, I heard, that Dostoevsky had lost his nerve and not explored the mind of a Raskolnikov who rejected the Christian answer of redemption through suffering, confession and forgiveness.

I suspect that one of the reasons why Alec checked anyone in Melbourne who came near was that he was out of sympathy with the dominant ethos in Melbourne intellectual circles, he eyeing socialism and equality with a jaundiced eye. He had no time for writers of history. History, he said at the time, was 'the anus of the human mind.' He believed in the role of the poets. He spoke of them as the chosen people. He was right to see himself as a very special person, but some of his disciples were corrupted by their assumption that they too were 'special'. He was an Australian Olympian. He sometimes reminded me of Goethe in his search for someone who would understand who he was, and why men of his gifts needed love and admiration without commitment. He was himself a most impressive representative of an Olympian's view of the world. He knew Russian, he was studying Arabic under Professor Goldman, the first Professor of Semitic Languages at the University of Melbourne. He was no narrow specialist, not a man who knew his Milton and little else.

At that time you did not talk with Alec. Like Auden, he spoke to you about Russian literature, Icelandic sagas, Homer, Freud, Jung and so on, but not about Marx or Lenin, or the Declaration of the Rights of Man, or the American Declaration of Independence. Melbourne was then full of believers in 1917, or one-time believers in 1917, and enthusiasts for the Australia that was coming to be. Unlike James McAuley who had once been a believer in 1917 and knew what it was like to be under the spell of 1917, I doubt if this touched Alec at all except as a threat to 'higher civilisation'.

In the Melbourne days Alec sang the most delightful and amusing arias for unaccompanied poet. Anyone misguided enough to make a bid for a duet would soon be silenced, politely but firmly. The obtuse, who did not pick up the message, soon learned the error of their ways. Yet to those in need of comfort he was a faithful server. He gave them the impression he had saved the afternoon for them.

He meant it. Men beamed, women purred, as the aria, a mixture of flattery, great wit, profound learning, and that air of belonging, as in one sense he did, to a higher order of being, moved from the statement of the theme into the variations (always very delightful), the cadenzas and the coda, followed by a pause in which he would ask the listener or listeners whether he could fill their glass again. The wisps of cigarette smoke in the room heightened the atmosphere: it was as though one were being initiated into a mystery cult. I always felt you got the most out of Alec by adopting the role of a novice or a supplicant. That was rewarding because he had so much to offer.

He never revealed who had been his teachers, either in the past or in the present. Even after listening to him for over forty years I still have no certainty on that point. I think the line would go something like this: Homer, the prophets of the Old Testament, the Norse and Icelandic sagas, Dante, Shakespeare, Milton, Dryden, Pope, Dostoevsky, Tolstoy, and so on, with all the writers and the painters in the radical or democratic tradition left out, they not touching him at all. I should add the 'elitism' in Goethe, Hölderlin, Freud and John Anderson – because Alec was in part a missionary for 'higher civilisation' in Canberra. This air of the Olympian was rendered palatable, even attractive, for those with no claims to be 'special' by charm and a lively interest in 'country matters' – a subject on which he was just as learned as he was on any problems of prosody or metaphysics.

So I was surprised one day in 1950 to receive a letter from him in which he told me he wanted to ask my advice on something next time I was in Melbourne. We met for a cup of tea in a tiny tea-room near Elizabeth Street. He put one question: did I find it was possible to work in Canberra? I said yes, it was. That was all he wanted to know. He told me then he would apply for the Chair of English at the University College. Years later he thanked me for the advice. I was surprised that he should either remember or want to thank me. That probably reveals something about me – I mean my failure to see earlier that there was this side to him, that the Olympian was a carer. That realisation will draw us together later, when differences of faith and values had ceased to keep us apart. I started to speak with him two years ago, and soon regretted that this had not begun years earlier. Perhaps it was my folly which kept us apart. Some discoveries are made when it is almost too late to enjoy them. Such is life.

It has been said that all storytellers are parasites: they feed on food grown by other people: they sustain themselves by picking and choosing from a haystack that they themselves did not build. Life, in the Flemish proverb, is a haystack; we take from it what we believe we need. Canberra was rich in food for parasites, rich for observers of the human scene, rich for anyone like myself who was hoping one day to impose an order on the chaos of life – a searcher then for what Henry James called 'the figure in the carpet'. There were so many people to observe, so many to listen to.

One was Murray Todd, later Professor of English at the University of Tasmania. He was a man of many parts. He was a New Zealander, a young man who had already made his mark with his book on Coleridge. He was a brilliant actor. I still remember his performance as Eilert Løvborg in Ibsen's *Hedda Gabler*. We used to '*jouer aux télégraphes*' (play at telegraphy) together. I remember feeling so close to him after his understanding so well what it was like to be Eilert Løvborg, that I sent him this telegram from Adaminaby:

Eilert Løvborg,
c/o Murray Todd,
Canberra University College.

Have discovered your manuscript at the bottom of Lake Adaminaby. Mrs Elvsted very pleased.

(Sgd) George Tesman.

Murray was delighted. He knew I had every reason to be fascinated by the Løvborg story. He knew that the editor of a volume of select documents was no George Tesman. Murray told me that one day I might hear the bell of salvation. Well, by the time I had heard a few tinkles on that bell, no louder than a bellbird calling miles and miles away, Murray had died of leukemia, and there would be no chance to tell him how far I had travelled in the quest for grace, or how much further I had to travel.

There was Alan Donagan, a lecturer in philosophy, a student in Melbourne during the Wittgenstein years, so much given to the sedentary life of a thinker that his wife, Barbara, a model of propriety and decorous behaviour, once said of him, with eyebrows fluttering like the wings of a delicate butterfly: 'Poor dear, he gets so tired if he can't spend the whole day in an armchair.' We all laughed. But we were in error if we assumed that Donagan was just an armchair philosopher. He spoke with wit and immense learning on subjects as diverse as the best half-back line Carlton had ever had – he was an enthusiast for Brown, Deacon and Clark – the behaviour of Sir John Falstaff ('Stand, Sir John?' I still hear him asking), the teaching of the Catholic

Church, the poetry of T. S. Eliot, and the philosophy of Collingwood. Donagan was never at ease with the mythology of Melbourne – either the Wittgenstein view of the world, or the mateship–equality duet. He will find a haven with the Anglo-Catholics and American high seriousness. That was Australia's loss. Our world was too narrow and too oppressive for a man with Donagan's range. It was a pity Donagan never knew the Australia that was coming to be. We were still victims of the giant of British philistinism. Donagan will leave for America just as the giant was about to receive a mortal wound.

Burgess Cameron, later a Professor of Economics, was a man who took many daring steps on the dance floor, but was cautious and responsible in the classroom. He will make his mark in the teaching of economics in Canberra.

There was Brian Beddie, a one-time member of the Department of External Affairs, who had resigned to start a new life as a teacher of political science. He was a man who had much to say. In politics he was at that time a conservative; in philosophy, art, music and literature he was a follower of John Anderson, the Professor of Philosophy at the University of Sydney. In those moments when we were both 'charioted by Bacchus and his pards', Brian sang a beautiful song about the Dionysian frenzy – that passion 'Lofty' Franklin had warned me years ago must be restrained if a man was to bear fruit.

Listening to Brian persuaded me to read the works of John Anderson. That was a let-down. His words touched me not at all. As a Melbourne man, I was suspicious of Anderson as the man who had betrayed the Left, a man who had gone over to the other side. Melburnians wanted Anderson to answer a simple question: was he or was he not interested in the fact that some were very rich and some very poor? Anderson replied that we were all bothered by different things. That finished him with the Melburnians. Out of his own mouth Anderson had shown himself to be wrong-headed and walnut-hearted. Exit John Anderson, that Fascist bastard, ha, ha, ha!

I heard John Anderson speak in Canberra at the philosophy conference in 1951, and was enchanted. Melburnians had warned me to be on my guard lest he get me in. The man, they said, was a mesmeriser, a man who got you in by giving you in the first five minutes of his talk high-minded reasons for wanting to 'kill' your father. Be on your guard, Melburnians warned, the bastard will convince you that if you do what you want to do you will not feel guilty. Yes, be careful, or he will persuade you that everything is allowable.

Well, I was carried away, though I did not know why. I disagreed with everything he said, but enjoyed the act he put on. Maybe it was the Scottish accent; maybe it was the capacity to toss off the right word or the lively image; maybe it was the man wearing Scottish tweed suits in sunny Australia, a man wearing a tie when most of his colleagues in philosophy and other intellectual sports were dressing much more casually. I was already convinced that the Bohemians of the heart wore suits, and that the new conformists stripped off all formal gear; maybe it was the thumbs under the waistcoat, and the twiddling fingers which explained the attraction; or maybe it was the light in the eye, a sign that there was a man within who was still alive.

I was soon disenchanted. At the end of the conference Bruce Benjamin, then a lecturer in philosophy and in the front row of the Melbourne philosophers' scrum, invited philosophers and hangers-on, such as Don Baker and myself, to a party at his house in Turner. Towards midnight, after many tongue-looseners, and conscience-quieteners, John Anderson put on a turn. Don Baker, who in the early 1950s had the appearance and the mien of a John the Baptist, though his behaviour made it quite clear that he had not been refreshing himself that night on a diet of locusts and wild honey, shook Anderson by the shoulders and told him he, Anderson, was the greatest academic in Australia. Anderson liked that. He offered to sing a song about the ascension of Christ – I do not remember any words now except the last line sung with Anderson waving his right hand towards the ceiling, 'Goodbye, goodbye.'

Don Baker nearly had convulsions. The acolytes were ecstatic. Geoffrey Fairbairn whispered to Dymphna, 'Promise me faithfully that when his time comes you will never let Manning go on like that.' Dymphna said not a word. She knew then it would be a long time before she or anyone could persuade me not to put on an act in public.

I was dismayed by what had come up from inside John Anderson – I mean the old-hat blasphemy, and black humour about Christianity which belonged to the age of Bradlaugh, to the age of believers in progress, and not to the age of the atomic bomb. Why was his humour directed against such a target? I could understand any serious-minded man or woman rejecting the virgin birth, the claim to be God's only son, the resurrection, the post-resurrection appearances (pleased though I was then and am now to notice that after the resurrection we are told Christ spoke to those he had loved, both male and female, that he went fishing, and that he drank wine and ate bread) and the ascension. What bothered me was that Anderson had neither reverence nor love for the man who had spoken the memorable words about love, belief, forgiveness and compassion. The previous day I had heard Anderson dismiss these words as trivial and superficial. So for me that night he was the man of infinite charm, infinite charisma, but not my type of man at all. But the picture of the man lived on in my mind, the man with the light in the eye. I thought of him later as a man of vast gifts who, for some reason I did not understand, devoted the last half of his life to swimming up-stream against the great river of life.

The conference of philosophers had one amusing effect in our family. Our son Axel (later the biographer of Christopher Brennan and Henry Handel Richardson) was, and still is, one who 'notices such things'. A week or so after the conference, his teacher at Ainslie Primary School set the class a test in measuring the dimensions of a door. All the boys and girls in grade three wrote down the answer – but not Axel. The teacher asked him, 'What's wrong with you?' Axel: 'How can you ever know the size of anything?' The teacher, I gather, had one thing in common with Pontius Pilate: he did not answer the question! Who could?

For some Canberra was a city without a soul. I came to the conlusion that its critics were talking about themselves. I loved it. For me Canberra was quite quickly the place where I heard memorable remarks about the human situation. I remember once picking up a man who was steering a very uneven course across Northbourne Avenue near the old Canberra Police Station, and offering to drive him home. He told me he wanted to get to heaven but feared the sin of drunkenness was a hurdle he would never leap over. He had, he said, a bank of merit – two sons being priests, and three daughters nuns. But what could that avail? I reminded him of the definition of drunkenness by the Council of Trent. No one was drunk unless he lost consciousness. That cheered him up. A smile of hope replaced the lugubrious looks. Heaven, he said, would be so wonderful. I asked him why. He replied, 'Because I'm going to take my super [super-annuation] with me.'

At a meeting of the local philosophers, at which I had no difficulty in obeying the command of the Melbourne team to be silent on all questions on which you cannot speak with certainty, I heard Guildford Young, the coadjutor Catholic Bishop of Canberra and Goulburn, read a paper on the natural law in which he spent much time on the church's teaching on procreation. Noel Ruth, one of the lecturers in economics at the College, asked Dr Young, 'My Lord [a way of declaring membership], why is an obstruction in time right, and an obstruction in space wrong?' Well, Dr Young was also like Pontius Pilate. He did not answer the question: he spoke for twenty minutes around it and about.

Years later the woman who was trying in vain to teach me Russian, Mila Gapanovich, a relative of Rimsky-Korsakov, said to me in her broken but very lively English,

Professor Clark, my daughter Svieta — she will — how do you tell? — marry Rob. My daughter when she came to Canberra, she believe nothing — nothing — absolutely nothing. But now Svieta, Professor Clark, she believe just a little bit. So she marry Church of England.

Our youngest son Benedict, then aged six, also illustrated the accuracy of the remark that 'out of the mouths of babes and sucklings hast thou ordained truth.' With many misgivings we took him to a play in the Playhouse Theatre, a play by Carson McCullers, *The Ballad of the Sad Café*. When the atmosphere became steamy, when a grandson made an improper suggestion to his grandmother, Benedict said to Dymphna, 'Mum, they need hobbies.'

In 1950 I had had the good fortune to go to a lunch in the old Hotel Canberra in honour of Bertrand Russell. Like his ancestor, Lord John Russell, physically he was a tiny man with a wizened face, and wisps of white hair. The eyes were the only outward and visible sign of the mighty spirit encased within this frail body. He did not treat his fellow-diners seriously. In his speech I remember he told us, laughing more than the audience at his own wit, that the members of the English aristocracy had been taxed out of existence, that some of them had become the mistresses of Hitler, and that he ought to know because many of them were his cousins. It was a period in his life when class loyalty had seduced him into advocating an immediate atomic war against the Russians to end the scourge of communism before the Russians discovered how to make the bomb. So we did not hear the thinker; we only heard the crusader for bourgeois civilisation, Russell the saviour, not Russell the philosopher, or Russell the lover of women, or Russell the wit. When leaving the Canberra Hotel I recalled a remark by Ottoline Morell about Russell: 'Bertie', she said, 'had a cold hand.'

He did drop one memorable remark about Australia. Just before he boarded the ship in Fremantle to take him back to 'old civilisation' he broadcast his message to the Australian people. Australia's task he said was as pioneers 'not only in the development of Australia but in pointing the way to a happier destiny for man throughout the centuries to come. This is a noble ambition. I am a firm believer in your capacity to play your part in this great work, and I leave your shores with more hope for mankind than I had when I came here.' Australians, he continued, were happier than Americans because they did not have the same restless itch always to be doing something else.

Was that true? Australia was a child of two revolutions – the American revolution and the French revolution. Had we, the Australians, achieved the aims of 1776 and 1789 – believing that all men were born equal, that they were endowed by their Creator with certain inalienable rights, that amongst these were life, liberty and the pursuit of happiness? Was there equality in Australia? Was there liberty? Was there happiness? Was it true, as Bertie Russell had said, that we Australians had already pointed the way to a happier destiny for man? Perhaps that could be a theme in a story about Australia. Were we all 'the sons of the Enlightenment'? What was this happiness to which Bertie Russell had referred? Was it the happiness of men and women who were still 'stifling the sorrow' they had experienced ever since the loss of the comforters of a loving, caring, forgiving God and the life of the world to come, or was it the happiness of people dwelling in a kingdom of nothingness?

I was feeling my way towards a story of Australia as a battlefield for the last days of the myths of Europe and America – the myth of Christendom, and the myth of the Enlightenment – but only vaguely, much of my time being spent dreaming of what was forever out of reach, or tempted to believe that a few hours in the bar of the Hotel Civic with Don Baker, David Campbell, Graeme Hughes, and Alec Hope might reveal the answers I was looking for. That which brought me so much pleasure at the time proved to be a cruel mirage. I was beginning to believe that the story of Australia might be a bible of wisdom for the living, that it may play a part in opening eyes to the field of the possible.

I was still a polyphon, a man of many voices. There was the man who saw human life as a tragedy in the Greek sense, saw the mighty men and women of renown as individuals who would not get what they wanted because of some flaw in their being. There was the man

197

who believed, or rather hoped, that a change in the ownership of the means of production, distribution and exchange would see the dawn of a new era for humanity: that was the millenarian, the man who believed in the O'Dowd words of Australia as a country where 'lurks millennial Eden 'neath thy breast'. There was the man who loved Mozart's *Magic Flute*, Mozart's piano concertos. There was the man who hoped for, yes who needed someone, somewhere, 'up above the sky so high', or here on Earth who would take pity on all of us for our folly, someone who could and would forgive all of us. There was the man who wanted to get on in the world but tormented himself, and punished himself for being such a prey to vulgar ambition. There was the man who believed he had something to say, but doubted whether he could find the words in which to say it.

Much of what I had seen in Canberra nourished the hopes of the Enlightenment inside me. That was one voice. Another voice, an antiphon, asked me to collect examples of human folly. The election debate in November and December 1949 provided many such examples. A Labor government brought in the army to crush a strike. The conservatives promised to 'put value back in the pound' and 'fill the bowsers'. The conservatives played on the fears of the greedy. Once again, as in April 1917 and December 1931, the electors of Australia, in a time of political crisis, voted for the conservatives, as they will again in December 1975. Did this mean we Australians were doomed to go on repeating the past, that we were chained to our past? I had read Werner Sombart's *Why Is There No Socialism in the United States?* I had digested his explanation, and had applied his pattern to Australia and found it fitted. (All historians pinch their ideas from other people.) We were a society of immigrants: we were all either immigrants or the descendants of immigrants – including the Aborigines. We all, save the Aborigines, had the dream of the block of land and a house of our own: we all had petit-bourgeois values or aspirations, there being no large propertyless proletariat in Australia. There was the same spread of middle-class affluence in Australia as in America.

Australians were standing in front of an unclimbable brick wall. Ever since 1910, and possibly earlier, it was clear that if Labor were either ideological or radical, or both, they would never win political power in Australia. So Labor became pragmatic, Labor became a machine for the capture of political power at the risk of becoming a prey to corruption, careerism, and a medium for demagogues. The elections of 1910, 1917, 1931 and 1949 demonstrated that for Labor the price of being even vaguely radical was electoral defeat. Did that mean the ballot box was not the way forward in Australia? Did that mean the only way forward was outside the ballot box – that there must be a 'lick on the lug', that in Australia either blood must stain the wattle, or Australians must join the British and the New Zealanders as the darling dodoes of the twentieth century? Like the hopes of 1929 the hopes of 1941 turned into a cruel mirage. There was a temptation then to give way to despair, to see us all as a people doomed to go on repeating the past, a people who would never face up to the causes of their dullness and mediocrity, a people who had opted for cosiness, a people so unprepared to face the truth about themselves that they lived in a world of make-believe.

Two events in my personal life provided food for pessimism and despair. In the years since my mother's death on 31 March 1943 I had drawn closer to my father. Each January we went fishing together either at Pyramid Rock, the Nobbies or Cape Schanck. We began at last to talk to each other over lunch. He was still dreaming of a day when he could drop his line in a deep hole in the ocean right opposite the Pyramid, a hole where huge blue-noses and deep-sea leather-johnnies fed when the tide was moving in. The man who had begun his life in the Church of England in Sydney believing, with Christ, that he would draw all manner of men unto him, was ending his days breeding ducks in the back yard of the vicarage at Mentone, ducks which laid the eggs no one wanted.

I sensed then sitting on the rocks at lunch-time, watching the waves roll in from Bass Strait, relentless, never-ending, forever changing but forever remaining the same, that my father had a story to tell, that there were things in his life so painful that he could never speak about them to anyone. I was not surprised to hear years later that he advised a young man who came to him for guidance in things spiritual to see the Catholic priest in Mentone. My father knew by then that the Catholic Church – despite all its imperfections and all the abominations it had committed in Christ's name – and not those Moore College miserables and those respectability mongers in the Church of England, had kept alive the image of Christ. But my father was too much a prisoner of his own past, too preoccupied with his future prospects from the Clergy Provident Fund to make that move. So he stood outside the doors urging others to enter, still not daring to let others close to him know what he was thinking, or the torment and the anguish of that burden from the past.

He was still a perfectionist in little things. If Dymphna served rabbit for the evening meal there was never any flesh left on the bones on his plate: and the bones were always arranged in a geometrical pattern. He still inhaled the smoke from his last cigarette for the day with the pleasure of a man who was having his first puff after weeks of abstinence. He still loved his post-fishing glass of 'sarsaparilla' or 'cold tea', as he sometimes called it with a naughty wink for any woman in the room likely to understand what the 'straiteners' had done to him. In church he still sang:

> Jesu, Lover of my soul,
> Let me to Thy Bosom fly,
> While the gathering waters roll,
> While the tempest still is high

with the fervour of a man whose great hunger, whose great thirst, was that there must be someone who would understand what men of his temperament are called on to endure. He still loved the words of the Communion Service in the Book of Common Prayer: 'If any man sin, we have an advocate ... Jesus Christ, the righteous', or 'Ye that truly and earnestly repent you of your sins and intend to lead a new life following the commandments of God ...' It was all there, if only it were true.

The liars, the fornicators, the drunkards, all those who could not stop, still turned to him for comfort. He was still saying from the pulpit the words he had used as the vicar at St Philip's Church, Cowes, words about the resurrection, 'I am as sure of that as I am of anything living.' But his eyes still clouded over, and his nostrils quivered if anyone presumed to ask him later to give one reason for his faith. He was still saying to me about the problem of who moved the stone: 'That's my favourite subject, boy.' He was still telling everyone 'Manning's the thoughtful customer'. By 1950 he had added Dymphna to his short list of 'thoughtful customers'. He still turned his back on you before he opened his wallet. Money, religion, love: he still did not speak about them. He was still a presence in any room. He still wanted us all to be kind to each other. He still said in moments when people were not being kind, 'Well at least we can all have a good laugh.' But he who had so much to say would not allow anyone to come near.

One day in January 1951 Dymphna, Sebastian, Katerina, Axel and I went fishing with my father on the back beach at Sorrento. All day my father was strangely silent: there were no stories about the golden years at Long Bay Gaol, none of his cheek and deference about the 'Arch', none of his blarney to Dymphna. (Two days earlier he had delighted Dymphna by telling her, 'I'm always happy when I'm with you.' Dymphna never forgot those words.) His line was caught in the kelp. For him that was a terrible affront to his pride. 'I tell you, boy, the difference between a fisherman and a mug is that a fisherman never gets his line caught.' That day he did not catch a fish. All the years I had been fishing with him since 1922 I had never known him not to catch a fish. In the car on the way back to the cottage we were renting in Sorrento he did not say a word. I wondered if someone had said the wrong thing to him during the day. His teeth fell on to the floor of the car. As he groped for them I saw his face, and knew there was something terribly wrong with 'Grandpa'. Katerina asked in fright, 'Why can't Grandpa speak?' I should have told her he would never speak again, but those were the days when some questions were never answered.

He died ten days later, on 16 January. Perhaps it was just as well that he never regained consciousness, as he would have thought of any bodily weakness or defect as evidence of some moral weakness. At the funeral service in St Augustine's Church – yes, that at least was appropriate, because my father strove all his life in vain to break with St Augustine's teaching that desire poisoned the soul – his fellow-clergymen spoke warmly of his humanity, of all those qualities which had endeared him to so many. But no one dwelt on the words which summed up the tragic grandeur of my father's life: 'My heart was hot within me ... the fire kindled ... I held my tongue though it was grief and agony to me.' At the graveside at Box Hill the tragic words were spoken, 'Man that is born of woman hath but a short time to live ...', as I, shaken within but trying not to show it, mused on how strange it was that my mother and father who in life were often so far apart were to be united in death. None of the words traditionally carved on headstones could come within coo-ee of the grandeur of their story.

The secular humanists of Melbourne made shallow remarks to me about death. One of them cracked a joke: 'Death of a father', he said, 'should be welcomed because it relieved a man of his desire to kill his father', ha, ha, ha! Well, that did not help. My soul was so 'disquieted within me' that I began to have bad dreams. I dreamed that I saw my father prising limpets off the flat rock to the left of the Nobbies. I told him that I wanted him to help me to row over to 'the other shore'. He paused in his bait-collecting, smiled at me as I had first seen him smile when he returned from the war in March 1919, and said to me, 'Boy, that is one journey you must make by yourself.' Well, I was not ready for a journey at that time. There had to be more suffering before I would risk taking my frail barque out on to the high seas.

First, sickness almost broke me. In December 1951, ill with rheumatic fever, with temperatures of just over 104°F, I lay for weeks in the Canberra Hospital, wondering whether I too, unprepared as I was, was about to set out on that last journey. Don Baker, Fin Crisp, and Alec Hope comforted me. Noel Ebbels came up from Melbourne to see me. Heinz and Ruth Arndt were very kind. The doctors in Canberra sent me to Melbourne for specialist treatment. Dymphna and I rested on the first night at Pinsent's Hotel in Wangaratta. On the stairway up to the bedroom the manager told me Noel Ebbels had died that day in the Gundagai Hospital after falling off the back of a semi-trailer five miles on the Yass side of Gundagai. I had no words with which to express my grief. I thought of the words of Thomas Hardy in the poem 'The Broken Appointment' – 'Grieved I.' But what could words do?

Years later I wrote about the loss in a foreword for a book of documents on the Labor movement which Noel had almost finished. It was a poem of friendship. My loss was so great that I risked revealing what mattered most to me in life. I confessed in public my love for Noel. The mockers of Melbourne had the evidence they wanted, 'I told you so . . . ha, ha, ha!' I also implied that the words of Christ and the Russian revolution were the great hopes for humanity. This statement was greeted with uproar. The apologists for Stalin were so angered by the references to Christ that they tried to suppress publication. The self-appointed defenders of 'higher civilisation' greeted the words with their traditional 'wintry sneers'.

From that time I must steel myself for the howls of disapproval every time words of mine were published. To anticipate twenty years: when it was suggested that I should give the Boyer Lectures for 1976, Keith Mackriel, a senior executive in the Australian Broadcasting Commission tried to censor the scripts, because he believed I may say something outrageous about Sir John Kerr. I was astounded. Mackriel had studied under me in Canberra in 1956. Conservatives in the Senate, such as Sir John Carrick, wanted to stop the lectures being given. They wanted to silence me, just as some of the teachers at Geelong Grammar School and politicians in Melbourne had tried to silence me.

There were compensations. In 1976 Senator Susan Ryan, later a creative minister in the Labor government which came into office in March 1983, spoke eloquently in my defence. The academics had a good wash of the hands. But one woman who lived west of Broken Hill sent me a sixpenny diary, explaining that was all she could afford. She wanted to thank me for helping her to understand Australia, helping her to understand who she was and where she came from. Such people, and many more, gave me the strength to endure, the faith to go on to the end.

The loss of Noel Ebbels and the angry words which greeted my hymn of love and praise happened to coincide with another event which taught me a lesson about power in Australia. My main work in the first two years at the Canberra University College was to teach the diplomatic cadets. For a while I enjoyed the work. In some ways the cadets reminded me of the students in Melbourne. They were perhaps more career-conscious because they were making the transition from seekers for what held the world together into young men and women who had an eye for what the 'higher ups' in External Affairs would think if they sang 'a rebel chorus'. The conservatives were again in power in Canberra: the twenty-three years of unleavened bread were about to begin.

The cadets soon learned how to please their new masters. It was a curious experience to lecture and tutor twelve young men and women about Australia who did not really want to hear what I had to say. They were warm to me as a person. I remember many of them with affection – cadets such as Nancy Gleeson-White, one of the few women in an otherwise almost all-male show; Jill Crichton, lively, irreverent, but sharp and shrewd; Dick Woolcott, exuberant, a man with the gift of being able to speak to anyone, a born 'fixer' of disputes; Nick Parkinson, full of jokes, a man who was always acting a part on the stage of life, but underneath the actor there was a man with a warm and understanding heart; Peter Henderson, who had so much of the manners of an English country gentleman that one was surprised to find how kind and understanding he was underneath all the drawing-room politeness; John Hoyle, who had the mind of an academic and knew he would have to conceal his insights if he were to do things pleasing in the eyes of the new men on top; and Ken Rogers, a gifted man with a great moral passion and a high seriousness which did not please 'the men in black'. Warmth of heart, goodwill, jokes, buffoonery, horseplay, none of the tricks of a teacher could succeed in this new atmosphere. There had been a great change. The eyes of the cadets were not on me, their ears were not on what I had to say. In the years of the cold war, believers in 1917 and the words of the Galilean fisherman were no longer relevant. They must be silenced.

So it was no surprise when Keith Waller, the new head of the Department of External Affairs, a gifted performer, who, like another scholarship boy, Bob Menzies, had dedicated his talents to serve the interests of the comfortable classes in Australia, told me at the end of 1953 that the department was reorganising the course for the diplomatic cadets. My services as a teacher would be no longer required. There was much soft soap – how grateful he was, indeed how grateful they all were that the cadets of 1950–53 had had the good fortune to attend my lectures on Australian history. They had all told him how privileged they felt to hear me – *but* . . . Years later I read in my Security file in the Commonwealth Archives the reasons for the change. The 'men in black' wanted me out of the way, and Keith Waller obeyed. Out Clark: in defenders of the old order.

What to do? I was a teacher, and a teacher must have an audience. Only three students had enrolled for Australian history at the College in 1950. Were they the two or three I had read about in childhood, the grain of mustard seed from which a huge tree would one day grow? To keep going one needed faith, the faith that would move mountains, but, at that time, it seemed to me that Mount Ainslie and Black Mountain were as immovable as the founder of the Christian religion was unsinkable. There was always Melbourne: there was that understanding (or did I have it all wrong?) that I could return whenever I asked. But when I did ask, I was told, any other time, of course, they would be delighted to have me with them again, but not just now. It reminded me of a remark in Noel Coward's *Private Lives*: it was 'not the right time of the year for Tunis'.

There was a temptation to blame others for disappointments brought on by my own folly. It was the time of the dark night of the soul – with the soul being deadened at least once a week clowning with Don Baker and David Campbell and Graeme Hughes in the bar of the Hotel Civic. It was a time to think what would go into a history of Australia if one ever were to write a history of Australia. That formed the subject of the inaugural lecture given in the Childers Street hall of the Canberra University College in 1953. It was a manifesto by a man who believed that history was the art of telling a story about the past. History, like all art, was a comforter for those then living. My lecture began by staking out a claim for history as an art. History, like music, could cause the evil spirit to depart from the mind. There was that passage in the first book of Samuel: 'And it came to pass when the *evil* spirit from God was upon Saul, that David took a harp, and played with his hand; so Saul was refreshed, and was well, and the evil spirit departed from him.' I made another bold proclamation. The history of Australia might help us to achieve what we are all after – 'to be there when everyone suddenly understands what it has all been for.' There were three tasks: to drop the comforters of the past, the myth of British civilisation, and so forth, to find something to say: to learn how to tell the story.

There was still the temptation to wield the whip on the backs of those who had gone before me. The whip had to be put back into the cupboard, it being far more difficult to tell the story than to wield the whip. There was the terror that if Old Mother Hubbard were to open the cupboard all she would find would be a collection of discarded whips. Something of what might be said was hinted at in the introductions to the various sections in volume two of *Select Documents in Australian History, 1851–1900*, published in 1955. The editorial remarks should have been a blast on the trumpet, but they often sounded like a wail on a foghorn by a man searching frantically for a way out of the fog in which he had been surrounded since boyhood.

The intellectual baggage accumulated at school, university, England, and Melbourne must be shed. The equation that material well-being equals happiness, and possibly even goodness, must be dropped. All history was not just the history of class struggles: the heart was the great battlefield for the conflict between good and evil: there was the problem of desert: there was the tragedy of men and women brought to their destruction by flaws in their clay: what mattered most in life could never be, and no change in the ownership of the means of production, distribution and exchange could mend that 'primal fault'. All I knew was that I was resuming a journey which had begun a long time ago. I was still seeking an answer to the puzzles of childhood.

In the early 1950s I found out the answer to one of these puzzles. I had wanted for years to find out what had happened to Marge Thompson, the maid who had worked for my mother at Kempsey in 1920–21, and then joined us again at Belgrave in 1923. I knew she had married Reg Goulter in 1933, that she had had a child. I had heard that in drunken rages, he had whipped her back and legs with barbed wire. Goulter had his own life-lie: he used to tell me in 1933 when he was courting Marge at the vicarage that if he could only get to the Soviet Union, the workers' paradise, as he called it, he would be able to get off the grog, because in Russia a worker was not treated as a beast. Well, we all have our delusions. Reg never got to the Soviet Union. He got to Yarra Glen, where he died early in the 1950s, blaming to the end capitalist society for his abominable behaviour to his wife and his child.

Marge wept when she saw me at Yarra Glen. So did I, though I had no idea of what she had lived through. She showed me the scars on her legs from the hidings Reg had given her with the barbed wire. 'Dad', she said, 'was a demon when the drink was inside him.' She had a surprise for me. There were two other females in the house: her daughter Bess, then a teenager, and another daughter Jane, then in her early thirties. Who was she? I had never heard of her before.

Years later Jane sought me out in Canberra, and began to tell me her story. She told me she was Marge's daughter. She was born in a hospital in Sydney on 25 June 1921, the day and the year on which my father left Kempsey. She told me my father and mother had paid for Marge's confinement in Sydney, had paid for Marge, her baby, and her mother, to move from Kempsey to South Melbourne in 1923, and had paid a small sum each week to help Marge. They had employed Marge as their maid in the vicarage at Belgrave.

Marge's daughter had suffered so much from thrashings and sexual assaults by Reg Goulter that she decided to accept the proposal of a woman friend that they should spend their lives together. She changed her name by deed poll to Margaret Reynolds, and joined Helen in a partnership which lasted till Helen died. Now I understood why Marge had made those journeys from Belgrave to Melbourne once a fortnight. Now I understood why my mother wore a worried expression on her face when Marge pressed close to the man she was dancing with in the Soldiers' Memorial Hall in Belgrave. Some things which had puzzled me in childhood began to become clear.

The Marge Thompson story was part of my life. I had loved her as a boy. She had people's wisdom: she had taught me the secrets of the heart. This knowledge of her past in Kempsey helped me to see my father and my mother in a new light. I wanted to speak to them. I wanted to tell them I now knew what they had lived through with great dignity and courage. It was too late: they were both dead. Marge also died before I had a chance to draw near to her again. The story was part of the canvas of life I must paint if I were to tell the story of Australia. So was Reg Goulter with his terrible delusion that all his cruelty, all his sadism and brutality, were not his fault, but the consequence of being a worker in a capitalist society. He too, must be viewed with the eye of pity, difficult though that would be. The drunkards, and all those who could not stop must be viewed with the eye of pity. It was not only the mighty men of renown whose life was a tragedy. The question was how to tell the story of a Marge Thompson, how to convey to a reader the tragic grandeur of life, with the sympathy refreshed by knowledge of such a life? Or so I began to think during those never-ending years of unleavened bread in Australia.

One other experience strengthened the vision of life which was beginning to take shape in my mind. In 1954 Dr Evatt, who was then leader of the Australian Labor Party, expressed a wish to ask me questions about Ian Milner. Someone had told Evatt that I had known Milner well in the mid-1940s. Evatt was a folk hero, a cult figure for the believers in the Enlightenment in Australia. He was the judge who had liberated Egon Kisch from his gaolers: he was a patron of the arts: he believed in the cultivation of Australian sentiment: he was a fine flower of the Labor movement, a man who believed the words in a couplet in the *Bulletin*: 'Heaven and Hell are priests' inventions / Trust the brotherhood of man.' He believed in the liberty of the individual, witness his heroic stand against the anti-communist bill and the ensuing referendum. He believed in the rule of reason: he was a 'great is truth and it will prevail' man. He was shocked, I was told, to hear that his colleague Jack Beasley had held a political meeting outside a hotel. Politics was part of the quest for truth, an act of the mind, not the plaything of the baser passions of humanity.

Before meeting him in his house near the Canberra Fire Station, Telopea Park, Pat Shaw, a close friend from Melbourne days, and then a man of ambassadorial rank, told me of the other side of Dr Evatt – Evatt the liar, Evatt the bully, Evatt the man who suspected

207

everyone as a potential traitor, the man who followed the advice Power, the bushranger, had given to Ned Kelly: 'Trust no man – and no woman either.' Years later I discovered to my delight that Bert Evatt had placed an absolute trust in the woman he loved, his wife Mary Alice. She had found her 'darling Bert' to be a 'most beautiful lover'; they had known 'the glory'; they twain had become one flesh. But Bert Evatt had probably never known such trust, faith and love with any other human being.

I met him in a Canberra suburban brick house. When I entered the room the one-time President of the General Assembly of the United Nations was sitting dressed in a woollen dressing gown with tiger-coloured stripes, his face ravaged, his eyes darting around the room, maybe in search of someone who would not let him down. He wanted to know all about Ian Milner from me, or so he said. But he had already made up his mind about Ian Milner, and nothing I told him had the slightest influence on him. By then he saw himself as the object of a gigantic conspiracy to destroy him. His mind was like a chessboard on which he had placed all the pieces in their places. The fact that the position of those pieces did not correspond with the facts did not cause him to change his mind. On that chessboard inside his teeming brain Milner was in one place in 1949: I happened to know he was nowhere near that place. But Evatt would not budge.

On that night and subsequent nights he talked of what he would do when he was Prime Minister of Australia after the next election. His wife, who never lost faith in her 'Bert, darling' would turn to me and say with the fervour of a recent convert (she had been converted to the perpetual adoration of her Bert more than thirty years earlier), 'Did you hear what he said? [long pause] That's what he'll do.' But it did not seem very likely that this man of many talents, and many flaws, who had years earlier been the white hope of those who believed in the mission of Labor in Australia, but was now in a state of decay, would ever win an election. What he had coveted so desperately was forever out of his reach, the flaws in his being having cheated him of his much-coveted prize. I wondered why a man of such gifts should 'walk into the night' rather than savour the fruit of all his dreams. Perhaps we were all like that. I wanted to know by whose strange laws that came to be. I began to spend much time looking at the paintings of Goya. He will teach me about the dreams which torment men deluded by 'the sleep of reason': he will teach me many things.

For Evatt worse was yet to come. In April 1954 Bob Menzies told the House of Representatives that it was his 'unpleasant duty to convey to the House some information: Vladimir Petrov, secretary in the Soviet Embassy in Canberra has asked for and been granted political asylum in Australia.' A day later he announced the government had appointed a Royal Commission of three judges to inquire into and report on Soviet espionage in Australia. Suspecting it was all part of a political conspiracy to discredit him and the Labor Party on the eve of an election, Evatt made wild accusations. Evatt's judgement faltered: in a moment of madness he wrote a letter to Molotov, the minister for foreign affairs in Moscow, asking him to deny that Petrov was a Soviet spy. The fatal flaw in Evatt, the poison of suspicion, was about to be followed by a cruel punishment. Menzies, his rival, solemnly passed judgement: Dr Evatt, he told the House, was not worthy of leading a great political party.

Events moved swiftly. The right wing of Labor broke with the Australian Labor Party to form first the anti-communist Labor Party. Such a split meant that Labor could not win an election. The Australian Labor Party lost the election on 10 December 1955, and went on losing until December 1972. Evatt resigned as leader of the Labor Party to take up the position of Chief Justice of New South Wales. It was too late. The decay within him leading him on to his destruction was not arrested. One day in Sydney I slipped into a seat in the court room of the Supreme Court of New South Wales. Evatt was scribbling away on a pad of paper. Evatt did not seem to know which case was before the Bench. His colleague, Mr Justice Sugerman, shielded him from the giggles of the barristers of Phillip Street. The man who wrote the words about liberty and equality was now a heap of ruins. Mary Alice persuaded him to resign. She took him back to Canberra where for a year or so he babbled, as Falstaff had also once babbled, about what he would do when he was Prime Minister of Australia. He was still dreaming of the prize which the world had withheld from him as he lapsed into unconsciousness on 2 November 1965.

I went to the funeral service at St John's Canberra, and stood the 'pace or two apart' the historian must observe. The Bishop of Canberra, K. Clements, took as his text for the eulogy that most difficult command by Christ, 'Judge not.' I remembered the words of Carlyle in *The French Revolution* about the eye of pity, and that every person in the past was worthy of a little love, difficult though that might be.

At the Canberra Cemetery on the same day I witnessed another scene which reinforced my conviction of what should be in any history of Australia. Menzies stood at the open grave looking down on the coffin containing the mortal remains of the man he had destroyed. He looked like the victor looking down on the vanquished. But I wondered then: maybe history will turn that scene upside down, and see Menzies as the vanquished. History may see Menzies as the man who put his vast talents at the service of a corrupt and doomed society and Evatt as a man who fell from his great height because of some faults in his own clay. Maybe history would decide that Evatt was pitifully equipped to steal fire from heaven.

The story of Dr Herbert Vere Evatt defined more clearly in my mind the tragic vision of life which had been planted there by experiences in childhood and during the riper years. I wanted to tell the story of human beings in Australia. In childhood I heard the wondrous stories my father told. I know what makes a story live on. As a child I learnt the story of Noah and the ark. Now I had some idea why that story lived on. The storyteller had a point of view on the human situation: 'And God *saw* that the wickedness of man was great in the earth, and that every imagination of the thoughts of his heart *was* only evil continually.' The storyteller knew of the wonder of a man with a maid: he knew about love and passion: 'the sons of God saw the daughters of men that they *were* fair; and they took them wives of all which they chose.' The storyteller could create another human being. Noah, he tells us, 'found grace in the eyes of the Lord.' We know the Noahs of this world, the men of 'professorial timber' or those destined for higher things in the bureaucracy in Canberra. The storyteller could create scenes. Here is Noah after he had lived through the ordeal of the flood: 'And he [Noah] drank of the wine, and was drunken; and he was uncovered within his tent.'

As Mr Passion I believed I had something to say. I believed I must report accurately what I had seen, and take no notice of what others might think. As Mr Passion I believed it must be *my* voice - a voice purged of mockery, sarcasm, and disgust with life. But Mr Passion still found it hard to break with the way of life which allowed him to tell his stories in bars and drawing-rooms, and so avoid the pangs of facing the blank page. Mr Passion still feared he might have nothing to say. Mr Passion still feared that like Old Mother Hubbard his cupboard might be bare. So Mr Passion still mocked on: still indulged in wild buffoonery: Mr Passion still enjoyed being a Falstaff of the Canberra suburbs. But another voice inside Mr Passion was speaking louder and louder, telling him: put the vision penned inside your breast down on paper; find out if you have anything to say; use your pitifully inadequate equipment to tell the story of Australia.

In 1952 Dymphna came up with a suggestion which provided me with a setting in which it would be possible for me to say something on paper, that is, if I really had something to say. With her gift of seeing there was something amiss, her concern to find a way of life in which I would have a chance to show what was inside me, she suggested we should build our own house in Canberra. I suggested we should ask Robin Boyd to design it. Dymphna asked why I had so suddenly become an enthusiast for the man she had tried in vain to interest me in for years. I told her I had met him in Brian Fitzpatrick's house in Clendon Road, Toorak, adding with my usual enthusiasm when I met someone with whom it is possible to talk, 'We understood each other.' So we asked Robin to design a house. Dymphna told him what we needed. As the bus taking him to the airport moved away from the curb outside the old Trans-Australia Airlines terminal in Civic I shouted to him, 'Robin, put one room upstairs.' So we moved into a house at 11 Tasmania Circle on 28 October 1953 which still delights us thirty-seven years later, and I have a study upstairs. Alec Hope stood with me in the study in the week it was finished but not furnished, looked out of the window at Mt Ainslie and Black Mountain and prophesied, 'I see books being written here.' But still I dillied and dallied.

There were more births in our family. Dymphna was more fruitful than my imagination. Rowland, named after Rowland Hassall, was born in Canberra on 14 October 1955, and Benedict, named after my Oxford supervisor Benedict Humphrey Sumner, on 31 January 1957. Like the other four they will give Dymphna and me much pleasure – the greatest of which being that they will speak to us about everything. Rowland will become a teacher, a farmer, and the only member of our family who can dismantle the engine of a motor car or truck and put it together again. Benedict will become a doctor, a painter of landscapes, and a brilliant mimic of his doting father.

The students in Canberra were just as stimulating, just as lively as the students during those golden three years in Melbourne. There was Alistair Davidson, later the Professor of Government at the University of Sydney, a young man with a lively mind and a fire in the belly. There was Alan Gilbert, later the Professor of History at the Australian Defence Force Academy, and pro-Vice Chancellor of the University of New South Wales, a young man of prodigious industry, a shrewd observer of the human scene, and an exile from God. Bill Gammage, who came to us as a boy from the bush, a lover of the Australia of mates, resource, courage and kindness, developed into the man who wrote a great book on the First World War, *The Broken Years*, became an adviser for the film *Gallipoli*, and wrote the prize-winning history of Narrandera. Bill had a well of sympathy so deep no one could ever fathom it. So did his wife Jan. There was Ron Fraser, a young man with a troubled brow who believed it must be possible to build a better world than the one he knew. George Martin, the boy from Tumbarumba, shared that view, but was determined to enjoy what this world, with all its imperfections, had to offer. He did so with great gusto. Ian McAlmain was different. He knew a lot. He was such a born teacher that he began to teach me in class – to my great benefit. Elizabeth Cowell had a face of astonishing beauty, on which she wore at times a becoming melancholy. She had that rare combination of a sharp mind and a lively imagination. Helen McCallum was one of the quiet ones. The story could never give her what she was looking for; she will go on a pilgrimage to India to find the answers. We, teachers and students, were all looking for those answers. There are moments in life when things go well. Canberra was like that in the years before the muddying of the waters of university life.

There were many minds: there were many hearts. There was Robert Moss, later author of books on contemporary politics and a writer of novels, but then a young man not certain whether to walk forever down the primrose path of pleasure or to write books which would survive for more than a generation. He will have a shot at both. There was Frank Sheehan, then a priest of the Order of the Sacred Heart, a man with infinite compassion for the least of the little ones, for all those who could not manage the world, all those who could not stop. Philippa Weekes was one of the silent members, like Geoffrey Blainey and Ken Inglis, who put what was in the mind into their essays rather than into frivolous tutorial discussions. There was Jill Waterhouse, who combined the gifts of the storyteller with the wisdom of women who know what is in a man. There was Caroline Turner who had a great enthusiasm for history. She was lucky. People liked her.

The return of Keith Hancock to the Australian National University in 1957 was another spur to be up and doing. Keith was not a man to suffer evaders gladly. He believed in collaboration between historians, and he asked me to supervise some of his Ph.D. students. I already had one very interesting student for an M.A. She was Ruth

Knight, a graduate in music from Vassar College in the United States, who had always wanted to do history. In music she had been a pupil of the composer Paul Hindemith. She was a pleasing combination of the American tradition of hard work and her own lively imagination. So she and Tim Suttor, Michael Roe, and later Lloyd Robson and John Barrett, became the members of a weekly seminar. They all had much to offer. There were some memorable exchanges. Tim Suttor, a convert to Rome, a man who believed the devil had played and was still playing an active role in Australian history, sat there in my room in the old workers' huts in Childers Street opposite Don Baker, who believed everything done by the Catholic Church had been disastrous for humanity. Michael Roe was the burrower for information, a man who could never be satisfied until he had put together all the pieces in the jigsaw puzzle of the human past. Lloyd Robson was a paradox: he had the mind of a poet, and the intellectual habits of a fact-finder. They were all fruitful. Their theses were all published: Ruth Knight's on Robert Lowe as *The Illiberal Liberal*; Michael Roe's as *Quest for Authority in Eastern Australia, 1835-1851*; Tim Suttor's as *Hierarchy and Democracy in Australia*; John Barrett's as *That Better Country: The Religious Aspect of Life in Eastern Australia, 1835–1850*; and Lloyd Robson's in his books on the convicts, the first A.I.F., and the history of Tasmania.

I began to talk to Bede Nairn, then a research fellow in history at the Australian National University and later a brilliant joint editor of the *Australian Dictionary of Biography*. He and Keith Hancock will defend me later when some attacked me for not writing a history I had neither the intention nor the capacity to write. Bede understood what I tried so imperfectly to put into words. Bede knew that my 'quantity of felt life' included a knowledge of failure and damnation. I will never forget his recognition of what my quest was all about.

The increase in the number of students gave me the chance to select teachers who could participate in a great debate about the past. Tim Suttor joined us as a brilliant, if somewhat eccentric, apologist for Catholic Christendom. Later Humphrey McQueen joined us as an apologist for Marxist history. He had much more to offer than the gifts of a missionary for a view of the past and the future of humanity. He was a brilliant teacher who quickly attracted a following among the students; he had already written the tract for his time on Australian history, *A New Britannia*. He was that rare phenomenon of a Marxist with a rapidly growing interest in and knowledge of the human heart.

He was like Don Baker and David Campbell. It was possible to speak with him. Bruce Kent and Daphne Gollan, both strong in the faith of Karl Marx, showed the students how the laws of history explained the French, the Russian and the Chinese revolutions.

Geoffrey Fairbairn joined us to tell Australian students about the world of the Buddha, of Hinduism and Islam, and about the insurgency movements in south-east Asia. Late at night he would tell me he feared he was the barren fig-tree. His published work belied that fear. He always was an incurable romantic. At great personal risk he flew to Saigon on the eve of its fall to ask his friends there to forgive him for not foreseeing their doom. He was one of Australia's great carers. He was also an antiphon to Humphrey McQueen's view of the world. Ian Hancock joined us to tell Australian students about Africa. As a balance to those who knew the answers there was Don Baker, the sceptic and the searcher. There were also two men who were distinguished representatives of the great liberal tradition of English-speaking universities. For an all-too-brief period there was Ken Inglis, who gave us all the clues, and did not pretend there were any answers. He was succeeded by C. M. (Mick) Williams, who had the gift of persuading students that what looked like a muddle could be construed into delightful patterns if they were prepared to work hard. John Ritchie became a brilliant lecturer in Australian history, and Dorothy Shineberg brought grace and wisdom into the teaching of Pacific history.

My world went well. But Mr Passion was still having trouble in putting pen to paper. The research assistants, and Mr Passion himself, went on collecting material in the National Library, the Mitchell Library, the archives in Hobart, and the Melbourne Public Library. Like my colleagues in the Department of History my research assistants were another stroke of good fortune. They were not only efficient, productive, and mind-readers of what was going on behind the mask, but people it was possible to talk to. I remember with gratitude and affection what I gained and learned from Barbara Donagan, Ailsa Zainu'ddin, Barbara Penny, Lyndall Ryan, Beverley Hooper, Susan Magarey, Sigrid McCausland, Elizabeth Cham and Roslyn Russell. Folder after folder was filled with notes, but still no words went down on the blank page. The secretaries in the History Department, Pat Romans, Shirley Bradley and 'Paddy' Maughan, made their own contribution to the hope that we were all participating in an exciting and high-minded quest to use the past to illuminate the present.

Dymphna stood firm when the wayward Mr Passion threatened to go overboard. She was like my mother. I only had to look at her face to learn when I had erred and strayed.

A chance event helped to get me going. There must always be someone to talk to. Canberra gave me that. One night in 1954 David Campbell and I made a vain attempt at a party to rescue Judith Wright from a monologue by Tom Inglis Moore, who was a man given to such performances. We decided it would be better to drink whisky than to attempt the impossible.

He and his wife Bonny were then living on the land as graziers at Wells Station in the Australian Capital Territory. Later they moved to a property called 'Palerang', halfway between Bungendore and Braidwood. I knew many David Campbells. He came down our drive in Tasmania Circle at all times of the day and the night. He came once at three in the morning, knocked loudly on the glass in our gallery, woke us up and asked whether we could lend him a jemmy. He wanted to prise open a window in the old Riverside Art Gallery, remove a picture painted by Sir Alan McNicoll, then a rear-admiral in the Australian Navy, to win a bet with the latter that its absence would not be noticed. Mr Handyman and his wife did not have a jemmy. So they offered him a chisel which Mr Campbell said would do. He won his bet. That was the daredevil Mr Campbell.

There was also David Campbell, the swashbuckler. One day he came down the drive to tell me he had had a gay time at a dance in a ballroom in Forrest. His hostess told me later that while David and his partner were swirling together, he fell into the big bass drum. They helped him to his feet. Next day his hostess had a phone call. 'Oh hello, it's Dave.' My God, she thought, David Campbell is going to apologise. But no, the voice on the phone was not that of a contrite heart. 'I want to thank you for last night,' he said, 'I found it very therapeutic.'

There was the man of delightful fancies. One day he walked down our drive to tell me he had just called on Tom Inglis Moore, the man who introduced a course in Australian literature at the Canberra University College in 1955. David asked Tom, 'Is there a gum tree in the house?' Somewhat startled, Tom asked him why he, David, wanted a gum tree. David replied that he had a great desire to hang his hat on a gum tree. I never had any difficulty in believing Mr Campbell had the dream about being in bed with Her Majesty – a dream which he recreated with such wit and panache in the poem to which he gave the cheeky and symbolical title, 'The Australian Dream'.

There was the magical David Campbell, the David Campbell who was larger than life. That was the man I got to know on the banks of the Goodradigbee, the rocks at Wapengo, at Palerang, The Run (on the Captain's Flat Road), and at Tasmania Circle. We spoke of many things. We talked about whom we would like to see on the resurrection morning – that is if there were to be a resurrection morning. I told him hosts of men and women would want to see him, as he had a generous heart, and that I might have to spend time avoiding the people I could not manage. We were entering the calm-down years. We were both only just managing to decline the invitation to come over on the wild side.

During those talks I got to know a very dear man – a man, like my father, who wanted everyone to enjoy the great banquet of life. He was an enlarger of life, not a straitener or a measurer, or a life-denier. He was chafed in the company of heart-dimmers. He went silent in the presence of the mockers of the literary world. Even when death was near he practised what he had commended in the couplet: 'Praise life while you walk and wake / It's only lent.' He belonged to no political group. He distanced himself from all political parties. He was proud of belonging by birth to what he called his tribe – the tribe of the country gentry – but was ill at ease with the lore of that tribe. He held a religious view of the world, but belonged to no church.

Perhaps the key to the magical David Campbell, the man with the wondrous eyes, can be found in the two books he re-read each year: *The Idiot* by Dostoevsky, and *The Aunt's Story* by Patrick White. David, I found to my delight, was both the innocent one and the man of action: he was both the lover and the fool in Christ. He could have said of Theodora Goodman in *The Aunt's Story*, 'She's more myself than I am.' He was both a pilgrim for the means of grace and John Bunyan's Mr Passion who wanted everything now. He was the war hero, the victor in the boxing ring, the strong man in the rugby scrum, the fisherman, the horseman, the polo player who knew all about Myshkin and Theodora Goodman. I saw him knock out a man in the bar at Delegate for casting doubts on his manhood. The next morning I saw him cast a fly with such delicacy that it landed on the waters of the Snowy River with the grace of a butterfly.

It was my good fortune to get to know this magical David Campbell, to see his face transfigured, his eyes dancing with life as he spoke to me about all the beauty in the world, the beauty of a woman's face, the 'Madonnas of the Paradise moment', the fragile beauty of Australia beneath its harsh exterior. I began to understand why in his poem, 'Night Sowing', he wrote:

> O gentle land, I sow
> The heart's living grain.
> Stars draw their harrows over,
> Dews send their melting rain:
> I meet you as a lover.

He was a great lover. It was my good fortune to get to know both the man of action and the poet, the man who came out of Old Australia, the man who, like me, loved to go 'down Kosciusko way'. That was the man I knew. That is the man I never forget.

In 1955, just when I was beginning to get to know David Campbell, the Council of the University College gave me one year's sabbatical leave. Dymphna travelled with me. All the children except Sebastian joined us in Bombay. I decided to go first to Jakarta to study the views held in south-east Asia before the coming of the European on what lay south of Java. In December 1955, with the help of Dymphna's gifts as a linguist, I unearthed a gold mine. I found the Hindu, Muslim and Chinese stories designed to deter sailors from venturing south of Java: there was the story of the Garuda bird; the story of the great hole in the ocean; there was the story of the kingdom of women. That material could be part of an early chapter in my story, if only I had the gift and the strength to tell it.

So on to Singapore, Rangoon, Delhi, Agra, Benares, Calcutta, Madras and Bombay, to collect more material, and in between collecting material to ponder over why those who lived in such poverty had a dignity and a reverence for life often singularly lacking in the two-car family sections of Australian society. On to Oxford, where Dick Southern and Christopher Hill were kind, so kind that I could almost tolerate the over-civilised chatter of the common-rooms.

In April Dymphna, Katerina, Axel, Andrew, Rowland and I drove to Whitby. Katerina, who was then deep in her Dad-must-be-a-phony years, asked me when we stopped at Eastwood, the birthplace of D. H. Lawrence, 'Which phony are you looking up this time, Dad?' We drove on in silence to Whitby where I stood beside the statue of Captain Cook, scrutinising his face in search of the clue to what 'kept him man alive'. I noticed on the hillside behind the statue the ruins of the Abbey of Whitby, which I took to be a symbol of the ruins of Catholic Christendom. The words of John Henry Newman came again into my mind: '[Protestant Christianity] had no intellectual basis; no internal idea, no principle of unity, no theology. Its adherents ... will melt away like a snow-drift ... it does not stand on intrenched ground, or make any pretence to a position.' There will be a 'stern encounter' between 'contending powers, Catholic Truth and Rationalism.' I remembered also Newman's prophecy of a coming age of unbelief.

In June Axel, then in his early teens, and I travelled to Ireland, where I discovered a society of people in whom compassion and the eye of pity were stronger than the ambition of 'gaining the whole world'. While searching the Irish newspapers in the Dublin Public Library for material on the Irish convicts I came across a cartoon on the famine of 1847. In the cartoon an Englishman, dressed in the clothes of the governing classes, was explaining to an Irish peasant why the laws of supply and demand made it impossible for the British government in Ireland to provide relief for starving potato farmers. The peasant, chewing a dry stalk of grass, gazed at the Englishman in wonder. As I walked out of the Library a picture of how to begin a history of Australia began to take shape in my mind. There was Catholic Christendom: there was Protestant Christianity: there were the sons of the Enlightenment. That reminded me of the experience in Whitby.

In September I travelled alone to Rome. Mr Gibbon has already taught me about the follies of human beings. I noticed on a pillar at the left of the entrance to St Peters a bronze plaque in honour of Charles Edward Stuart, on which were inscribed in Latin the words, 'Blessed are those who die in the Lord'. I seemed to remember reading that Charles Edward Stuart died of alcoholic poisoning. I also remembered then that in the first ceremony in February 1788 under the gum tree beside the blue waters of Sydney Harbour Governor Arthur Phillip, himself an unbeliever, swore on the Bible that he would not attempt to restore Charles Edward Stuart to the throne of England – he not knowing then that Bonnie Prince Charlie was dead. That scene would have to be created in any history of Australia.

A few days later I stood in front of the statue of Moses by Michelangelo in the church of St Peter in Chains. Freud had interested me in the work. Michelangelo, Freud argued, was making the point that a man such as Moses must learn to curb the passions of anger, or disgust with the worshippers of the golden calf, and channel such passions into creation rather than destruction.

It was time to begin. It was time to call on that 'quantity of felt life' which I had begun to accumulate in my Swanee River years on Phillip Island, in Belgrave, in the fiery ordeal of 'Grammar and that sort of thing', at the University of Melbourne, in Cologne Cathedral, from the harangues of Dr Busslei in Bonn, in Oxford, in the dark days at Geelong Grammar, the enthusiasms of post-war Melbourne, and the wisdom acquired from watching the drama of Menzies and Evatt, of watching my colleagues, of watching myself, and those conversations with David Campbell.

So in Oxford in the summer of 1956, with Rowland, our youngest child, doing a carry-on in his cot, I wrote the sentence, 'It was all there in the beginning . . .' and stopped because I did not know what I meant by 'it'. There had to be another start. So a few weeks later I wrote the fateful words: 'Civilisation did not begin in Australia until the last quarter of the eighteenth century.' I was a child of my age, and paid a great penalty for that, because I missed out on one of the great tragedies in the history of Australia. I saw it as the coming of 'civilisation' to the ancient and barbarous continent: I failed to see it through the eyes of the original occupants of Australia – the Aborigines.

But the story had begun. There was still much to do. A visit to Moscow in November 1958 with Judah Waten and James Devaney influenced the chapter on 'The Sons of the Enlightenment'. Judah's faith was as strong as ever. I remember that one night in the foyer of the Hotel Ukraine in Moscow Judah said to me, with tears of joy in his eyes, 'Communism will shit it in.' Jim Devaney believed in the resurrection of the dead and the life of the world to come. They represented my two shy hopes. I was still a child of unbelief, who had never lost the thirst to believe. Russia was filling with culture the vacuum where God had once been. I went to a performance of Chekhov's *Three Sisters* in the Moscow Arts Theatre, and was exalted when Vershinin professed his faith in the capacity of human beings to build a better society. I felt the tears pricking at the back of the eyes when Vershinin confessed his love to Masha. But a week later at the Bolshoi Theatre in Moscow, I heard Onegin in Tchaikovsky's opera *Eugene Onegin*, the man who has transgressed against the lore of his class, put at the end of the opera the question to which I wanted to know the answer: How can I escape my cruel fate? And I knew then that the faith of a Vershinin, the hopes of a man of the Enlightenment, were a superficial response to the human situation.

In 1959, a few months after my return to Australia, I was talking to Jim McAuley in George Street, Sydney, when a man with a face which will haunt me for days walked up to us. It was one of those epiphanies in life. It was Patrick White. Once again I was in the presence of a mighty spirit. Once again I was in the presence of a man who wanted something which no human being could give him. We were all inadequate: we would all let him down. We began in the street a conversation which will be resumed later at Castle Hill, and later still in Centennial Park. He knew that the tormented are often the ones who understand. He was an inspiration to keep going.

The writing was not easy. The first draft was appalling, the second not much better, and the third closer to the story I wanted to tell. On 29 December 1960 I posted the manuscript of volume one of *A History of Australia* to the Melbourne University Press, where it received the brilliant editing of Gwyn James and Barbara Ramsden. Dymphna made many rough places smooth, and she will do that generously for all the other volumes too. She had shielded me from the world, and the world from me. I went on fiddling with the words, but I was never able to do justice to the tragic grandeur I wanted to convey. Life is immense.

On 7 September 1962 Max Crawford launched volume one in the Melbourne University Union, and quoted this passage about Governor William Bligh:

So chance and circumstance connived to ensure once again in the history of human affairs that the man who was angry without cause bequeathed no monument of achievement to posterity, and tasted deep damnation on earth as the fruit of his disquiet.

My words had said something about life to another human being. Max Crawford, Keith Hancock, Mark Oliphant and Bede Nairn helped me not to lose faith in my capacity to tell the story of Australia. Music, fishing, talks with David Campbell on the banks of the Goodradigbee River, provided the boosters I needed when the onslaught began. From that time each morning I asked for strength, for faith in my own powers, and for the eye of pity for all the people I tried to recreate.

Volume two was published in 1968, volume three in 1973, volume four in 1978, volume five in 1981, and volume six in 1987. At the launching of volume six in University House, Canberra, David Malouf told the audience, 'We are here to celebrate the conclusion to a great undertaking'. It had been my good fortune to grow up at a time when Australians wanted to be told the story of how they came to be. There were many flaws in the way in which I told the story. In the telling something was added to me. It was over fifty years since I had read the words by Dostoevsky, 'I want to be there when everyone suddenly understands what it has all been for. All the religions of the world are built on this longing, and I am a believer.' I have not reached that level of understanding, but during the long quest I experienced moments of grace.

PENGUIN – THE BEST AUSTRALIAN READING

OTHER BOOKS BY MANNING CLARK

The Puzzles of Childhood Manning Clark

The Puzzles of Childhood takes us on a journey through the early life of Manning Clark as he follows the confused path to self-understanding, signposted by attempts to understand others.

Collected Short Stories Manning Clark

Growing up at Phillip Island, solemn moments in church, memories of school, confrontations in academe, fishing with a son – this is the stuff of Manning Clark's short stories.

'These are rare treasures from a writer of subtle eloquence – witty and compassionate observations on the human condition which give a lingering pleasure.' — Mary Lord

A Short History of Australia Manning Clark

In this lively, very readable book, the eminent and controversial historian Manning Clark portrays the evolution of Australia with remarkable breadth of vision. With a provocative style the author describes convicts and settlers, architecture, exploration, immigrants and squatters, politics and culture, the gold rushes, radicals and nationalists, the world wars. The incisive concluding chapter deals with the years from 1969 to 1986 – Manning Clark's 'age of ruins'.

This elegantly written and well-illustrated book brings to life the people and events that have shaped Australia's history.

The Education of Young Donald   Donald Horne

This is the classic autobiography of Donald Horne, the famous Australian who coined the term 'the lucky country'. It is both the personal story of one man in the 1920s and 30s and that of an entire generation.

First published twenty years ago, this edition, revised by the author, is now volume one of an autobiographical trilogy. It provides a perspective on the man who became best-selling writer, innovative editor, university professor, Chairman of the Australia Council, and trenchant social critic.

Confessions of a New Boy   Donald Horne

In this second volume Donald Horne gives a vivid portrait of Australia in the 1940s and his life as an *enfant terrible* at the University of Sydney; in the brutalising environment of the army; in Canberra where bleak 'provincial inferiorities' dictated things; and finally in the lively world of Sydney journalism, with its myths, legends and heroic figures. Young Donald falls in love, learns how to make mayonnaise, and what shoes to wear with a dark suit; friendships form and fall apart. At the same time we follow his journeyings through the world's greatest novels as he tries to make sense of his life through literature.

He is sometimes foolish, often pretentious or difficult to get along with, but always deeply committed to the priorities of the mind.

Portrait of an Optimist   Donald Horne

This third volume of Donald Horne's memoirs portrays a young man of the 1940s and 50s whose many enthusiasms are awkwardly counterbalanced by an instinct for self-parody. He shifts readily from novelist and Tory activist in an English village to tough and rumbustious Sydney newspaperman. He sees his life as 'a dream where you think you are running but your legs don't work'.

In presenting the uncertainties and triumphs of his younger self, Horne's 'saga of pratfalls' traces the onset of maturity with a sharp eye for the period.

PENGUIN – THE BEST AUSTRALIAN READING

Stirring the Possum   James McClelland

From his days as a young Trotskyist in the 1940s – secretly in love with an enemy Stalinist – to his role in the 1980s as commissioner in an inquiry into the Maralinga nuclear tests, Jim McClelland has been known as a stirrer.

In his autobiography he offers us a perspective on Australian politics that spans 50 years. His critical assessment of public figures and events is both humorous and acerbic; his account of a distinguished and varied career reflects his energy, his sharp mind and his unfailing capacity to 'liven things up.'

An Angel Bit the Bride   James McClelland

Within days of publication, James McClelland's autobiography *Stirring the Possum* established itself on the bestseller lists. It also reinforced 'Diamond Jim's' reputation among readers of his column in the *Sydney Morning Herald* as a stylish, acerbic and entertaining writer.

An Angel Bit the Bride draws on that column to bring together a selection of his 'less familiar jottings' as his earthy and irreverent pen ranges over politics, travel, law, the media, the environment, friends, foes and canines.

The Penguin Book of Australian Autobiography
Edited and introduced by John and Dorothy Colmer

Who am I? What makes me an Australian?

These are two of the questions that the writers in this richly rewarding anthology of Australian autobiography seek to answer. They celebrate the magic world of childhood; the painful struggle towards self-discovery and self-realisation; the impact of two World Wars and the Great Depression; the artist's conflicting loyalties to European and Australian culture and the joys and disappointments of worldly success.

A lively and stimulating introduction to more than forty Australians who write of their own lives. They include Kylie Tennant, Patrick White, Joan Lindsay, David Malouf, Henry Lawson, Judah Waten, Charles Perkins, Donald Horne, Albert Facey, Clive James, George Johnston and Mary Gilmore.

PENGUIN – THE BEST AUSTRALIAN READING

Solid Bluestone Foundations
Memories of an Australian Girlhood   Kathleen Fitzpatrick

This 'magnificent book of memories', as Manning Clark has called it, represents the life of Melbourne historian Kathleen Fitzpatrick. Growing up in Australia in the 1920s, in a world fragmented by religion and class differences, Kathleen came to associate the bluestone foundations of her grandparents' home with the security and abundance she needed. Later the University of Melbourne with its bluestone foundations became her source of 'constant enrichment'. Kathleen Fitzpatrick's delightful autobiography is itself a rich source of wisdom and wit.

George Johnston   Garry Kinnane

The award-winning biography of the Australian writer – his marriage, his friends, his time in Greece, his work. Garry Kinnane's book is a fascinating account of the development of a creative mind, set against the wider backdrop of Australian post-war culture. It traces the complex connections between Johnston's art and his life.

Katherine Mansfield   Gillian Boddy

Katherine Mansfield was not only an extraordinary writer, devoted to her work, she was also a woman of great vivacity and strength, who led a brief but fascinating life from her birth in New Zealand to the literary circles of England and Europe. The leading writers of her age, people like Virginia Woolf and D. H. Lawrence, were a constant part of her life.

Gillian Boddy has drawn on her years of research to introduce to us a new Katherine Mansfield, not ethereal as has been the myth, but substantial, alive.

No Place for a Nervous Lady
Voices from the Australian Bush   Lucy Frost

A fascinating collection of previously unpublished, intimate letters and diary entries by thirteen women in nineteenth-century Australia. It captures the fearful isolation of life in the bush and the marvellous friendships that developed between correspondents.

A McPhee Gribble/Penguin Book

Autobiography of My Mother   Meg Stewart

An unusual biography of Australian artist Margaret Coen, written by her daughter, that provides a portrait of an independent woman determined to be a painter in difficult times. It is set in the lively artistic and literary worlds of Australia in the 1930s and 40s.

Accidental Chords   Patricia Thompson

In a style both earthy and urbane, Partricia Thompson tells a simple story: her childhood in staid Auckland: her youth in 'jazz age' Sydney; the adventures of young womanhood in brilliant London; the grey world of maddeningly complacent Perth and, finally, her discovery of Paddington, Sydney, which she and her poet husband John set about rescuing from the urban dumps. Through the book runs a vein of outrageous fun, especially in the figure of her zany mother Grace, and her four husbands. But there is a darker side to Patricia's life, the shadow cast by her dominating mother, the shadow she never quite managed to overcome.

A Foreign Wife   Gillian Bouras

In 1980 Australian-born Gillian Bouras set off with her Greek husband to live in Greece. Her fellow-villagers fondly regarded her, a migrant in their midst, as something of a curiosity. They in turn were the source of admiration and curiosity to her. This is her account of her experience in a 'small quiet world' which caused her so much perplexity and pleasure.